Copyright © 2024 by Lindsay M. Thompson (Author)
All rights reserved. This book or any portion thereof may not be reproduced or used in any manner whatsoever without the express written permission of the publisher except for the use of brief quotations in a book review.

This book is copyright protected. This is only for personal use. You cannot amend, distributor, sell, use, quote or paraphrase any part or the content within this book without the consent of the author.

Please note the information contained within this document is for educational and entertainment purposes only. Every attempt has been made to provide accurate, up to date and reliable complete information. No warranties of any kind are expressed or implied. Readers acknowledge that the author is not engaging in the rendering of legal, financial, medical or professional advice. The content of this book has been derived from various sources. Please consult a licensed professional before attempting any techniques outlined in this book.

By reading this document, the readers agree that under no circumstances are the author responsible for any losses, direct or indirect, which are incurred as a result of the use of information contained within this document, including but not limited to errors, omissions or inaccuracies.

Thank you very much for reading this book.

Title: Global High School Classrooms: Unveiling the Tapestry of Learning
Subtitle: Challenges, Triumphs, and the Future of Education Worldwide

Author: Lindsay M. Thompson

Table of Contents

Introduction 7
Overview of Global High School Education 7
Importance of Assessing Education Globally 11
Scope and Structure of the Book 17

Chapter 1: Geographic Variation in High School Education 23
Continental Perspectives 23
Regional Disparities 29
Country-specific Challenges 36
Global Education Goals and Disparities 42

Chapter 2: Educational Systems Around the World . 49
Structure of High School Education 49
Curriculum Variations 56
Grading Systems 62
Teaching Methodologies 68

Chapter 3: Cultural Influences on High School Education 74
Societal Attitudes Towards Education 74
Cultural Impact on Aspirations 80
Cultural Barriers to Education 86
Success Stories in Diverse Cultural Contexts 92

Chapter 4: Economic Disparities and Education 99
Economic Conditions and Access 99
Socio-economic Factors in Educational Success 108
Impact of Income Inequality 118
Government Initiatives to Address Economic Disparities 125

Chapter 5: Government Policies and High School Education 132
Policy Frameworks Globally: Navigating the Educational Landscape 132
Educational Reforms: Transforming High School Education Globally 142

Effectiveness of Government Initiatives: Navigating Impact and Outcomes..148
Challenges in Policy Implementation: Navigating the Complexities of Educational Reform..158

Chapter 6: Technology Integration in High School Education **165**

Global Perspectives on Educational Technology: A Window into the Digital Classroom..165
Digital Divide and Its Implications: Bridging Gaps in Access and Opportunity 171
Innovations in EdTech: Transforming Learning Landscapes 177
Challenges and Opportunities in Technology Integration: Navigating the Digital Frontier 183

Chapter 7: Transition to Higher Education **189**

Challenges in Transitioning to Universities: Navigating the Bridge to Higher Learning 189
Vocational Education and Training: Forging Alternative Paths to Success 194
Role of High School Education in Career Paths: Charting Futures through Academic Foundations 199
Global Trends in Higher Education Admission: Navigating the Evolving Landscape of College Entrances........................... 206

Chapter 8: Success Stories and Innovations in Education **213**

Educational Initiatives Making a Difference: Transformative Pathways to Learning Excellence 213
Innovative Approaches to Educational Challenges: Pioneering Solutions for 21st-Century Learning..............................219
Lessons Learned from Success Stories: Guiding Principles for Educational Transformation.. 224
Scalability and Replicability of Educational Innovations: Unlocking Global Potential... 229

Chapter 9: Global Assessments in High School Education 234
Overview of International Assessments: Benchmarking Educational Excellence 234
Role of PISA and TIMSS: Unveiling Educational Landscapes 239
Standardized Testing Practices Globally: Navigating Assessment Landscapes 245
Alternative Assessment Methods: Beyond Standardized Testing 251

Chapter 10: Standardized Testing: Pros and Cons ... 257
Advantages of Standardized Testing: Illuminating Educational Landscapes 257
Limitations and Criticisms: Navigating the Complexities of Assessment 261
Impact on Educational Policy: Shaping Systems and Priorities 265
Evolving Trends in Standardized Testing: Navigating the Future of Assessment 270

Chapter 11: Quality Indicators in Education 275
Key Indicators of Educational Quality: Navigating the Path to Excellence 275
Correlation with Academic Success: Unraveling the Impact of Educational Quality Indicators 280
Infrastructure, Spending, and Educational Outcomes: Unveiling the Nexus 285
Challenges in Implementing Quality Indicators: Navigating the Roadblocks to Educational Excellence 289

Chapter 12: Global Educational Rankings 294
Overview of Ranking Systems: Decoding the Metrics of Educational Excellence 294
Criteria Used in Educational Rankings: Unveiling the Metrics of Excellence 299

Implications for Educational Policy: Guiding Decision-Making in a Globalized Landscape *304*
Criticisms and Alternatives to Ranking Systems: Navigating the Complexities of Assessment *309*
Chapter 13: Emerging Trends and Future Prospects 314
Evolving Landscape of High School Education: Navigating Change and Embracing Innovation *314*
Anticipated Changes and Challenges: Navigating the Path Forward in High School Education *319*
Opportunities for Global Collaboration: Building Bridges in High School Education *323*
Vision for the Future of High School Education: Shaping Tomorrow's Global Learners *327*
Conclusion **331**
Key Findings and Takeaways: Unveiling the Essence of Global High School Education *331*
Implications for Policymakers and Educators: Navigating the Path Forward in Global High School Education *336*
Call to Action for Improving Global High School Education: Inspiring Change on a Global Scale *341*
Glossary **346**
Potential References **349**

Introduction
Overview of Global High School Education

Education is a fundamental right, a cornerstone for personal development, and a key driver of societal progress. As we embark on a journey to explore the disparities in high school education levels globally, we are compelled to unravel the intricacies of a complex tapestry that defines the learning experiences of millions of students worldwide. In this exploration, we delve into the heart of classrooms across the globe, seeking to understand the variances, challenges, and triumphs that shape the educational landscape.

Overview of Global High School Education

At the core of our inquiry lies the global high school education system, a mosaic of diverse institutions, each contributing to the intellectual, social, and emotional growth of students within their respective contexts. Understanding the broader framework within which high school education operates is crucial to deciphering the disparities that exist and the implications they have on the future of individuals and societies.

Defining the Landscape

High school education, often considered the bridge between primary schooling and higher education or the workforce, takes on myriad forms across different continents, regions, and countries. The structures, curricula, and methodologies employed in high schools worldwide are reflective of unique cultural, economic, and historical factors that have shaped the educational systems within each locale.

Educational Structures and Variations

High school education structures vary significantly, with different countries adopting diverse models. Some adhere to a more traditional approach with a fixed curriculum, while others embrace flexibility and student-centered learning. This chapter will illuminate these structural differences, providing insights into how they impact the overall educational experience for students.

Curriculum Diversity

The curriculum is the backbone of any education system, influencing what students learn, how they learn, and the skills they acquire. In our exploration, we will traverse the globe to uncover the vast array of high school curricula. From STEM-focused programs to those emphasizing humanities and arts, each curriculum reflects not only the educational priorities of a nation but also its vision for the future.

Grading Systems Across Borders

Grading systems serve as a universal language of assessment, yet the criteria and methods can vary widely. Some nations rely on rigorous standardized testing, while others place greater emphasis on continuous assessment. By dissecting these grading systems, we gain insights into the cultural and educational values that underpin them and their implications for students' future trajectories.

Teaching Methodologies: A Spectrum of Approaches

High school education is not just about what is taught but also how it is taught. Teaching methodologies vary globally, ranging from traditional lecture-based approaches to more innovative, student-driven methods. Examining these diverse approaches unveils the adaptability of education to cultural norms and the evolving demands of the 21st-century workforce.

Contextualizing Disparities

The disparities in high school education are not arbitrary; they are embedded in the historical, cultural, and socio-economic contexts of each region and nation. To comprehend these differences, we embark on a journey through continental perspectives, regional disparities, and the specific challenges faced by students in different corners of the world.

This contextualization sets the stage for a nuanced understanding of the global educational landscape.

Continental Perspectives

The continents themselves serve as broad canvases upon which educational narratives unfold. From the rigorous academic expectations of Asian countries to the inclusive and experiential approaches in European nations, the continent plays a significant role in shaping the character of high school education. By examining these continental perspectives, we can discern patterns and contrasts that inform our understanding of global education.

Regional Disparities

Within each continent, regional disparities further compound the complexities of high school education. Urban and rural divides, economic disparities, and access to resources create unique challenges for educators and students alike. Unraveling these regional intricacies provides a granular understanding of the obstacles and opportunities that exist at a local level.

Country-specific Challenges

Zooming in even further, we confront the specific challenges faced by individual countries. These challenges may stem from historical legacies, socio-economic inequalities, or systemic issues deeply rooted in a nation's educational history. By examining case studies, we gain insights into the multifaceted nature of global high school education challenges.

Global Education Goals and Disparities

As nations strive to meet global education goals, disparities persist. Discrepancies in achieving universal access, gender parity, and quality education become apparent when scrutinizing the progress made by different countries. This section explores the tension between global aspirations and the stark realities on the ground, setting the tone for our exploration into the nuances of high school education disparities.

In the chapters that follow, we will navigate through the educational landscapes of different continents, explore the intricacies of varied curricula, and uncover the cultural influences that shape students' aspirations and barriers. Through this comprehensive journey, we aim to shed light on the disparities in high school education globally, offering valuable insights for educators, policymakers, and anyone passionate about the transformative power of education.

Importance of Assessing Education Globally

As we embark on the ambitious journey of exploring the disparities in high school education levels globally, it becomes imperative to underscore the profound significance of assessing education on a global scale. The importance of this assessment extends beyond the realm of academia; it holds the key to understanding, addressing, and ultimately rectifying the disparities that plague high school education systems around the world. In this section, we delve into the reasons why a global perspective on education is not just desirable but essential for shaping the future of individuals, communities, and nations.

Understanding the Interconnected World

In an era characterized by unprecedented connectivity and interdependence, the consequences of disparities in high school education reverberate far beyond national borders. The skills and competencies acquired by students in one corner of the globe impact their ability to contribute meaningfully to a globalized workforce. As economies become increasingly intertwined, and information flows seamlessly across continents, the educational disparities between nations become a collective challenge that requires a collaborative and informed approach.

Economic Implications of Global Education Disparities

The global economy operates on the premise of a skilled and adaptable workforce. Disparities in high school education levels translate into variations in the quality of human capital available to nations. This, in turn, influences economic productivity, innovation, and competitiveness on the global stage. Assessing education globally becomes a strategic imperative for nations seeking sustainable economic development and resilience in an ever-evolving economic landscape.

Societal Impact Beyond Borders

High school education is not merely a conduit for transmitting knowledge; it is a powerful socializing agent that shapes individuals' values, perspectives, and civic responsibilities. Disparities in educational access and quality can exacerbate social inequalities, fostering conditions ripe for unrest and instability. A global assessment of education allows us to comprehend how these societal dynamics transcend national boundaries, influencing regional and global stability.

Equity and Social Justice

Assessing education globally is fundamentally linked to the pursuit of equity and social justice. Education is often hailed as the great equalizer, providing individuals with the tools to overcome socio-economic barriers. However, when disparities persist, the promise of education as an equalizing force remains unfulfilled. A global perspective allows us to identify patterns of inequality, from gender disparities in access to education to the impact of socio-economic status on academic achievement. By understanding these patterns, we can advocate for policies and interventions that foster greater equity within and between nations.

Gender Disparities in High School Education

Girls and young women, in many parts of the world, still face barriers to accessing quality education. These barriers can be rooted in cultural norms, economic constraints, or systemic biases. A global assessment enables us to unravel the complexities of gender disparities in high school education, highlighting both progress and persistent challenges. It empowers us to champion initiatives that break down gender-based barriers, ensuring that education is truly accessible to all.

Socio-economic Factors and Educational Opportunities

The socio-economic background of students often determines their access to educational resources and opportunities. By assessing education globally, we can discern the impact of economic conditions on educational outcomes. Understanding how socio-economic factors intersect with educational disparities allows for targeted interventions that aim to level the playing field, ensuring that every student, regardless of their background, has a fair chance at success.

Cultural Diversity and Educational Pluralism

Culture plays a pivotal role in shaping educational systems and practices. Each society brings a unique set of values, traditions, and expectations to the realm of education. A global assessment allows us to appreciate this cultural diversity and understand how it influences not only the structure of high school education but also the aspirations and challenges faced by students.

Cultural Impact on Aspirations

In many cultures, the value placed on education is deeply ingrained, influencing students' aspirations and career choices. Conversely, cultural factors can also create barriers to education, perpetuating stereotypes and limiting opportunities for certain groups. By assessing education globally, we gain insights into the dynamic interplay between culture and education, enabling us to celebrate cultural strengths while addressing cultural barriers.

Cultural Barriers to Education

Certain cultural norms and expectations may inadvertently hinder educational access and success. For instance, gender roles or expectations around vocational pursuits can limit the choices available to students. A global perspective allows us to identify and understand these cultural barriers, fostering a nuanced approach to education that respects cultural diversity while promoting inclusivity.

Informing Policy and Educational Reform

The importance of assessing education globally becomes particularly evident when considering its impact on policy formulation and educational reform. By comparing systems, identifying best practices, and understanding the outcomes of various policy interventions, nations can make informed decisions that enhance the quality and inclusivity of their education systems.

Policy Frameworks and International Benchmarks

Global assessment serves as a yardstick against which nations can measure the effectiveness of their policy frameworks. International benchmarks, such as global education goals and standardized assessments, provide a common language for evaluating educational outcomes. Understanding how different nations align with these benchmarks informs policymakers about the areas where improvement is needed and highlights successful strategies that can be emulated.

Effectiveness of Government Initiatives

Governments worldwide invest substantial resources in educational initiatives. Assessing the impact of these initiatives on a global scale allows for a comparative analysis of their effectiveness. Whether focused on improving access, enhancing teacher training, or implementing technology in classrooms, understanding what works and what doesn't provides valuable insights for refining policies and optimizing resource allocation.

Challenges in Policy Implementation

Educational policies are not one-size-fits-all solutions. The challenges faced in policy implementation can vary significantly across nations. A global assessment enables policymakers to learn from the successes and failures of their counterparts, anticipating potential challenges and devising strategies for overcoming them. This collaborative approach to policy implementation contributes to the development of resilient and adaptive education systems.

Preparing Students for a Globalized World

In an interconnected world, students need to be equipped with skills and perspectives that transcend geographical and cultural boundaries. Global assessments of education shed light on the strengths and weaknesses of educational systems in nurturing these global competencies, guiding educators in preparing students for the challenges and opportunities of the 21st century.

Global Competencies and 21st-century Skills

The demands of the modern workforce extend beyond traditional academic knowledge. Employers seek individuals with skills such as critical thinking, communication, collaboration, and cultural competence. A global assessment allows us to evaluate how well high school education systems foster these skills, ensuring that students are not only academically proficient but also equipped for success in a globalized economy.

Language Proficiency and Intercultural Communication

Language is a powerful tool for communication and understanding. High school education plays a pivotal role in developing language proficiency and intercultural communication skills. By assessing education globally, we can identify successful strategies for language education, explore the challenges faced by students in multilingual environments, and promote educational practices that enhance cross-cultural understanding.

Conclusion: A Call to Global Action

In conclusion, the importance of assessing education globally cannot be overstated. It is not merely an academic exercise but a moral imperative, a strategic necessity, and a catalyst for positive change. As we journey through the chapters that follow, exploring geographic variations, educational systems, cultural influences, economic disparities, government policies, technological integration, and more, we do so with the understanding that each revelation contributes to a collective understanding of the challenges and opportunities that define high school education on a global scale.

By assessing education globally, we move beyond isolated narratives and embrace a holistic perspective that transcends borders. We recognize that the disparities in high school education are not insurmountable obstacles but challenges that demand collaborative solutions. It is a call to action for educators, policymakers, and advocates of education to join hands in shaping a future where every student, regardless of their geographical location or socio-economic background, has access to a high-quality education that prepares them for a world of endless possibilities. The journey begins with the acknowledgment of the importance of global assessment—an acknowledgment that paves the way for informed decisions, equitable policies, and a shared commitment to the transformative power of education.

Scope and Structure of the Book

As we embark on the exploration of global high school education, it is essential to delineate the scope and structure of this comprehensive journey. This section serves as a guide, providing readers with a roadmap to navigate the intricate terrain of disparities, challenges, and innovations in high school education worldwide. By understanding the scope and structure of the book, readers can anticipate the depth and breadth of insights that await them in each chapter.

Scope of the Book

The scope of "Global High School Classrooms: Unveiling the Tapestry of Learning" transcends geographic boundaries and delves into the heart of educational disparities, seeking to unravel the multifaceted layers that define high school education on a global scale. The book aims to be a compendium of knowledge, offering readers a panoramic view of the challenges and opportunities that students encounter in their high school journeys across continents and cultures.

Geographic Variation and Global Context

The exploration begins with a macroscopic view of high school education, examining geographic variations in educational systems, policies, and outcomes. From continent to continent, region to region, the book traverses the diverse landscapes of high school education, uncovering the unique challenges and triumphs that contribute to the global tapestry of learning.

Cultural, Economic, and Policy Perspectives

A significant aspect of the book's scope is its holistic examination of cultural, economic, and policy influences on high school education. Beyond mere statistics and academic outcomes, we aim to illuminate the cultural nuances that shape educational aspirations, the economic factors influencing access to quality education, and the policies that either bridge or widen educational disparities.

Technology Integration and Future Prospects

Technology, a transformative force in the 21st century, occupies a prominent place in the book's scope. We delve into the global perspectives on educational technology, exploring how it bridges gaps and, at times, exacerbates disparities. Moreover, the book projects into the future, envisioning the evolving landscape of high school education and anticipating the challenges and opportunities that lie ahead.

Assessment Practices and Educational Quality

The scope extends to the realm of assessment, examining global practices and their impact on educational quality. From standardized testing to alternative assessment methods, the book provides a comprehensive understanding of how assessments shape educational policies and contribute to the overarching goal of improving educational outcomes globally.

Global Collaboration and Success Stories

In highlighting success stories and innovations in education, the book showcases instances where concerted efforts have made a tangible difference. The scope encompasses collaborative initiatives that transcend borders, emphasizing the potential for global cooperation in addressing the challenges faced by high school education worldwide.

Structure of the Book

The structure of "Global High School Classrooms" is carefully designed to unfold a coherent narrative, guiding readers through a systematic exploration of the myriad facets of high school education. Each chapter serves as a building block, contributing to a comprehensive understanding of the global educational landscape.

Chapter 1: Geographic Variation in High School Education

The journey commences with an examination of geographic variations in high school education. By providing continental perspectives, dissecting regional disparities, and delving into country-specific challenges, this chapter lays the foundation for understanding how the global context shapes the educational experiences of high school students.

Chapter 2: Educational Systems Around the World

Building on the geographical exploration, this chapter delves into the structures of high school education globally. From the organization of curricula to the intricacies of grading systems and teaching methodologies, readers gain insights into the diverse approaches that nations adopt in shaping the educational journeys of their students.

Chapter 3: Cultural Influences on High School Education

Recognizing the profound impact of culture on education, this chapter explores societal attitudes towards education, the cultural influences on aspirations, and the barriers that cultural norms may pose to educational access. Success stories in diverse cultural contexts offer a nuanced understanding of the complex interplay between culture and high school education.

Chapter 4: Economic Disparities and Education

Economic conditions significantly influence educational opportunities. This chapter analyzes the relationship between economic disparities and access to education, examines socio-economic factors in educational success, and assesses the impact of income inequality. Government initiatives to address economic disparities are explored, providing a holistic perspective on the role of economics in shaping high school education.

Chapter 5: Government Policies and High School Education

Policy frameworks play a pivotal role in shaping educational outcomes. This chapter scrutinizes global educational policies, evaluates the effectiveness of educational reforms, and addresses the challenges in policy implementation. By understanding the role of governments in education, readers gain insights into the mechanisms driving change in high school systems worldwide.

Chapter 6: Technology Integration in High School Education

The integration of technology in education is a dynamic and transformative process. This chapter explores global perspectives on educational technology, analyzes the digital divide and its implications, and assesses innovations in EdTech. Challenges and opportunities in technology integration are examined, providing a forward-looking perspective on the role of technology in high school education.

Chapter 7: Transition to Higher Education

Transitioning from high school to higher education is a critical juncture. This chapter unravels the challenges students face during this transition, examines vocational education and training as alternative paths, and explores the role of high school education in shaping diverse career paths. Global trends in higher education admission shed light on the evolving landscape beyond high school.

Chapter 8: Success Stories and Innovations in Education

Amidst challenges, this chapter introduces readers to educational initiatives that have made a difference. Innovations in addressing high school education challenges are explored, offering lessons learned from success stories. The scalability and replicability of these innovations are scrutinized, providing inspiration and practical insights for educators and policymakers.

Chapter 9: Global Assessments in High School Education

Assessment practices serve as benchmarks for educational quality. This chapter provides an overview of international assessments, explores the role of entities like PISA and TIMSS, and examines standardized testing practices globally. Alternative assessment methods are also considered, offering a holistic view of the varied ways in which educational success is measured.

Chapter 10: Standardized Testing: Pros and Cons

The use of standardized testing is a subject of debate and scrutiny. This chapter critically evaluates the advantages and limitations of standardized testing, analyzes its impact on educational policy, and explores evolving trends in this assessment methodology. By presenting a balanced perspective, the chapter contributes to informed discussions on the role of standardized testing in high school education.

Chapter 11: Quality Indicators in Education

Quality indicators are essential for assessing the effectiveness of educational systems. This chapter identifies key indicators of educational quality, explores their correlation with academic success, and addresses challenges in implementing quality indicators. By focusing on infrastructure, spending, and educational outcomes, the chapter provides a nuanced understanding of what defines a high-quality education.

Chapter 12: Global Educational Rankings

Educational rankings influence perceptions and policies. This chapter provides an overview of ranking systems, analyzes the criteria used in educational rankings, and explores the implications for educational policy. Criticisms and alternatives to ranking systems are considered, encouraging readers to critically evaluate the significance of global educational rankings.

Chapter 13: Emerging Trends and Future Prospects

The book concludes with a forward-looking chapter that explores the evolving landscape of high school education. Anticipated changes, challenges, and opportunities are examined, offering a glimpse into the future of high school classrooms. Global collaboration is envisioned as a key component of the future of high school education, emphasizing the potential for collective action in shaping a positive trajectory.

Conclusion: Key Findings and Call to Action

The concluding chapter synthesizes the key findings from each exploration, providing readers with a comprehensive understanding of the disparities, challenges, and innovations in global high school education. Implications for policymakers and educators are highlighted, and a compelling call to action is issued. The aim is to inspire readers to contribute actively to the ongoing dialogue on improving high school education globally, recognizing it as a shared responsibility and an investment in the future of individuals and societies.

As readers navigate through the chapters of "Global High School Classrooms," the scope and structure serve as guiding principles, ensuring a coherent and insightful exploration of the intricate tapestry of high school education worldwide. Each chapter contributes a unique perspective, building a holistic narrative that transcends borders and invites readers to be active participants in the collective endeavor to unveil the true potential of global high school classrooms.

Chapter 1: Geographic Variation in High School Education
Continental Perspectives

As we embark on a journey to explore the disparities in high school education levels globally, our first destination is an examination of high school systems through the lens of continental perspectives. The diverse continents of our world serve as distinct arenas where education is shaped by unique cultural, historical, and socioeconomic factors. Each continent's approach to high school education reflects a mosaic of influences, contributing to a rich tapestry of learning experiences for students.

North America: A Tapestry of Diversity

North America, comprising the United States and Canada, presents a complex tapestry of high school education. While sharing similarities, the two nations exhibit nuanced differences in their approaches. In the United States, a decentralized education system allows for significant state-level variations. The curriculum, graduation requirements, and even the structure of high school education can differ markedly from one state to another.

Canada, with its federal structure, manages to strike a balance between national standards and provincial autonomy. The emphasis on inclusivity and multicultural education is a defining feature, reflecting the nation's commitment to acknowledging and celebrating diversity. High school education in North America is also characterized by a strong vocational education component, providing students with alternative pathways to success.

The continent grapples with challenges such as educational inequality, particularly in the United States, where disparities between urban and rural schools and socio-economic factors impact access to quality education.

Understanding the dynamics of North American high school education requires navigating through these complexities and appreciating the ongoing efforts to address disparities.

Europe: Balancing Tradition and Innovation

Europe, a continent steeped in history and cultural diversity, showcases a high school education landscape that balances tradition with innovation. The European education system is characterized by a strong emphasis on academic rigor and a broad-based curriculum. Countries such as Germany and the United Kingdom have distinct pathways, with students often making early decisions about their educational trajectories.

The Bologna Process, initiated to create a unified European Higher Education Area, has influenced high school education by fostering standardization and mobility. However, continental disparities persist. Western European nations often boast well-established and well-funded educational systems, while Eastern European countries may face challenges related to infrastructure and resources.

Europe's approach to high school education reflects a commitment to preparing students for both academic and vocational pursuits. The continent's educational landscape is evolving, with a growing emphasis on digital literacy and adaptability in response to the demands of the modern workforce. Examining the continental perspectives of Europe unveils a delicate balance between preserving educational traditions and embracing innovation to address contemporary challenges.

Asia: A Hub of Academic Excellence and Intense Competition

Asia stands as a hub of academic excellence, marked by a strong emphasis on educational achievement and rigorous examination systems. Countries like China, South Korea, and

Japan have gained international recognition for their high-performing students in global assessments. The Confucian tradition of valuing education as a means of societal advancement is deeply ingrained in the region's cultural ethos.

High school education in Asia is often characterized by intense competition, with students facing rigorous entrance exams to access prestigious institutions. The curriculum places a heavy emphasis on STEM (Science, Technology, Engineering, and Mathematics) subjects, reflecting an alignment with economic priorities. However, this focus can sometimes lead to concerns about the neglect of broader skill sets such as creativity and critical thinking.

While countries like Singapore and China excel in global education rankings, disparities exist within nations. Urban-rural divides, economic disparities, and pressures on students to succeed in competitive environments contribute to challenges. Exploring Asia's continental perspectives necessitates a nuanced understanding of the delicate balance between academic excellence and the well-being of students.

Africa: Navigating Challenges with Resilience

Africa, a continent known for its diversity of cultures and languages, faces unique challenges in the realm of high school education. The legacy of colonialism has left a lasting impact on education systems, with disparities existing between nations and regions. While some African countries boast vibrant educational landscapes, others grapple with issues such as limited access to quality education, inadequate infrastructure, and linguistic diversity.

In many African nations, high school education is not only a pathway to personal development but also a means of addressing broader societal challenges. Efforts to overcome disparities include initiatives to enhance access to education, particularly for girls, and a focus on vocational training to meet the demands of local economies.

The continent's diverse educational approaches highlight the resilience of communities in navigating challenges. Understanding African perspectives on high school education requires acknowledging both the progress made and the ongoing efforts needed to ensure equitable access and quality education for all.

South America: Embracing Cultural Diversity

South America, with its rich cultural diversity and varying economic landscapes, presents a fascinating exploration of high school education. Countries like Brazil, Argentina, and Chile exhibit unique approaches shaped by their histories, indigenous influences, and economic structures.

In South America, education is often seen as a tool for social mobility, with a focus on inclusive policies to address historical inequalities. Some nations prioritize bilingual education to preserve indigenous languages, fostering a connection between cultural heritage and contemporary learning. However, challenges persist, including economic disparities and rural-urban divides that impact access to quality education.

South America's educational landscape is undergoing transformations, with a growing emphasis on innovation, technology, and international collaboration. The continent's commitment to embracing cultural diversity while addressing educational disparities provides a lens through which we can appreciate the complexities of high school education in the region.

Oceania: Nurturing Education in the Pacific Breeze

Oceania, comprising Australia and New Zealand along with numerous Pacific island nations, offers a distinctive perspective on high school education. Australia and New

Zealand boast well-established and comprehensive education systems that prioritize inclusivity and cultural awareness. Indigenous perspectives are increasingly integrated into curricula, acknowledging the historical context and contributing to a more holistic educational experience.

In the Pacific island nations, high school education often faces unique challenges, including geographical isolation, limited resources, and the impact of climate change on educational infrastructure. Efforts to address disparities involve a blend of traditional knowledge and contemporary educational practices.

Oceania's continental perspectives illustrate the delicate balance between nurturing education in well-established systems and addressing the specific challenges faced by smaller nations in the Pacific. The region's commitment to inclusivity, cultural sensitivity, and environmental sustainability shapes the narrative of high school education in Oceania.

Conclusion: Navigating the Global Tapestry

Continental perspectives on high school education provide a crucial foundation for understanding the complexities and diversities that shape learning experiences across the globe. From the intense competition in Asia to the resilience in overcoming challenges in Africa, each continent contributes unique insights to the global tapestry of high school education.

As we traverse these continental landscapes, it becomes evident that the disparities and challenges are as diverse as the nations themselves. Recognizing the strengths, acknowledging the challenges, and understanding the cultural contexts are essential steps toward formulating global strategies that enhance the quality and inclusivity of high school education. The journey through continental perspectives sets the stage for deeper explorations into regional disparities, country-specific challenges, and the overarching global goals that guide the future of high school education.

Regional Disparities

In our exploration of high school education on a global scale, the canvas of regional disparities emerges as a critical focal point. Regions, defined by geographical, cultural, and economic contexts, manifest distinct educational landscapes that contribute to the intricate tapestry of global learning experiences. As we delve into the regional disparities, we unravel the challenges and opportunities faced by high school students across different parts of the world.

Latin America: Striving for Inclusive Education

Latin America, a region known for its vibrant cultures and histories, grapples with regional disparities in high school education. Countries like Mexico, Brazil, and Argentina coexist with nations facing economic challenges and limited resources. Urban-rural divides, coupled with socio-economic inequalities, contribute to disparities in educational access and quality.

In Latin America, high school education is often perceived as a means of overcoming historical inequalities. Initiatives focus on inclusive policies, including efforts to bridge the gap between urban and rural educational opportunities. However, challenges persist, including a need for improved infrastructure, teacher training, and the incorporation of technology to enhance learning experiences.

Navigating through Latin America's regional disparities offers insights into the complex dynamics of balancing cultural richness with the imperative of providing equitable high school education. The region's commitment to inclusive education stands as a testament to ongoing efforts to address disparities and empower students from diverse backgrounds.

Sub-Saharan Africa: Navigating Educational Challenges

Sub-Saharan Africa, a vast and diverse region, grapples with unique challenges in high school education. The legacy of colonialism, linguistic diversity, and economic constraints contribute to disparities in educational access and outcomes. Regional variations in infrastructure, teacher quality, and curriculum implementation further underscore the complexities faced by Sub-Saharan African nations.

Efforts to address regional disparities in Sub-Saharan Africa include initiatives to improve access to education, particularly for girls, and the promotion of vocational training to meet local economic needs. The region's commitment to education as a tool for societal development is evident, but persistent challenges such as limited resources and political instability shape the high school landscape.

Exploring Sub-Saharan Africa's regional disparities sheds light on the resilience of communities in navigating challenges. The region's commitment to education as a catalyst for societal progress stands as an inspiration amidst the multifaceted complexities faced by high school education in diverse African nations.

Middle East and North Africa: Balancing Tradition and Modernization

The Middle East and North Africa (MENA) region, characterized by rich histories and cultural diversity, grapples with regional disparities in high school education. Nations like Saudi Arabia, Egypt, and the United Arab Emirates exhibit distinct approaches shaped by cultural traditions, economic structures, and geopolitical considerations.

In MENA, high school education often balances the preservation of cultural values with the demands of a globalized world. Regional disparities emerge in the availability of resources, quality of infrastructure, and gender-based educational access. Initiatives in the region aim to modernize educational systems, incorporate technology, and empower youth for the challenges of the 21st century.

Navigating through the Middle East and North Africa's regional disparities provides insights into the delicate balance between tradition and modernization. The region's commitment to high-quality education, even amidst regional complexities, reflects a vision for equipping students with the skills necessary for a rapidly evolving global landscape.

East Asia: Excellence and Intensity

East Asia, comprising economic powerhouses such as China, Japan, and South Korea, stands as a region known for educational excellence and intense academic competition. Regional disparities in high school education are influenced by cultural values, economic development, and societal expectations.

Countries in East Asia often prioritize STEM subjects, and students face competitive entrance exams for prestigious institutions. While the region excels in global education rankings, disparities exist within nations, including urban-rural divides and pressures on students to succeed. Regional initiatives focus on addressing these challenges, promoting creativity, and nurturing a more holistic approach to education.

Exploring regional disparities in East Asia unveils the intense academic culture, innovative teaching methodologies, and ongoing efforts to strike a balance between academic excellence and the well-being of students. The region's commitment to educational innovation and adaptability stands as a testament to its vision for shaping global citizens.

South Asia: Addressing Educational Inequalities

South Asia, a region marked by diversity and contrasts, grapples with regional disparities in high school education. Nations like India, Pakistan, and Bangladesh exhibit variations in educational access, quality, and cultural influences. Economic conditions, linguistic diversity, and historical legacies contribute to the complexities faced by South Asian nations.

In South Asia, disparities are evident in access to education, with rural areas facing challenges compared to urban centers. Efforts to address regional disparities include initiatives to enhance access, improve teacher quality, and bridge the gap between traditional and modern education. The region's commitment to education as a tool for social change is reflected in ongoing efforts to address historical inequalities.

Navigating through South Asia's regional disparities provides insights into the diverse cultural influences, economic challenges, and innovative educational approaches. The region's commitment to inclusive and accessible high school education emerges as a pivotal force in addressing disparities and fostering societal progress.

Europe: Bridging Eastern and Western Approaches

Europe, a continent marked by cultural richness and historical legacies, navigates regional disparities in high school education. Western European nations, such as Germany and France, coexist with Eastern European countries, each exhibiting unique educational approaches shaped by historical contexts and economic structures.

While Western European nations often prioritize comprehensive and inclusive educational systems, Eastern European countries may face challenges related to resources and infrastructure. Efforts to bridge regional disparities include initiatives to standardize education through the Bologna Process and promote cross-cultural understanding.

Exploring regional disparities in Europe provides insights into the delicate balance between Eastern and Western educational approaches. The region's commitment to fostering collaboration, cultural exchange, and educational standardization reflects a vision for a unified European educational landscape.

North America: Balancing Autonomy and National Standards

North America, comprising the United States and Canada, grapples with regional disparities influenced by the continent's vast geographical expanse and cultural diversity. While sharing similarities, the two nations exhibit nuanced differences in their approaches to high school education. The United States, with its decentralized education system, allows for significant state-level variations, contributing to regional disparities.

In Canada, a federal structure strikes a balance between national standards and provincial autonomy. The emphasis on inclusivity and multicultural education is a defining feature, reflecting the nation's commitment to acknowledging and celebrating diversity. Regional disparities emerge in the availability of resources, linguistic diversity, and urban-rural divides.

Navigating through North America's regional disparities provides insights into the intricate dynamics of balancing autonomy with national standards. The region's commitment to diversity, innovation, and inclusivity reflects ongoing efforts to address disparities and shape a high school education system that caters to the needs of diverse communities.

Oceania: Synthesizing Indigenous and Contemporary Education

Oceania, comprising Australia, New Zealand, and numerous Pacific island nations, faces regional disparities influenced by the continent's geographical diversity and cultural richness. Australia and New Zealand boast well-established and comprehensive education systems, while Pacific island nations may encounter challenges related to limited resources, geographical isolation, and the impact of climate change.

Efforts to address regional disparities involve synthesizing indigenous knowledge with contemporary educational practices. In Australia and New Zealand, there is a growing emphasis on incorporating indigenous perspectives into curricula, fostering cultural awareness and sensitivity. In the Pacific islands, initiatives focus on overcoming geographical challenges and promoting sustainable education.

Navigating through Oceania's regional disparities provides insights into the delicate balance between preserving indigenous knowledge and embracing contemporary educational approaches. The region's commitment to inclusivity, cultural sensitivity, and environmental sustainability shapes the narrative of high school education, reflecting a vision for a harmonious coexistence of diverse perspectives.

Conclusion: Unveiling Regional Dynamics

Regional disparities in high school education encapsulate the diverse challenges and opportunities that shape the educational experiences of students across the globe. From Latin America's pursuit of inclusive education to East Asia's excellence and intensity, each region contributes a unique chapter to the global narrative of learning.

As we unveil the regional dynamics, it becomes evident that regional disparities are not merely challenges to be overcome but reflections of the intricate interplay between cultural, economic, and historical factors. The commitment of regions to address disparities, foster inclusivity, and provide quality education stands as a testament to the shared vision of creating a world where every student has the opportunity to thrive.

The journey through regional disparities sets the stage for delving deeper into country-specific challenges, global education goals, and the collective efforts needed to shape a future where high school education is truly a gateway to empowerment, irrespective of geographical boundaries. The regional dynamics enrich our understanding of the complexities and nuances that define the global tapestry of high school education.

Country-specific Challenges

Embarking on a journey to understand the global landscape of high school education, it is crucial to dissect the unique challenges faced by individual countries. Within each geographical region, nations grapple with distinct socio-economic, cultural, and historical factors that mold their educational systems. Examining country-specific challenges unveils the intricacies that contribute to the broader disparities in high school education globally.

United States: The Quandary of Educational Inequality

In the United States, a nation often seen as a beacon of opportunity, high school education faces the perennial challenge of educational inequality. Despite strides towards inclusivity, socio-economic disparities persist, resulting in divergent educational experiences for students based on their economic backgrounds, geographical locations, and racial demographics.

Urban schools, especially those in economically disadvantaged areas, often grapple with limited resources, outdated infrastructure, and a dearth of qualified teachers. The digital divide exacerbates these challenges, as students from low-income families may lack access to essential technology for modern learning.

Moreover, the U.S. educational system's decentralized nature contributes to disparities. Each state operates with a degree of autonomy, shaping its curriculum, graduation requirements, and educational standards. Consequently, students' experiences can vary significantly depending on their geographic location.

Addressing country-specific challenges in the United States necessitates a comprehensive approach that includes targeted investments in underprivileged communities, equitable distribution of resources, and policy reforms to bridge the gap in educational outcomes.

Canada: Balancing Bilingualism and Cultural Diversity

Canada, with its commitment to bilingualism and cultural diversity, grapples with the challenge of balancing inclusivity with the preservation of cultural identities. The coexistence of English and French as official languages adds complexity to the educational landscape, requiring tailored approaches to cater to diverse linguistic backgrounds.

Indigenous communities in Canada face unique challenges, including historical injustices, insufficient resources, and the need for culturally sensitive education. Efforts to address these challenges involve integrating Indigenous perspectives into the curriculum, enhancing teacher training on cultural awareness, and fostering partnerships between Indigenous communities and educational institutions.

Canada's commitment to inclusivity is evident, but ongoing efforts are needed to ensure that high school education caters to the diverse needs of students from different linguistic and cultural backgrounds. Striking a balance between national unity and cultural diversity remains a persistent challenge.

Germany: The Dual Education Dilemma

In Germany, the dual education system, which combines vocational training with academic learning, presents both strengths and challenges. While the system is praised for its emphasis on practical skills and early integration into the workforce, it also perpetuates a perceived hierarchy between academic and vocational pathways.

Students in the vocational track may face societal stereotypes and limited opportunities for advancement. Addressing these challenges involves destigmatizing vocational education, creating pathways for seamless transitions between vocational and academic tracks, and ensuring that students have access to comprehensive career guidance.

Germany's dual education system requires ongoing reforms to adapt to the evolving demands of the global economy while maintaining its commitment to providing students with practical skills for successful careers.

China: Striving for Equality Amidst Intense Competition

China, with its globally recognized emphasis on academic achievement, faces challenges related to intense competition and the pursuit of educational equality. The Gaokao, the national college entrance examination, is a high-stakes test that plays a decisive role in determining students' academic trajectories.

The intense competition for limited spots in prestigious universities can result in immense pressure on students, leading to mental health concerns. Additionally, rural-urban divides in educational resources and opportunities contribute to disparities in academic outcomes.

China's educational policymakers are striving to address these challenges by reforming the examination system, promoting holistic education, and investing in rural education infrastructure. The goal is to ensure that every student, regardless of their background, has equal access to quality high school education and the opportunity for higher education.

India: Navigating Vast Diversity and Access Challenges

India, with its vast cultural and linguistic diversity, faces the complex challenge of providing inclusive and equitable high school education. Disparities in educational access between urban and rural areas persist, with rural schools often lacking infrastructure, qualified teachers, and access to technology.

The caste system and socio-economic inequalities further contribute to disparities in educational opportunities. Marginalized communities, including Dalits and tribal populations, often face discrimination, limiting their access to quality education. Gender-based disparities also exist, with girls encountering barriers to education in certain regions.

India's approach to addressing these challenges involves initiatives such as the Sarva Shiksha Abhiyan (Education for All) program, which aims to enhance access to primary and secondary education. However, sustained efforts are required to ensure that high school education reaches every corner of this diverse nation.

South Africa: Overcoming the Legacy of Apartheid

South Africa, with its tumultuous history of apartheid, confronts the enduring challenges of addressing historical injustices and building an inclusive high school education system. The legacy of apartheid has left a lasting impact on educational disparities, with significant gaps in resources, infrastructure, and educational outcomes.

Historically disadvantaged communities, primarily composed of Black South Africans, often face substandard educational conditions. Efforts to overcome these challenges include initiatives to redress historical imbalances, improve teacher training, and enhance infrastructure in underserved areas.

While progress has been made, addressing the legacy of apartheid requires sustained commitment to dismantling systemic inequalities and ensuring that every student in South Africa has access to a high-quality education.

Brazil: The Struggle for Quality Education

In Brazil, the struggle for quality high school education is evident in the disparities between urban and rural areas, as well as the challenges posed by economic inequality. Urban schools in affluent neighborhoods often enjoy better resources, infrastructure, and qualified teachers, while rural schools face limitations in access to educational facilities.

The economic divide contributes to variations in the quality of education, with students from lower-income backgrounds encountering barriers to academic success. Additionally, cultural and linguistic diversity within the country presents challenges in crafting an inclusive curriculum that reflects the nation's rich heritage.

Brazil's commitment to addressing these challenges involves targeted investments in rural education, initiatives to bridge economic disparities, and reforms to enhance the overall quality of high school education. The nation's educational policymakers are navigating the complexities of cultural diversity and economic inequality to shape a more equitable educational landscape.

Australia: The Indigenous Education Imperative

Australia, with its commitment to inclusivity and cultural awareness, grapples with the imperative of providing quality education to Indigenous communities. The historical injustices faced by Indigenous Australians, including forced removal of children from their families, have left a legacy of educational disparities.

Efforts to address these challenges involve initiatives to incorporate Indigenous perspectives into the curriculum, enhance teacher training on cultural sensitivity, and foster partnerships between educational institutions and Indigenous communities. However, persistent disparities in educational outcomes and access to resources highlight the need for ongoing reforms.

Australia's commitment to Indigenous education reflects a broader national aspiration for inclusivity and acknowledgment of the rich cultural heritage of the continent. Bridging the gaps in Indigenous education remains a priority for shaping a more equitable high school education system.

Conclusion: Unveiling Diversity in Educational Challenges

Country-specific challenges in high school education unveil the remarkable diversity of issues faced by nations across the globe. From the pursuit of educational equality in the United States to the dual education dilemma in Germany, each country grapples with unique circumstances that shape its approach to high school education.

As we navigate through the complexities of educational challenges, it becomes evident that a one-size-fits-all solution is insufficient. Tailored approaches, rooted in an understanding of each country's socio-economic, cultural, and historical context, are essential to addressing disparities and fostering inclusive high school education.

The collective commitment of nations to overcome these challenges reflects a shared vision for a future where every student, regardless of their background, has the opportunity to access quality education and realize their full potential. The journey through country-specific challenges sets the stage for a deeper exploration of global education goals and the collaborative efforts needed to shape a more equitable and empowering high school education landscape.

Global Education Goals and Disparities

In the vast tapestry of global high school education, the pursuit of common goals unites nations, yet disparities persist, creating challenges on the path to achieving universal access, quality, and inclusivity. This exploration delves into the shared aspirations and persistent inequities that characterize the global landscape of high school education.

Common Aspirations: United Nations' Sustainable Development Goals

The pursuit of global education goals is encapsulated in the United Nations' Sustainable Development Goals (SDGs), with Goal 4 specifically dedicated to "Quality Education." The SDGs aim to ensure inclusive and equitable quality education for all by 2030. This overarching goal recognizes education as a fundamental human right and a catalyst for sustainable development.

Under Goal 4, the targets include universal access to free primary and secondary education, elimination of gender disparities in education, and ensuring equal access to vocational training. The SDGs provide a comprehensive framework that encourages countries to address disparities, improve educational quality, and promote lifelong learning opportunities.

Despite these admirable aspirations, the global high school education landscape reveals persistent disparities that challenge the realization of these goals. Examining these disparities in the context of specific regions and countries unveils the intricate dynamics that shape the journey towards achieving universal education.

Access Disparities: Barriers to Enrollment and Completion

One of the primary challenges in achieving global education goals is the persistent disparity in access to high school education. While the SDGs advocate for universal access, barriers such as economic inequalities, geographical remoteness, and gender-based discrimination often impede enrollment and completion.

In many developing nations, economic conditions force families to prioritize immediate needs over education, leading to high dropout rates, especially at the high school level. Geographical challenges, including the lack of schools in remote areas, contribute to unequal access, particularly in regions with dispersed populations.

Gender disparities further compound the issue, with cultural norms, societal expectations, and economic factors limiting girls' access to education. Despite progress in some regions, girls, especially in rural areas, still face barriers to completing high school.

Addressing access disparities requires multifaceted strategies, including targeted interventions to alleviate economic barriers, infrastructure development in remote areas, and initiatives to challenge gender stereotypes and promote girls' education.

Quality Disparities: Varied Standards and Resource Allocation

While access is a critical concern, the quality of high school education is equally pivotal in achieving global goals. Disparities in the quality of education often arise from variations in standards, curriculum, teacher training, and resource allocation.

Countries with well-established education systems may have rigorous standards and comprehensive curricula, providing students with a holistic learning experience. However, in regions facing economic challenges or political instability, the quality of education may be compromised due to insufficient resources, outdated curricula, and inadequate teacher training.

Resource allocation disparities are evident in urban-rural divides, with urban schools often benefiting from better infrastructure, qualified teachers, and access to technology. In contrast, rural schools may lack essential resources, impacting the overall quality of education.

Bridging quality disparities requires a concerted effort to standardize curricula, enhance teacher training programs, and ensure equitable distribution of resources. Additionally, embracing innovative teaching methodologies and integrating technology can contribute to enhancing the overall quality of high school education.

Inclusivity Disparities: Addressing Diverse Learning Needs

Inclusivity is a cornerstone of global education goals, emphasizing the need to accommodate diverse learning needs, including those of students with disabilities and those from marginalized communities. Despite progress, disparities persist in creating truly inclusive high school environments.

Students with disabilities often face physical and attitudinal barriers that limit their participation in mainstream education. While inclusive education policies exist in many countries, implementation challenges, lack of specialized support, and societal stigmas hinder the full integration of students with disabilities into high schools.

Marginalized communities, including ethnic minorities and indigenous populations, may encounter cultural biases, linguistic challenges, and insufficient representation in educational materials. Achieving true inclusivity requires not only policy changes but also cultural sensitivity, teacher training, and efforts to address systemic biases.

Creating inclusive high school environments involves adapting teaching methodologies to accommodate diverse learning styles, providing necessary support services, and promoting a culture of acceptance and diversity within educational institutions.

Global Collaboration Challenges: Navigating Political and Cultural Realities

The pursuit of global education goals requires collaboration and shared commitment from nations worldwide. However, challenges arise in navigating the political, cultural, and economic realities that shape each country's approach to education.

Political factors, including geopolitical tensions, diplomatic relations, and national priorities, can influence the willingness of nations to collaborate on educational initiatives. Cultural differences may impact the reception and implementation of global educational frameworks, requiring a nuanced understanding of diverse perspectives.

Economic disparities among nations contribute to variations in the financial commitment to education. While some countries may allocate substantial resources to achieve global education goals, others may face economic constraints that limit their capacity to invest in education infrastructure and programs.

Overcoming these challenges necessitates diplomatic efforts to foster collaboration, cultural sensitivity in the design of global educational frameworks, and targeted financial support to nations facing economic challenges. International organizations, non-governmental entities, and diplomatic forums play a crucial role in facilitating global collaboration for education.

Technology Divide: Implications for Learning Opportunities

The integration of technology in education is a key aspect of achieving global education goals. However, a significant global divide in access to technology, known as the digital divide, poses challenges to ensuring equal learning opportunities for all students.

In developed nations, students often have access to advanced technology, including laptops, tablets, and high-speed internet, facilitating digital learning experiences. In contrast, students in developing nations, especially those in remote areas, may lack access to basic technology, limiting their exposure to digital learning resources.

The implications of the technology divide go beyond access to hardware and connectivity. It also influences students' digital literacy, their ability to adapt to technological advancements, and their preparedness for the demands of a technology-driven workforce.

Addressing the technology divide requires concerted efforts to provide infrastructure, digital devices, and internet connectivity to all schools globally. Additionally, digital literacy programs and initiatives to incorporate technology into teaching methodologies can help bridge the gap and ensure that all students have equal access to the benefits of digital learning.

Language and Cultural Relevance: Enhancing Learning Experiences

The language of instruction and the cultural relevance of educational content significantly impact the learning experiences of students. Disparities in language and cultural representation can hinder effective communication, understanding, and engagement in the learning process.

In multilingual countries, the choice of the language of instruction can be a source of disparities, with students from different linguistic backgrounds facing challenges in accessing and comprehending educational content. This issue is particularly pronounced in regions with numerous indigenous languages.

Cultural relevance in educational materials is equally crucial. A curriculum that reflects the diversity of cultures and perspectives enhances students' sense of identity and connection to the content. However, disparities may arise when educational materials favor certain cultural narratives, leading to a lack of representation for diverse backgrounds.

Efforts to address language and cultural disparities involve inclusive language policies, the incorporation of indigenous languages in curricula, and the development of culturally relevant educational materials. These initiatives contribute to creating an inclusive and empowering learning environment for all students.

Conclusion: Navigating the Global Educational Landscape

The pursuit of global education goals is a shared endeavor that requires acknowledgment of the diverse challenges and disparities shaping the high school education landscape. While the United Nations' Sustainable Development Goals provide a comprehensive framework, the complexities of access, quality, inclusivity, and global collaboration demand tailored approaches.

As nations navigate the intricate dynamics of their educational systems, it is essential to recognize the interplay of socio-economic, cultural, and political factors that contribute to disparities. Bridging these gaps requires a commitment to equity, innovative solutions, and international cooperation.

The global educational landscape is a mosaic of diverse challenges and aspirations, each contributing to the evolving narrative of high school education. Understanding and addressing these disparities pave the way for a future where every student, regardless of their geographical location or socio-economic background, can access quality education and contribute to a more equitable and sustainable world.

Chapter 2: Educational Systems Around the World
Structure of High School Education

The structure of high school education varies significantly across the globe, reflecting diverse educational philosophies, cultural values, and societal expectations. This exploration delves into the intricate details of how high school education is structured in different countries, shedding light on the duration, curriculum, and pathways that shape the learning journey of students worldwide.

United States: A Varied Landscape of Secondary Education

In the United States, high school education typically spans four years, starting in the 9th grade and concluding with the 12th grade. The structure is designed to provide a comprehensive educational experience, covering a broad range of subjects in the initial years and allowing for more specialized study in the later years.

The core curriculum often includes subjects such as English, mathematics, science, and social studies. Students are required to accumulate a certain number of credits in various subjects to graduate. Additionally, elective courses enable students to explore specific areas of interest, fostering a well-rounded education.

Extracurricular activities, including sports, arts, and community service, are integral to the American high school experience, emphasizing holistic development beyond academic achievement. The flexibility of the system allows for diverse learning pathways, including honors classes, Advanced Placement (AP) courses, and vocational education programs.

The culmination of high school education in the U.S. is marked by graduation ceremonies, and students are awarded a high school diploma upon successful completion of the requirements. Post-graduation, students often pursue higher education or enter the workforce.

United Kingdom: Specialization through GCSEs and A-Levels

The United Kingdom follows a distinct structure for high school education, emphasizing specialization in the later years. The process begins with General Certificate of Secondary Education (GCSE) examinations typically taken at age 16. Students choose subjects for their GCSEs, laying the foundation for further specialization.

After GCSEs, students can choose between different educational paths. One prominent option is the pursuit of A-Levels (Advanced Levels), a two-year program that allows for in-depth study of a smaller number of subjects. A-Levels are a crucial determinant for university admissions in the UK.

Another pathway is the completion of vocational qualifications, such as BTECs (Business and Technology Education Council) or apprenticeships. These options provide practical, skills-based education and cater to students with diverse learning preferences.

The culmination of high school education in the UK is marked by A-Level examinations, and successful students can proceed to university or other higher education institutions. The British system's emphasis on specialization early in the education journey provides students with a focused and in-depth understanding of their chosen subjects.

Germany: The Dual System and Vocational Training

In Germany, high school education takes a unique form with the integration of the dual education system. The dual system combines academic learning with practical, on-the-job training, offering students a blend of theoretical knowledge and real-world application.

High school education in Germany typically concludes with the Abitur examination, which is a prerequisite for university admission. However, a significant proportion of German students opt for vocational training programs after completing their compulsory education.

Vocational education in Germany involves apprenticeships, where students work in a company while simultaneously attending vocational school. This hands-on approach equips students with practical skills and prepares them for specific careers. The emphasis on vocational training is a distinctive feature of the German education system, contributing to the nation's robust workforce.

The dual system allows students to choose between an academic path leading to university or a vocational path leading to skilled employment. This flexibility caters to diverse career aspirations and ensures that students receive education tailored to their individual strengths and preferences.

China: Gaokao and the Academic Gauntlet

In China, high school education culminates in the gaokao, the national college entrance examination. The structure of high school education is geared towards preparing students for this high-stakes examination, which plays a pivotal role in determining university admissions.

Chinese high school education typically spans three years, starting from the 10th grade. The curriculum is standardized and focuses on subjects such as Chinese, mathematics, foreign languages, and sciences. Students are required to accumulate a certain number of credits in specific subjects to qualify for the gaokao.

The intensity of academic competition in China is a defining characteristic of the high school experience. Students often attend additional classes, known as "cram schools," to supplement their regular studies and enhance their chances of success in the gaokao.

The gaokao is administered annually, and students' performance in this examination determines their eligibility for admission to universities. The structure of high school education in China is designed to prepare students rigorously for this academic gauntlet, reflecting the societal emphasis on educational achievement as a pathway to success.

Japan: The Rigorous Journey to University

In Japan, high school education follows a three-year structure, with the final year being particularly crucial for university entrance examinations. The curriculum is standardized, covering subjects such as Japanese language, mathematics, science, social studies, and foreign languages.

The culmination of high school education in Japan is marked by the National Center Test for University Admissions, a standardized test that assesses students' academic abilities. Additionally, individual universities may conduct their own entrance examinations, focusing on specific subjects relevant to their programs.

The emphasis on rigorous academic preparation is a hallmark of the Japanese education system. High school students often attend "juku" or private tutoring schools to supplement their studies and enhance their performance in university entrance examinations. The competition for admission to prestigious universities is intense, reflecting the societal value placed on educational attainment.

Upon successful completion of high school and university entrance examinations, students can pursue higher education or enter the workforce. The Japanese education system's structured approach prepares students for the challenges of university-level studies and beyond.

South Korea: The Suneung and Academic Pressures

South Korea's high school education structure revolves around the College Scholastic Ability Test, known as suneung. Similar to China's gaokao, the suneung is a high-stakes examination that determines university admissions and, consequently, plays a pivotal role in shaping students' academic journeys.

High school education in South Korea spans three years, and the curriculum is standardized, covering subjects such as Korean language, mathematics, sciences, and foreign languages. The intensity of academic competition is heightened by the societal expectation that success in the suneung opens doors to prestigious universities and promising careers.

The suneung is administered annually, and students devote significant time and effort to preparing for this crucial examination. The competitive nature of the South Korean education system has led to concerns about the well-being of students, prompting discussions about potential reforms to alleviate academic pressures.

Upon successful completion of the suneung, students can pursue higher education or enter the workforce. The structured nature of high school education in South Korea reflects a societal emphasis on academic excellence as a pathway to success.

India: A Diverse Landscape of High School Education

In India, the structure of high school education varies across different states and education boards. However, a common framework involves a 10+2 system, where students complete ten years of basic education followed by two years of higher secondary education.

The higher secondary stage, often referred to as the 11th and 12th grades, is crucial as it prepares students for higher education or entry into the workforce. Students typically choose between three streams: Science, Commerce, and Arts, each offering a specialized curriculum aligned with specific career pathways.

The Central Board of Secondary Education (CBSE) and the Indian Certificate of Secondary Education (ICSE) are prominent education boards in India, each with its own curriculum and examination system. State boards also play a significant role, contributing to the diversity in the structure of high school education.

The culmination of high school education is marked by board examinations, and successful students receive a higher secondary certificate. Post-high school, students can pursue undergraduate studies or opt for vocational training programs, contributing to the diverse educational landscape in India.

Brazil: Ensino Médio and the Path to Higher Education

In Brazil, high school education is referred to as "Ensino Médio" and typically spans three years. The curriculum is comprehensive, covering subjects such as Portuguese, mathematics, sciences, humanities, and foreign languages. High school education in Brazil aims to provide students with a well-rounded education and prepare them for higher education or vocational pathways.

The structure of Ensino Médio includes a common core curriculum along with elective subjects, allowing students to tailor their education based on their interests and career aspirations. Additionally, vocational education programs are available for students who prefer a more skills-focused approach.

The culmination of Ensino Médio is marked by the Exame Nacional do Ensino Médio (ENEM), a standardized test used for university admissions. Successful completion of high school and a satisfactory performance in the ENEM open doors to higher education opportunities.

The diversity in Brazil's education system allows students to choose between academic and vocational paths, contributing to a flexible and inclusive high school education structure.

Conclusion: Navigating Educational Pathways

The structure of high school education worldwide reflects a rich tapestry of approaches, each shaped by cultural values, societal expectations, and educational philosophies. From the flexible and diverse system in the United States to the specialization-focused paths in the United Kingdom, Germany, and Japan, each country's approach provides unique insights into the priorities and goals of their education systems.

Understanding the structure of high school education is essential for appreciating the diverse pathways available to students globally. The emphasis on academic rigor, vocational training, or a combination of both reflects the broader societal values and economic needs of each nation.

As nations navigate the complexities of their educational systems, the continuous evolution of high school education underscores the importance of adaptability and responsiveness to the changing needs of students and society. The exploration of educational pathways sets the stage for further examination of curriculum variations, grading systems, and teaching methodologies, contributing to a comprehensive understanding of global high school education.

Curriculum Variations

The curriculum is the heart of any educational system, shaping the knowledge, skills, and perspectives that students acquire during their high school journey. Across the globe, diverse approaches to curriculum design reflect cultural values, educational philosophies, and societal needs. This exploration delves into the variations in high school curricula, providing insights into how different countries structure their educational content to prepare students for the challenges of the future.

United States: Flexibility and Electives

The curriculum in the United States is characterized by its flexibility and emphasis on choice. High school students have the opportunity to explore a wide range of subjects before deciding on a more focused academic path. The core curriculum typically includes English, mathematics, science, and social studies, providing a foundation for future studies.

One notable feature of the American high school system is the availability of elective courses. These courses allow students to tailor their education to their interests and aspirations. Whether it's delving into the arts, participating in vocational programs, or exploring advanced topics through Advanced Placement (AP) courses, students can shape their educational experience according to their preferences.

The flexibility of the curriculum is complemented by a credit system, where students earn credits for completing courses. This system allows for individualized learning paths and accommodates diverse student needs. The emphasis on a broad yet customizable curriculum aligns with the American belief in fostering well-rounded individuals ready for the challenges of an ever-changing world.

United Kingdom: Specialization through GCSEs and A-Levels

In the United Kingdom, the curriculum is structured to allow students to specialize in specific subjects as they progress through high school. The General Certificate of Secondary Education (GCSE) marks the first significant stage, where students choose subjects they wish to study in depth.

GCSEs cover a range of subjects, including core subjects such as English, mathematics, and science, along with optional subjects like history, geography, or foreign languages. The flexibility of GCSEs sets the stage for the next phase of specialization.

Post-GCSE, students can opt for A-Levels (Advanced Levels) or vocational qualifications. A-Levels offer an in-depth study of a smaller number of subjects, providing a pathway to university. The emphasis on specialization aligns with the British approach to preparing students for higher education or specific career paths.

The structured nature of the curriculum ensures that students acquire a deep understanding of their chosen subjects, fostering expertise and knowledge in areas that align with their interests and aspirations.

Germany: Dual System Integrating Theory and Practice

Germany's curriculum reflects the unique dual education system, which integrates theoretical learning with practical, on-the-job training. The high school curriculum, leading to the Abitur examination, includes a mix of academic subjects and vocational training.

Academic subjects encompass a broad range, including languages, mathematics, sciences, and humanities. Simultaneously, vocational training involves hands-on experience in a chosen field through apprenticeships. This dual approach prepares students for both academic pursuits and skilled employment.

The emphasis on practical skills and real-world application distinguishes the German curriculum. The integration of vocational training ensures that students develop not only theoretical knowledge but also the practical skills needed for successful careers. This approach aligns with Germany's commitment to a strong and versatile workforce.

China: Gaokao-driven Academic Rigor

China's high school curriculum is designed with a singular focus – preparing students for the gaokao, the national college entrance examination. The curriculum is standardized, covering subjects such as Chinese, mathematics, foreign languages, and sciences.

The intensity of the curriculum is heightened by the gaokao's role in determining university admissions. Students undergo rigorous preparation, often attending additional classes to supplement their studies and enhance their chances of success in the examination.

While the curriculum is comprehensive, the emphasis on exam-oriented education has led to discussions about the potential drawbacks, including concerns about student well-being and creativity. Balancing academic rigor with holistic development remains a topic of ongoing debate within the Chinese education system.

Japan: Preparation for University Entrance Examinations

Japan's high school curriculum is structured to prepare students for the demanding university entrance examinations. The curriculum covers a range of subjects, including Japanese language, mathematics, sciences, and foreign languages.

The culmination of high school education in Japan is marked by the National Center Test for University Admissions, along with individual university entrance examinations. The structured nature of the curriculum aligns with the academic pressures associated with the pursuit of higher education.

Supplementary education, including attendance at private tutoring schools (juku), is common, reflecting the societal expectation of academic excellence. While the curriculum provides a strong academic foundation, concerns about student well-being and the need for a more balanced approach continue to shape discussions on educational reforms in Japan.

South Korea: Suneung-focused Intensity

Similar to China, South Korea's high school curriculum centers around preparing students for the suneung, the College Scholastic Ability Test. The curriculum covers subjects such as Korean language, mathematics, sciences, and foreign languages, aligning with the content tested in the suneung.

The intense focus on academic achievement, driven by the importance of the suneung in university admissions, has led to discussions about the well-being of students. Efforts to address the pressures associated with high-stakes examinations include discussions about potential reforms to create a more balanced and holistic approach to education.

While the curriculum provides a solid foundation for academic success, ongoing discussions within South Korea's education system emphasize the importance of fostering creativity, critical thinking, and overall well-being.

India: 10+2 System with Stream Specialization

India's high school curriculum follows a 10+2 system, with ten years of basic education followed by two years of higher secondary education. The higher secondary stage allows students to choose between three streams: Science, Commerce, and Arts.

The Science stream typically includes subjects such as physics, chemistry, mathematics, and biology. Commerce focuses on subjects like accounting, economics, and business studies. Arts encompasses a range of subjects, including literature, history, and the social sciences.

The curriculum is designed to provide students with a strong foundation in their chosen streams, preparing them for higher education or vocational pathways. The flexibility within the 10+2 system caters to diverse career aspirations, allowing students to align their education with their interests and goals.

Brazil: Comprehensive Ensino Médio

Brazil's high school curriculum, known as Ensino Médio, is comprehensive and covers a wide range of subjects. The curriculum includes Portuguese, mathematics, sciences, humanities, and foreign languages, providing students with a well-rounded education.

Ensino Médio incorporates both a common core curriculum and elective subjects, allowing students to tailor their education based on their interests. Vocational education programs are also available, offering a more specialized and skills-focused approach.

The culmination of Ensino Médio is marked by the Exame Nacional do Ensino Médio (ENEM), a standardized test used for university admissions. The diverse nature of the curriculum ensures that students receive a balanced education, providing a foundation for future academic and career pursuits.

Comparative Analysis: Diverse Philosophies, Common Goals

Examining these diverse curricular approaches highlights the varying philosophies that underpin high school education across the globe. The United States emphasizes flexibility and choice, allowing students to explore a broad range of subjects before committing to more specialized areas. In contrast, countries like China and South Korea place a significant emphasis on standardized testing, guiding the curriculum towards preparation for high-stakes examinations.

Germany's integration of vocational training reflects a commitment to practical skills, aligning with the nation's strong emphasis on workforce development. The United Kingdom's focus on specialization through A-Levels prepares students for in-depth study in their chosen subjects, while Japan and India's structured systems gear students towards university entrance examinations.

Despite these differences, there are common threads woven into the fabric of high school curricula globally. The emphasis on providing students with a well-rounded education, fostering critical thinking skills, and preparing them for future academic or vocational pursuits transcends cultural and national boundaries.

Moreover, ongoing discussions within each education system reflect a shared awareness of the need to balance academic rigor with the holistic development of students. The evolving nature of curricular approaches underscores the dynamic relationship between education, societal values, and the ever-changing demands of the global landscape.

As the exploration of high school education continues, the focus will shift towards examining grading systems, teaching methodologies, and the cultural influences that shape the educational experience for students worldwide. The comparative analysis of curricular variations sets the stage for a deeper understanding of the complexities and nuances that define global high school education.

Grading Systems

Grading systems play a crucial role in assessing and communicating student performance, providing a quantitative measure of academic achievement. However, the methods and scales used to evaluate students vary widely across different educational systems globally. This exploration delves into the diverse grading systems employed in high schools around the world, shedding light on the approaches, implications, and cultural nuances that shape the assessment of student learning.

United States: Letter Grades and GPA

In the United States, the grading system commonly employs letter grades, with corresponding grade point averages (GPA) providing an overall assessment of academic performance. The letter grades typically range from A to F, with A indicating excellent performance and F representing failure.

The GPA is calculated on a scale of 0 to 4, with an A contributing 4 points, B contributing 3 points, and so on. Advanced Placement (AP) courses and honors classes often carry additional weight, allowing students to earn more than 4.0 on a weighted scale.

This system provides a standardized and easily understandable method for evaluating students' performance. It also allows for a nuanced assessment, considering the rigor of courses taken. The emphasis on GPA in the U.S. is significant, as it plays a crucial role in college admissions.

United Kingdom: Grades and UCAS Points

In the United Kingdom, the grading system is often based on letter grades, with corresponding numerical values. At the high school level, the General Certificate of Secondary Education (GCSE) and A-Level examinations utilize this system.

GCSEs are graded from A* to G, with A* being the highest grade. A-Levels use letter grades from A* to E. Each grade corresponds to a specific number of Universal College Admissions System (UCAS) points, which are crucial for university admissions.

The UCAS point system allows universities to assess applicants' overall academic achievement. It also considers the specific grades achieved in relevant subjects. This method provides a standardized way to evaluate students across a variety of examination boards and subjects.

Germany: Numerical Grading Scale

In Germany, the grading system relies on numerical scores ranging from 1 to 6, with 1 being the best and 6 indicating failure. This system is used throughout primary and secondary education, including high schools.

Grades 1 to 4 are considered passing, while grades 5 and 6 denote failure. The numerical grading scale provides a clear and straightforward way to assess student performance. It is used in both academic and vocational settings, contributing to the nation's emphasis on clear and transparent evaluation.

China: Gaokao-driven Standardized Assessment

China's high-stakes examination system, particularly the gaokao, employs a unique grading system. The gaokao is a standardized test with a maximum score of 750 points. It assesses students in subjects such as Chinese, mathematics, foreign languages, and sciences.

The grading system is closely tied to university admissions, with different score ranges determining eligibility for various institutions. The competition is intense, and students strive for high scores to secure a place in prestigious universities.

While the gaokao's grading system is clear and objective, concerns have been raised about the pressure it places on students and its potential limitations in capturing a comprehensive view of their abilities.

Japan: Scores and Percentages

In Japan, the grading system is based on scores and percentages. Students receive scores for individual assignments and exams, and these scores are often converted into percentages. The percentage system provides a detailed breakdown of students' performance in various assessments.

Grades are often given on a scale of A to F, with A indicating excellent and F representing failure. This system offers a nuanced evaluation, allowing teachers to provide specific feedback on students' strengths and areas for improvement.

Japanese high schools may also use a point system, where students accumulate points based on their performance in different subjects. This system helps determine class rankings and provides an additional layer of assessment.

South Korea: Numeric Scores and Class Rankings

In South Korea, the grading system utilizes numeric scores on a scale of 0 to 100, with 100 being the highest score. Students are ranked within their classes based on these scores, and class rankings are often prominently displayed.

The emphasis on numeric scores and rankings reflects the competitive nature of South Korea's education system, where academic achievement is closely linked to future opportunities. While the system provides a clear indication of students' relative performance, it has been criticized for contributing to excessive competition and stress.

India: Percentage-based Grading System

India's high school grading system is largely percentage-based. Students receive grades based on the percentage of marks obtained in examinations. The grading scale typically ranges from A to F, with A indicating excellent performance and F representing failure.

The percentage system provides a straightforward way to communicate academic achievement. It is widely used in both board examinations and internal assessments. While the system offers clarity, there have been discussions about its limitations in capturing the nuances of students' abilities.

Brazil: Numeric Grades and Descriptive Assessments

In Brazil, the grading system often uses numeric scores on a scale of 0 to 10, with 10 being the highest score. Descriptive assessments are also common, providing qualitative feedback on students' performance.

The numeric grading system allows for precise evaluation, and the inclusion of descriptive assessments enhances the feedback provided to students. This combination aligns with Brazil's emphasis on holistic education, recognizing the importance of both quantitative and qualitative assessments.

Comparative Analysis: Cultural Context and Educational Philosophy

Analyzing these diverse grading systems reveals the intersection of cultural context and educational philosophy. In the United States and the United Kingdom, the emphasis on letter grades and corresponding point systems aligns with the importance placed on standardized assessments for college admissions. These systems provide a clear and comparable measure of academic achievement.

In Germany, the use of a numerical grading scale reflects the nation's commitment to transparency in evaluation. The simplicity of the scale allows for easy communication of student performance.

China and South Korea's reliance on numeric scores and rankings mirrors the competitive nature of their education systems. These systems provide a quantifiable measure of success but have been critiqued for contributing to intense academic pressures.

Japan's use of scores, percentages, and rankings offers a detailed assessment of student performance, emphasizing precision in evaluation. The system aligns with Japan's commitment to academic excellence.

India's percentage-based system and Brazil's use of numeric grades highlight the clarity provided by quantitative assessments. While offering transparency, discussions persist about the ability of these systems to capture the full spectrum of students' abilities.

The inclusion of descriptive assessments in Brazil demonstrates a commitment to providing qualitative feedback, acknowledging the importance of a holistic understanding of student performance.

Conclusion: Navigating Assessment Diversity

The diversity in grading systems across the globe underscores the complexity of assessing and measuring student achievement. Cultural values, societal expectations, and educational philosophies all contribute to the unique approaches adopted by different nations.

While numeric or letter grades provide a standardized way to assess students, the implications of these assessments extend beyond academic achievement. They influence university admissions, shape career opportunities, and contribute to the overall educational experience.

As high school education continues to evolve, the discussion around grading systems will likely evolve as well. Balancing the need for objective assessments with the recognition of diverse talents and skills remains a challenge. The comparative analysis of grading systems sets the stage for further exploration into teaching methodologies, cultural influences, and the broader factors that shape the educational landscape globally.

Teaching Methodologies

Teaching methodologies represent the diverse approaches educators use to impart knowledge, foster critical thinking, and engage students in the learning process. These methodologies are shaped by cultural influences, educational philosophies, and the goals of each nation's education system. This exploration delves into the varied teaching methodologies employed in high schools around the world, offering insights into the methods and practices that contribute to effective and meaningful learning experiences.

United States: Student-Centered Learning and Project-Based Approaches

In the United States, teaching methodologies have evolved over time to emphasize student-centered learning and project-based approaches. The shift away from traditional teacher-centric models towards more interactive and collaborative methods is a hallmark of American high school education.

Student-centered learning encourages active student participation, critical thinking, and problem-solving skills. Teachers act as facilitators, guiding students in exploring topics, conducting research, and presenting their findings. Project-based approaches involve students in real-world projects, fostering creativity and practical application of knowledge.

The use of technology is also prominent in American classrooms, with interactive whiteboards, online resources, and educational apps enhancing the learning experience. This dynamic and interactive teaching methodology aligns with the broader goal of preparing students for the challenges of the 21st century.

United Kingdom: Lecture-Based Teaching and Tutorial Systems

In the United Kingdom, teaching methodologies often involve a combination of lecture-based instruction and tutorial systems, especially at the A-Level stage. Lectures provide a structured presentation of information, while tutorials offer small-group discussions and personalized guidance.

University-style tutorials, where students engage in discussions, debate ideas, and receive individualized feedback, are integral to the UK's higher education preparation. This approach fosters critical thinking, independent research skills, and a deeper understanding of subjects.

The emphasis on subject-specific knowledge and examinations also influences teaching methodologies, with educators focusing on preparing students for high-stakes assessments. The balance between lecture-based learning and tutorials reflects the UK's commitment to academic rigor and specialization.

Germany: Dual Education System and Practical Training

Germany's teaching methodologies are closely tied to its unique dual education system. The emphasis on integrating theoretical learning with practical, on-the-job training is a defining feature of German high school education.

Classroom instruction is complemented by vocational training, where students gain hands-on experience in a chosen field. This dual approach allows students to apply theoretical knowledge in real-world settings, fostering a strong connection between education and the workforce.

Teachers in Germany play a pivotal role in guiding students through both academic and vocational components of their education. This practical and applied teaching methodology aligns with Germany's commitment to producing a skilled and versatile workforce.

China: Exam-Oriented Teaching and Rote Learning

China's teaching methodologies are often characterized by an exam-oriented approach, particularly in high school. The gaokao, the national college entrance examination, exerts a significant influence on teaching methods.

Rote learning, the memorization of facts and formulas, is prevalent in Chinese classrooms as students prepare for standardized exams. Teachers focus on covering extensive content, and students often attend additional classes, known as "cram schools," to reinforce their knowledge.

While the emphasis on exam results has been criticized for potential drawbacks, such as limited creativity and critical thinking, Chinese teaching methodologies are evolving. There is a growing recognition of the need for a more holistic approach to education that nurtures diverse skills.

Japan: Didactic Teaching and Whole-Class Instruction

In Japan, teaching methodologies often involve didactic instruction and whole-class learning. Teachers play a central role in delivering content, and students are expected to listen attentively and take notes.

Whole-class instruction allows for a collective learning experience, fostering a sense of unity and shared understanding. Teachers often use visual aids, such as diagrams and illustrations, to enhance comprehension.

Japanese classrooms also emphasize group activities and collaborative learning. While the teaching style may be more didactic, there is a recognition of the importance of social interaction and teamwork in the learning process.

South Korea: Intensive Classroom Instruction and Private Tutoring

South Korea's teaching methodologies are characterized by intensive classroom instruction and a strong reliance on private tutoring, known as "hagwon." In the classroom, teachers cover a significant amount of content, and students are expected to diligently absorb information.

The competitive nature of South Korea's education system drives students to seek additional support through private tutoring. These supplementary classes often focus on exam preparation and reinforcing classroom lessons.

While the intensity of classroom instruction and private tutoring has been credited with academic excellence, there are ongoing discussions about the potential impact on student well-being and the need for a more balanced approach.

India: Lecture-Based Teaching and Emphasis on Examinations

In India, teaching methodologies often involve lecture-based instruction, where teachers deliver content to a large group of students. The emphasis is placed on covering the prescribed curriculum to prepare students for board examinations.

Examinations play a central role in the Indian education system, influencing teaching methodologies. Teachers often tailor their instruction to align with examination patterns, and students engage in extensive exam preparation.

There is a growing recognition of the need for more interactive and student-centric teaching methods in India. Initiatives promoting experiential learning, project-based approaches, and the integration of technology aim to enhance the overall educational experience.

Brazil: Student-Centered Learning and Multidisciplinary Approaches

In Brazil, teaching methodologies have shifted towards student-centered learning and multidisciplinary approaches. Educators aim to engage students actively in the learning process, encouraging critical thinking and collaboration.

Multidisciplinary projects, where students explore topics from various perspectives, are common in Brazilian classrooms. This approach promotes a holistic understanding of subjects and helps students connect theoretical knowledge to real-world applications.

The use of technology, including digital resources and online platforms, is becoming more prevalent in Brazilian classrooms. This integration aligns with the global trend towards leveraging technology to enhance educational experiences.

Comparative Analysis: Balancing Tradition and Innovation

The comparative analysis of teaching methodologies across these diverse educational systems reveals a balance between traditional practices and innovative approaches. In the United States and Brazil, student-centered learning and project-based methods reflect a commitment to fostering creativity and critical thinking, aligning with global trends in education.

In the United Kingdom and Japan, the integration of lecture-based teaching and tutorials emphasizes a structured approach to subject-specific knowledge. The tutorial system in the UK and collaborative learning in Japanese classrooms provide students with a more personalized and interactive educational experience.

Germany's dual education system, rooted in practical training, stands out for its emphasis on hands-on learning and workforce preparation. Similarly, South Korea's intensive classroom instruction and private tutoring highlight the dedication to academic excellence, though concerns about student well-being persist.

China's exam-oriented teaching methods, centered around rote learning, demonstrate the influence of high-stakes examinations on educational practices. The ongoing shift towards a more holistic approach reflects evolving perspectives on education in China.

India's focus on lecture-based teaching and examination-centric approaches is gradually evolving to incorporate more interactive and student-centric methods. The acknowledgment of the need for a balanced and holistic education is driving initiatives to enhance teaching methodologies.

The teaching methodologies across these nations reflect not only the diversity of cultural and educational philosophies but also the shared goals of preparing students for the challenges of the future. As education systems continue to evolve, striking a balance between tradition and innovation remains a key consideration in shaping effective teaching practices globally.

Chapter 3: Cultural Influences on High School Education

Societal Attitudes Towards Education

Societal attitudes towards education play a pivotal role in shaping high school experiences, influencing students' motivation, aspirations, and the overall approach to learning. Cultural values, traditions, and expectations intertwine to create a unique educational landscape in each nation. This exploration delves into the diverse societal attitudes towards education across the globe, shedding light on the cultural nuances that contribute to the shaping of high school education.

United States: The Pursuit of Individual Excellence

In the United States, societal attitudes towards education are often characterized by a strong emphasis on the pursuit of individual excellence. The American Dream, a cultural ethos that permeates society, associates education with upward mobility and success.

Parents, educators, and students alike view education as a pathway to personal and professional achievements. The competitive nature of the education system is reflected in the pursuit of high grades, participation in extracurricular activities, and the drive to gain admission to prestigious universities.

The diversity of American society also influences attitudes towards education, with a recognition of the value of a well-rounded education that includes both academic and extracurricular achievements. This emphasis aligns with the broader societal belief that education is a transformative force, empowering individuals to reach their full potential.

United Kingdom: Tradition, Prestige, and Class Distinctions

In the United Kingdom, societal attitudes towards education are influenced by a sense of tradition, prestige, and historical class distinctions. The education system has been shaped by centuries-old institutions such as Eton and Oxford, contributing to a cultural reverence for certain educational paths.

The pursuit of a prestigious education, often associated with private schools and elite universities, is deeply ingrained in British society. Attending institutions with historical significance is viewed not only as a means of acquiring knowledge but also as a symbol of social status and success.

Class distinctions, rooted in the historical divide between public and private education, continue to influence societal perceptions. While efforts have been made to address educational inequalities, the echoes of class-based attitudes persist in shaping the aspirations and expectations of students and their families.

Germany: Vocational Pragmatism and Technological Excellence

In Germany, societal attitudes towards education are marked by a pragmatic approach that values vocational training alongside academic pursuits. The dual education system, which combines theoretical learning with practical, on-the-job training, reflects the societal belief in the importance of acquiring real-world skills.

The emphasis on vocational education is rooted in Germany's commitment to producing a skilled workforce capable of contributing to its robust industrial sector. This pragmatic perspective recognizes that success in the workforce is not solely dependent on academic achievements but also on practical skills and competencies.

Additionally, Germany's focus on technological excellence aligns with the nation's position as an industrial and technological powerhouse. The cultural appreciation for precision and innovation is reflected in the education system's emphasis on science, technology, engineering, and mathematics (STEM) subjects.

China: The Gaokao and Familial Expectations

In China, societal attitudes towards education are profoundly influenced by the gaokao, the national college entrance examination. Education is viewed as a key avenue for social mobility, and the gaokao is regarded as the primary determinant of future opportunities.

Familial expectations play a central role in shaping students' attitudes towards education. Parents often invest significant resources in their children's education, viewing academic success as a pathway to a better life. The one-child policy, which was in place for several decades, intensified the focus on a single child's academic achievements.

The competitive nature of the gaokao fosters a culture of intense academic pressure and dedication to exam preparation. Success in the gaokao is not only a personal achievement but also a source of pride for families and communities. The cultural importance placed on education as a means of societal advancement underscores the significance of the gaokao in shaping attitudes towards learning.

Japan: Academic Rigor, Group Harmony, and Social Conformity

In Japan, societal attitudes towards education are characterized by a commitment to academic rigor, group harmony, and social conformity. The cultural value of diligence and hard work is reflected in the rigorous nature of the education system.

Students in Japan often face long hours of study and preparation for high-stakes examinations. The emphasis on academic achievement is deeply ingrained in societal expectations, with success in exams seen as a prerequisite for a successful future.

Group harmony, or "wa," is a cultural concept that influences education by promoting cooperation, teamwork, and a sense of collective responsibility. The value placed on social conformity extends to the education system, where students are expected to adhere to established norms and traditions.

While these cultural attitudes contribute to a disciplined and focused approach to education, there are ongoing discussions about the need to balance academic rigor with the promotion of individual creativity and critical thinking.

South Korea: Educational Achievement as a National Priority

In South Korea, societal attitudes towards education reflect a national priority placed on educational achievement. The pursuit of academic excellence is deeply ingrained in the culture, with success in high-stakes examinations perceived as essential for future success.

Parents, students, and educators invest significant time and resources in academic preparation, including private tutoring and supplementary classes. The intensity of the education system is viewed as a reflection of national aspirations for economic prosperity and global competitiveness.

Educational achievement is often seen as a source of national pride, with successful students celebrated as role models for the entire society. While the dedication to academic success has contributed to South Korea's impressive educational outcomes, there are ongoing discussions about the potential drawbacks, including stress and mental health concerns among students.

India: Academic Performance and Career Opportunities

In India, societal attitudes towards education are shaped by a strong emphasis on academic performance as a gateway to career opportunities. The competitive nature of the education system, coupled with a population size that exceeds a billion, creates intense competition for limited university spots and job opportunities.

The societal expectation for academic success influences students' aspirations and choices from a young age. Engineering and medical professions, often associated with prestige and financial stability, are particularly sought after. The pressure to excel academically is a common experience for many Indian students, driven by societal expectations and the pursuit of secure and well-paying careers.

While there is a growing recognition of the need for a more holistic approach to education, including the development of soft skills and creativity, the cultural emphasis on academic achievement remains a significant influence on societal attitudes towards education.

Brazil: Inclusive Education and Cultural Diversity

In Brazil, societal attitudes towards education are shaped by a commitment to inclusive education and the celebration of cultural diversity. The Brazilian education system recognizes the importance of catering to diverse learning needs and fostering an inclusive environment.

Cultural diversity is a central aspect of Brazilian society, and this is reflected in the education system's emphasis on valuing and respecting different cultural backgrounds. The promotion of multiculturalism is woven into the curriculum, fostering an appreciation for Brazil's rich heritage and the contributions of various ethnic groups.

The societal view of education as a tool for social inclusion aligns with Brazil's broader commitment to reducing inequalities and creating opportunities for all. The emphasis on inclusive education and cultural diversity contributes to a more holistic and equitable educational experience.

Comparative Analysis: Balancing Tradition and Progress

The comparative analysis of societal attitudes towards education across these diverse nations reveals a balance between traditional values and evolving perspectives on education. In the United States and Brazil, a focus on individual excellence and inclusive education reflects a commitment to progress and diversity.

In the United Kingdom and Japan, the influence of historical traditions and the importance placed on academic rigor highlight the persistence of cultural values. Germany's pragmatic approach to education, China's emphasis on familial expectations and the gaokao, and South Korea's national priority on educational achievement underscore the intricate relationship between societal attitudes and cultural values.

India's emphasis on academic performance as a gateway to career opportunities reflects the complex interplay between societal expectations and economic realities. In Brazil, the celebration of cultural diversity and the promotion of inclusive education demonstrate a commitment to addressing social inequalities.

As education systems continue to evolve globally, navigating the delicate balance between preserving cultural values and embracing progress remains a challenge. The cultural influences on high school education extend beyond the classroom, shaping the aspirations, motivations, and identities of students as they navigate their educational journeys within diverse societal contexts.

Cultural Impact on Aspirations

The cultural fabric of a society weaves a complex tapestry that profoundly influences the aspirations of its youth. High school education serves as a critical juncture where students develop and shape their dreams, ambitions, and goals. Cultural norms, values, and expectations play a pivotal role in defining these aspirations, guiding students on paths that align with the collective ethos of their societies. This exploration delves into the diverse cultural impact on aspirations in high school education across the globe, providing insights into how societal values shape the dreams of the next generation.

United States: The Pursuit of Individual Success

In the United States, cultural influences on aspirations are marked by a strong emphasis on individual success and personal fulfillment. The American Dream, deeply ingrained in the national psyche, fosters aspirations centered around achieving economic prosperity, social mobility, and personal happiness.

In high schools across the country, students are encouraged to pursue their passions, explore diverse career paths, and envision a future where personal fulfillment aligns with professional success. The emphasis on extracurricular activities, leadership roles, and community engagement reflects the cultural belief that a well-rounded individual is better equipped to navigate the complexities of the modern world.

The diversity of American society further contributes to a broad spectrum of aspirations, recognizing and celebrating different cultural backgrounds, talents, and ambitions. High school education in the U.S. serves as a platform where students are empowered to dream big and forge paths uniquely tailored to their individual aspirations.

United Kingdom: Tradition, Class, and Academic Prestige

In the United Kingdom, cultural influences on aspirations are intertwined with traditions, class distinctions, and a reverence for academic prestige. Historical institutions, such as Oxford and Cambridge, cast a long shadow, shaping aspirations towards academic excellence and a certain social standing.

Aspirations in British high schools often reflect the cultural value placed on achieving success within the established social hierarchy. Students may aspire to attend prestigious universities or follow traditional career paths associated with societal expectations.

Class distinctions persist in shaping aspirations, with societal perceptions often influencing the types of careers and educational paths deemed desirable. However, ongoing efforts to promote social mobility and diversify opportunities are challenging these traditional influences, opening up new avenues for aspirations beyond historical norms.

Germany: Vocational Excellence and Practical Skills

In Germany, cultural impacts on aspirations are characterized by a pragmatic approach that values vocational excellence and practical skills. The cultural appreciation for precision, engineering, and technical prowess influences students to aspire to careers that align with these values.

High school education in Germany often prepares students for diverse vocational paths, fostering aspirations towards becoming skilled professionals in fields such as engineering, manufacturing, and technology. Apprenticeships, a prominent feature of the education system, provide practical experiences that shape aspirations towards hands-on, applied learning.

The German cultural emphasis on the integration of theoretical knowledge with practical skills guides students towards careers that contribute to the nation's industrial strength. Aspirations in German high schools often revolve around achieving mastery in a specific trade or technical field.

China: Filial Piety, Academic Achievement, and Social Contribution

In China, cultural impacts on aspirations are deeply rooted in Confucian values, including filial piety, academic achievement, and a sense of social contribution. Aspirations in Chinese high schools are often shaped by the cultural expectation of honoring one's family through academic success.

Students aspire to excel academically, not only for personal accomplishment but also as a means of contributing to the well-being and status of their families. Filial piety, the respect and devotion to one's parents, influences career aspirations that align with societal expectations of stability and success.

Additionally, the cultural emphasis on the collective good encourages aspirations that contribute to social and economic development. Careers in science, technology, medicine, and other fields seen as beneficial to society are often highly esteemed, reflecting a broader cultural value of social contribution.

Japan: Group Harmony, Professional Dedication, and Innovation

In Japan, cultural influences on aspirations are shaped by values such as group harmony, professional dedication, and a commitment to innovation. Aspirations often align with the cultural expectation of contributing to the collective success of the group, whether it be a family, company, or society.

Students in Japanese high schools aspire to careers that allow them to embody values like loyalty, dedication, and precision. Professions that contribute to the overall well-being of society, such as those in science, technology, and traditional arts, are often highly regarded.

The cultural appreciation for innovation also influences aspirations towards careers that contribute to technological advancements and economic progress. As Japan continues to balance tradition with a quest for cutting-edge advancements, high school students' aspirations reflect a dynamic blend of cultural values and a forward-looking mindset.

South Korea: Academic Excellence, Global Competitiveness, and Technological Advancements

In South Korea, cultural impacts on aspirations are marked by a strong emphasis on academic excellence, global competitiveness, and technological advancements. Aspirations in South Korean high schools are often deeply intertwined with the cultural expectation of achieving top academic rankings.

Students aspire to secure positions in prestigious universities, both domestically and globally, as a means of ensuring future success. The competitive nature of the education system influences aspirations towards careers in fields such as science, technology, engineering, and mathematics (STEM).

The cultural focus on global competitiveness encourages aspirations towards careers that position South Korea as a leader on the world stage. Advancements in technology and innovation play a significant role in shaping aspirations, reflecting the cultural value placed on staying at the forefront of global developments.

India: Academic Achievement, Professional Stability, and Social Status

In India, cultural influences on aspirations are often centered around academic achievement, professional stability, and the attainment of social status. The cultural belief in the transformative power of education shapes aspirations towards securing a strong academic foundation as a pathway to future success.

Students in Indian high schools often aspire to pursue careers in fields such as engineering, medicine, and information technology, which are traditionally associated with professional stability and social prestige. Aspirations are influenced by the cultural expectation of achieving financial security and upward mobility through education.

Furthermore, the societal importance placed on family and community plays a role in shaping career aspirations. Professions that contribute to societal well-being and uphold cultural values are often highly esteemed, reflecting the broader cultural ethos of collective progress.

Brazil: Inclusive Opportunities, Cultural Diversity, and Social Impact

In Brazil, cultural impacts on aspirations emphasize inclusive opportunities, cultural diversity, and a desire to make a positive social impact. Aspirations in Brazilian high schools often reflect a commitment to leveraging education for personal growth and societal betterment.

The cultural celebration of diversity shapes aspirations towards careers that honor and represent Brazil's rich cultural heritage. Students aspire to professions that contribute to the inclusive and multicultural fabric of Brazilian society, reflecting a cultural value placed on unity within diversity.

The emphasis on social impact influences aspirations towards careers that address societal challenges and promote positive change. As Brazil strives to reduce inequalities and create opportunities for all, high school students' aspirations align with cultural values that prioritize collective well-being.

Comparative Analysis: Cultural Values Shaping Aspirations

The comparative analysis of cultural impacts on aspirations across these diverse nations reveals the intricate interplay between societal values and individual dreams. In the

United States and Brazil, a focus on individual fulfillment and inclusive opportunities reflects cultural values that celebrate diversity and personal growth.

In the United Kingdom and Japan, the persistence of historical traditions and cultural values shapes aspirations towards academic excellence and contributions to societal well-being. Germany's pragmatic approach influences aspirations towards vocational excellence and applied skills, aligning with a cultural appreciation for precision and innovation.

China's cultural emphasis on filial piety and social contribution shapes aspirations towards academic achievement and careers that benefit society. In South Korea, aspirations are influenced by a cultural commitment to academic excellence, global competitiveness, and technological advancements.

India's cultural focus on academic achievement and professional stability shapes aspirations towards careers associated with financial security and social prestige. In Brazil, cultural influences on aspirations prioritize inclusive opportunities, cultural diversity, and a desire to make a positive social impact.

As education systems evolve globally, understanding the nuanced ways in which cultural values shape aspirations is essential for creating educational environments that empower students to pursue paths aligned with their individual and societal goals. High school education serves as a crucial stage where cultural influences play a defining role in shaping the aspirations of the next generation.

Cultural Barriers to Education

The cultural landscape within which high school education operates is not only a source of inspiration for students' aspirations but also a terrain marked by various challenges. Cultural barriers to education are intricate and multifaceted, reflecting societal norms, traditions, and expectations that can hinder or facilitate the learning process. This exploration delves into the diverse cultural barriers to education across the globe, offering insights into the challenges students face in navigating their educational journeys within specific cultural contexts.

United States: Socioeconomic Disparities and Educational Inequities

In the United States, cultural barriers to education are often intertwined with socioeconomic disparities and systemic educational inequities. Despite the cultural value placed on the importance of education, students from marginalized communities face challenges that hinder their academic success.

Socioeconomic factors, such as access to quality educational resources, extracurricular opportunities, and experienced teachers, contribute to disparities in educational outcomes. Cultural barriers may emerge from a lack of representation in the curriculum, inadequate support for English language learners, and limited access to advanced placement courses, perpetuating educational inequalities.

Cultural stereotypes and biases can also create barriers, impacting the experiences of minority students. Addressing these cultural barriers requires a comprehensive approach that considers not only academic support but also the broader sociocultural context in which education is situated.

United Kingdom: Class-Based Disparities and Traditional Expectations

In the United Kingdom, cultural barriers to education are influenced by class-based disparities and traditional expectations that shape students' experiences in high school. The historic divide between private and public education can contribute to inequalities in access to resources and opportunities.

Students from lower socioeconomic backgrounds may face cultural barriers related to a lack of resources, limited access to extracurricular activities, and fewer opportunities for educational enrichment. Additionally, traditional expectations associated with class distinctions can influence aspirations and limit the perceived possibilities for students from certain backgrounds.

The influence of cultural norms and expectations can create challenges for students striving to overcome class-based barriers. Efforts to address these cultural barriers involve promoting inclusivity, diversifying curriculum content, and providing targeted support for students facing socioeconomic challenges.

Germany: Vocational Stigma and Perceptions of Academic Paths

In Germany, cultural barriers to education are shaped by the stigma associated with vocational paths and societal perceptions of academic versus non-academic trajectories. While the dual education system is designed to integrate practical training with theoretical learning, cultural biases may favor traditional academic routes.

Students who opt for vocational training may encounter cultural barriers in the form of societal expectations and perceptions that undervalue non-academic paths. The emphasis on academic achievement can create challenges for those pursuing vocational careers, impacting their self-esteem and societal recognition.

Addressing these cultural barriers involves challenging stereotypes, promoting the value of vocational education, and creating pathways that validate diverse career choices. Fostering a cultural shift that recognizes the importance of both academic and vocational paths is essential for creating an inclusive educational environment.

China: Academic Pressure and High-Stakes Examinations

In China, cultural barriers to education are closely tied to the intense academic pressure and the influence of high-stakes examinations, particularly the gaokao. The cultural expectation for academic excellence places a significant burden on students, contributing to stress, anxiety, and mental health challenges.

The focus on rote learning and memorization, driven by the demands of high-stakes examinations, may hinder critical thinking and creativity. The cultural perception that success in the gaokao is the primary determinant of future opportunities can create a narrow definition of achievement, limiting students' exploration of alternative paths.

Addressing cultural barriers in China involves reevaluating the education system's emphasis on examination results, fostering a more holistic approach to learning, and promoting mental health and well-being. Recognizing diverse forms of success beyond academic achievements is crucial for mitigating cultural pressures.

Japan: Conformity and the Pressure to Excel

In Japan, cultural barriers to education are influenced by the emphasis on conformity, the pressure to excel academically, and the expectations for group harmony. The cultural value of conformity may discourage individual expression and creativity, hindering students who thrive in more diverse and dynamic learning environments.

The intense pressure to excel academically, driven by entrance examinations and societal expectations, can lead to stress and mental health challenges. Cultural norms that prioritize group harmony may discourage students from challenging traditional expectations or pursuing non-traditional paths.

Addressing these cultural barriers involves fostering an educational environment that values diversity, promotes individual expression, and recognizes success beyond academic achievements. Encouraging a more balanced approach to learning that considers students' well-being is essential for overcoming cultural pressures.

South Korea: Intensive Competition and Private Education

In South Korea, cultural barriers to education are characterized by intensive competition and the prevalence of private education, known as "hagwon." The highly competitive nature of the education system can create intense academic pressure, leading to stress, burnout, and mental health challenges among students.

The reliance on private education institutions, often seen as essential for academic success, can exacerbate inequalities, as not all students have equal access to such resources. Cultural expectations for academic excellence may limit students' exploration of diverse interests and talents.

Addressing these cultural barriers involves reevaluating the emphasis on intense competition, promoting a more balanced approach to education, and addressing the role of private education in perpetuating disparities. Fostering a cultural shift towards valuing well-rounded development is crucial for creating a more equitable educational landscape.

India: Exam-Centric Culture and Socioeconomic Disparities

In India, cultural barriers to education are influenced by an exam-centric culture and persistent socioeconomic disparities. The cultural emphasis on high-stakes examinations, such as board exams and competitive entrance tests, can create an environment of intense academic pressure and competition.

Socioeconomic disparities contribute to cultural barriers as students from marginalized backgrounds may face challenges related to access to quality education, resources, and support. Cultural expectations surrounding certain professions and traditional views on gender roles may further limit students' choices.

Addressing these cultural barriers involves reimagining assessment practices, promoting inclusivity, and addressing socioeconomic inequalities. Efforts to diversify educational opportunities and challenge traditional expectations contribute to a more inclusive and equitable educational environment.

Brazil: Inequality and Limited Access to Resources

In Brazil, cultural barriers to education are often rooted in inequality and limited access to resources. Socioeconomic disparities contribute to challenges such as inadequate infrastructure, insufficient educational resources, and disparities in the quality of education between urban and rural areas.

Cultural norms that perpetuate social and economic inequalities can create barriers for students from marginalized backgrounds. Limited access to extracurricular activities, advanced courses, and educational support may hinder the educational experiences of certain groups.

Addressing these cultural barriers involves addressing systemic inequalities, investing in educational infrastructure, and promoting inclusive policies. Recognizing and valuing cultural diversity within the educational system is essential for creating a more equitable learning environment.

Comparative Analysis: Navigating Cultural Barriers

The comparative analysis of cultural barriers to education across these diverse nations highlights the common challenges faced by students and the unique ways in which cultural factors shape educational experiences. Socioeconomic disparities emerge as a prevalent theme, impacting students in the United States, the United Kingdom, India, and Brazil, albeit in different contexts.

Traditional expectations and societal perceptions create barriers in the United Kingdom, Germany, and India, where cultural norms around class distinctions, vocational paths, and traditional professions influence students' choices and opportunities. The intense academic pressure and focus on high-stakes examinations in China, Japan, and South Korea reflect shared cultural values that prioritize academic achievement.

Efforts to address cultural barriers involve challenging stereotypes, promoting inclusivity, and fostering a cultural shift towards valuing diverse forms of success. Creating an equitable educational environment requires a nuanced understanding of the cultural factors at play, as well as a commitment to promoting diversity, equity, and inclusion within the educational system.

Success Stories in Diverse Cultural Contexts

Success stories in high school education transcend cultural boundaries, showcasing the resilience, determination, and innovation of students within diverse contexts. These narratives not only illuminate the triumphs of individuals but also provide valuable insights into the cultural factors that contribute to educational success. This exploration delves into inspiring success stories from various cultural contexts, highlighting the common threads of motivation, support, and adaptability that propel students to excel in high school education.

United States: Overcoming Adversity and Achieving Academic Excellence

In the United States, success stories abound, illustrating how students from diverse backgrounds overcome adversity and achieve academic excellence. One such inspiring tale is that of Jasmine, a first-generation immigrant facing language barriers and financial constraints. Despite these challenges, Jasmine's unwavering determination and the support of dedicated teachers propelled her to academic success.

Jasmine's story reflects the cultural value placed on resilience and the belief that education can be a transformative force. In the U.S., success is often measured not just by academic achievements but also by the ability to overcome obstacles and contribute meaningfully to one's community.

The cultural diversity within the U.S. education system is mirrored in success stories that celebrate achievements across various ethnic, socioeconomic, and linguistic backgrounds. These narratives underscore the importance of fostering inclusive educational environments that recognize and celebrate diverse forms of excellence.

United Kingdom: Breaking Class Barriers through Academic Achievement

Success stories in the United Kingdom often involve individuals who break class barriers through academic achievement. The tale of Sarah, a student from a working-class background, defying societal expectations by gaining admission to a prestigious university, exemplifies the cultural impact of educational success.

Sarah's journey challenges traditional perceptions about who can excel academically and reinforces the transformative power of education. Success stories in the U.K. frequently revolve around individuals who navigate class-based challenges, highlighting the importance of creating educational opportunities that bridge socioeconomic divides.

The cultural narrative of success in the U.K. is evolving to embrace a more inclusive definition that recognizes achievements beyond academic accolades. These stories inspire a cultural shift towards valuing diverse pathways to success, fostering environments where students from all backgrounds can thrive.

Germany: Pioneering Innovation in Vocational Education

In Germany, success stories often emerge from individuals who pioneer innovation within the vocational education system. The narrative of Klaus, an apprentice who developed a groundbreaking solution in collaboration with his industry mentors, showcases the cultural emphasis on practical skills and applied learning.

Klaus's success story reflects the German commitment to fostering a skilled workforce capable of driving technological advancements. In a cultural context that values vocational excellence, success is not solely defined by academic achievements but also by the ability to contribute to industry innovation.

Germany's success stories highlight the importance of cultivating a culture that appreciates and rewards practical skills, creativity, and entrepreneurship. These narratives challenge stereotypes about vocational paths and contribute to reshaping societal perceptions of success within the German education landscape.

China: Navigating Academic Rigor and Pursuing Passion

In China, success stories often revolve around students who navigate intense academic rigor while pursuing their passions. The narrative of Li, a student who excelled academically while actively participating in extracurricular activities, exemplifies the cultural expectation of academic excellence coupled with a holistic approach to education.

Li's success story challenges the notion that academic achievement requires sacrificing other pursuits and highlights the importance of a balanced educational experience. In a cultural context where academic pressure is high, success stories like Li's contribute to redefining success as a multifaceted concept that includes personal growth and fulfillment.

China's evolving education landscape is witnessing a shift towards recognizing diverse forms of success beyond traditional academic metrics. Success stories that celebrate well-rounded individuals inspire a cultural reevaluation of the pursuit of passion and balance in education.

Japan: Balancing Tradition and Innovation in Educational Pursuits

Success stories in Japan often involve individuals who successfully balance tradition and innovation in their educational pursuits. The narrative of Hiroshi, a student who integrated traditional arts with modern technology, exemplifies the cultural emphasis on preserving heritage while embracing innovation.

Hiroshi's success story reflects the Japanese commitment to fostering creativity and adaptability within a framework of cultural traditions. In a society that values both academic rigor and individual expression, success is not confined to conventional pathways but encompasses innovative approaches that contribute to cultural preservation and evolution.

Japan's success stories contribute to shaping a cultural narrative that encourages students to explore diverse interests and integrate traditional values with contemporary perspectives. These narratives celebrate individuals who navigate the delicate balance between tradition and progress within the Japanese education system.

South Korea: Excelling Academically while Nurturing Soft Skills

In South Korea, success stories often highlight individuals who excel academically while actively nurturing soft skills and personal development. The narrative of Ji-eun, a student who not only achieved top academic rankings but also demonstrated leadership and interpersonal skills, reflects the cultural emphasis on holistic education.

Ji-eun's success story challenges stereotypes about the singular focus on academic achievement in South Korea and underscores the cultural value placed on developing well-rounded individuals. Success in the South Korean context extends beyond exam results to encompass qualities such as teamwork, communication, and adaptability.

South Korea's evolving education landscape is witnessing a shift towards recognizing the importance of nurturing students' interpersonal skills alongside academic prowess. Success stories like Ji-eun's contribute to fostering a cultural environment that values a comprehensive approach to education.

India: Striving for Academic Excellence and Social Impact

Success stories in India often revolve around individuals who strive for academic excellence while also making a significant social impact. The narrative of Ayesha, a student who not only excelled academically but also initiated community projects, exemplifies the cultural expectation of combining individual success with contributions to society.

Ayesha's success story reflects India's cultural emphasis on education as a means of societal betterment. Success in the Indian context is not solely measured by individual achievements but also by the ability to use education for the greater good, aligning with the cultural values of social responsibility and community engagement.

India's success stories contribute to shaping a cultural narrative that encourages students to envision success as a platform for positive societal change. These narratives inspire a cultural shift towards recognizing the interconnectedness of individual success and social impact within the Indian education system.

Brazil: Overcoming Challenges and Embracing Cultural Diversity

Success stories in Brazil often center around individuals who overcome challenges and embrace cultural diversity in their educational journeys. The narrative of Carlos, a student from an underprivileged background who excelled academically while promoting cultural exchange, exemplifies the cultural value placed on resilience and inclusivity.

Carlos's success story challenges stereotypes and underscores the importance of creating educational environments that celebrate Brazil's rich cultural diversity. Success in the Brazilian context involves not only individual achievement but also the ability to contribute to a more inclusive and culturally vibrant society.

Brazil's success stories contribute to shaping a cultural narrative that recognizes the strength in diversity and encourages students to overcome challenges while embracing their unique cultural identities. These narratives inspire a cultural shift towards fostering inclusive educational spaces that celebrate Brazil's multicultural heritage.

Comparative Analysis: Common Themes in Success Stories

A comparative analysis of success stories across diverse cultural contexts reveals common themes that transcend national boundaries. The importance of resilience, determination, and support emerges as universal factors contributing to educational success. Regardless of cultural differences, students who overcome challenges, receive mentorship, and pursue their passions consistently feature in these narratives.

The evolving definition of success is another common theme, with many success stories challenging traditional notions and expanding the cultural understanding of achievement. Whether it involves breaking class barriers, pioneering innovation in vocational education, or balancing tradition and innovation, these narratives contribute to reshaping cultural perceptions of success within the global educational landscape.

Furthermore, the recognition of holistic education is evident in success stories that emphasize the importance of soft skills, personal development, and community engagement alongside academic achievements. The cultural shift towards valuing well-rounded individuals reflects a shared understanding that success extends beyond exam results to encompass a broader spectrum of skills and qualities.

These success stories not only inspire individuals within their respective cultural contexts but also contribute to a global dialogue on the transformative power of education. By highlighting the diverse pathways to success, these narratives foster a more inclusive and nuanced understanding of achievement within the complex interplay of cultural influences on high school education.

Chapter 4: Economic Disparities and Education
Economic Conditions and Access

The nexus between economic conditions and access to education is a critical lens through which to examine the disparities in high school education globally. Economic factors play a pivotal role in shaping the educational landscape, influencing access to resources, opportunities, and the quality of learning experiences. This exploration delves into the multifaceted relationship between economic conditions and access to high school education, examining the challenges and opportunities faced by students across diverse economic contexts.

Global Overview: Economic Disparities as Educational Barriers

At a global level, economic disparities stand as formidable barriers to accessing quality high school education. The World Bank estimates that millions of children and adolescents worldwide are still out of school, with economic conditions being a major determinant. Poverty, lack of infrastructure, and unequal distribution of resources contribute to a stark divide in educational access.

In low-income countries, economic challenges often manifest as insufficient funding for schools, inadequate teacher training, and limited access to learning materials. High school education is a distant dream for many in these regions, perpetuating a cycle of poverty where economic conditions hinder educational opportunities, further limiting future economic prospects.

Conversely, high-income countries may grapple with different but equally impactful economic disparities. While the infrastructure and resources may be more abundant, the cost of education, including tuition fees and associated expenses, can create barriers for certain socio-economic groups. In this context, economic conditions influence not only access to high school education but also the quality of educational experiences.

United States: Socioeconomic Disparities in Educational Opportunities

In the United States, economic conditions profoundly impact access to high school education, creating disparities that persist along socio-economic lines. Students from low-income families often face challenges related to inadequate funding for their schools, limited access to extracurricular activities, and fewer educational enrichment opportunities.

Economic disparities can manifest in several ways, including disparities in the quality of schools and educational resources. Schools in economically disadvantaged neighborhoods may struggle to attract and retain highly qualified teachers, resulting in a potential impact on the overall quality of education provided.

Additionally, the digital divide, exacerbated by economic disparities, has become increasingly relevant. Students from affluent families may have access to the latest technology, internet connectivity, and educational software, while those from lower-income households may lack these resources. This technological gap can further hinder educational access and achievement.

Efforts to address economic disparities in the U.S. education system involve targeted interventions such as increased funding for schools in economically disadvantaged areas, initiatives to bridge the digital divide, and scholarship programs to support students from low-income families.

United Kingdom: Class-Based Inequalities and Educational Access

In the United Kingdom, economic conditions contribute to class-based inequalities that impact educational access, particularly in high school. The historic divide between private and state-funded schools reflects economic disparities that shape the educational experiences of students from different socio-economic backgrounds.

Private schools, often attended by students from affluent families, may benefit from better facilities, smaller class sizes, and a wider range of extracurricular activities. In contrast, state-funded schools in economically deprived areas may struggle with limited resources, impacting the overall learning environment.

Economic conditions also influence access to additional educational support, such as private tutoring and exam preparation resources. Students from more economically advantaged backgrounds may have greater access to these resources, potentially affecting their academic performance and future educational opportunities.

Addressing economic disparities in the United Kingdom involves not only enhancing funding for state-funded schools but also exploring policies that promote equal access to educational resources and support services. Initiatives to reduce the influence of socio-economic factors on educational outcomes are crucial for creating a more equitable high school education system.

Germany: Vocational Pathways and Economic Mobility

In Germany, economic conditions are closely linked to educational pathways, particularly in the context of vocational education. The German dual education system, which combines classroom learning with practical apprenticeships, reflects a cultural emphasis on vocational training as a viable and respected pathway.

Economic conditions influence the choices students make regarding their educational paths. Those from families with limited financial resources may see vocational training as a more accessible and pragmatic option, offering a direct entry into the workforce without incurring the financial burden associated with higher education.

The dual education system contributes to economic mobility by providing students with practical skills and industry-specific knowledge. Apprenticeships, often sponsored by companies, enable students to earn while they learn, offering a financially viable alternative to traditional academic routes.

However, economic conditions can also create disparities within the vocational education system. Students from more affluent backgrounds may have the flexibility to pursue higher education, potentially leading to managerial or specialized roles. Addressing economic disparities in the German context involves ensuring equal access to vocational opportunities and fostering a culture that values the diverse pathways available to students.

China: Urban-Rural Disparities and Educational Access

In China, economic conditions intersect with urban-rural disparities, significantly influencing access to high school education. Economic growth in urban centers has led to the development of well-equipped schools with access to advanced educational resources. In contrast, rural areas may experience a shortage of qualified teachers, outdated infrastructure, and limited access to educational technologies.

Economic conditions can create barriers for rural students, affecting their ability to pursue high school education. Financial constraints may force some families to prioritize other necessities over education, leading to higher dropout rates and limited access to quality learning environments.

Efforts to address economic disparities in China often involve targeted policies aimed at improving educational infrastructure in rural areas, providing financial assistance to families, and implementing initiatives to attract qualified teachers to underserved regions. These measures aim to create a more equitable educational landscape by addressing the economic challenges faced by rural students.

Japan: Educational Costs and Affordability

In Japan, economic conditions impact educational access through the cost of education, including tuition fees and associated expenses. While high school education in Japan is generally considered more affordable than higher education, economic considerations can still create disparities in access.

The cost of attending private high schools, which may offer additional educational resources and extracurricular activities, can be a significant barrier for families with limited financial means. Economic conditions influence the choices families make regarding the type of high school their children attend, potentially impacting the quality of education and opportunities available.

Government initiatives in Japan often focus on making education more accessible by providing financial assistance, scholarships, and support for families facing economic challenges. Ensuring that economic conditions do not limit educational opportunities remains a priority for creating a more inclusive high school education system.

South Korea: Private Education Costs and Academic Pressure

In South Korea, economic conditions are intricately tied to the costs of private education, known as "hagwon." While high school education in public schools is relatively affordable, the prevalence of private education institutions can create economic disparities in access to additional academic support and exam preparation resources.

Families with greater financial resources may afford extensive private education for their children, potentially leading to advantages in academic performance and university admissions. Economic conditions can thus influence the competitiveness of students in the high-stakes education system, where academic success is often a determinant of future economic prospects.

Government efforts in South Korea aim to address the influence of private education costs on economic disparities. Policies may include regulations on hagwon fees, financial assistance programs for low-income families, and initiatives to provide equal access to academic resources for all students.

India: Socioeconomic Barriers and Educational Inequities

In India, economic conditions contribute to significant disparities in access to high school education, particularly in rural and economically disadvantaged areas. While efforts have been made to improve primary education, economic challenges persist at the secondary level.

Families facing economic hardships may prioritize immediate needs over education, leading to higher dropout rates, especially among girls. Limited access to transportation and the absence of nearby high schools can further hinder students' ability to continue their education.

Government initiatives, such as scholarship programs and the provision of free textbooks, aim to alleviate economic barriers and promote high school education. However, addressing economic conditions requires a comprehensive approach that considers infrastructure development, community engagement, and targeted support for families facing financial challenges.

Brazil: Inequality in Educational Resources and Economic Disparities

In Brazil, economic conditions contribute to inequality in educational resources, impacting access to high school education. Economic disparities between urban and rural areas, as well as between affluent and impoverished neighborhoods, can create stark differences in the quality of schools and available educational resources.

Students from economically disadvantaged backgrounds may face challenges related to inadequate infrastructure, limited access to qualified teachers, and insufficient learning materials. Economic conditions can thus create barriers that hinder the educational experiences and outcomes of certain groups.

Government efforts in Brazil often involve policies aimed at reducing economic disparities in education, including targeted investments in infrastructure, teacher training programs, and initiatives to improve the overall quality of education in underserved areas.

Comparative Analysis: Common Challenges and Potential Solutions

A comparative analysis of the intersection between economic conditions and access to high school education across these diverse contexts reveals common challenges and potential solutions. Economic disparities consistently emerge as a significant barrier to educational access, impacting students' opportunities, the quality of education, and the overall educational experience.

Common challenges include inadequate funding for schools in economically disadvantaged areas, limited access to educational resources, and disparities in the quality of teaching staff. The digital divide, private education costs, and the affordability of additional academic support also represent shared challenges that stem from economic conditions.

Addressing these challenges requires a multifaceted approach that combines targeted policies, community engagement, and international collaboration. Potential solutions include:

1. Increased Funding and Resource Allocation: Governments can prioritize increased funding for schools in economically disadvantaged areas to ensure access to quality educational resources, infrastructure, and well-qualified teachers.

2. Scholarship Programs and Financial Assistance: Implementing scholarship programs and financial assistance initiatives can help alleviate economic barriers for students, ensuring that they can pursue high school education regardless of their financial circumstances.

3. Regulations on Private Education Costs: In contexts where private education costs create economic disparities, governments can consider implementing regulations on fees charged by private education institutions, ensuring that access to additional academic support is not limited by financial means.

4. Infrastructure Development in Underserved Areas: Targeted infrastructure development in rural and economically disadvantaged areas can enhance access to high school education by reducing transportation barriers and improving the overall learning environment.

5. Community Engagement and Awareness Programs: Initiatives that engage communities and raise awareness about the importance of education can help overcome cultural and economic barriers, encouraging families to prioritize high school education.

6. International Collaboration and Knowledge Sharing: Countries facing similar economic challenges can benefit from international collaboration and knowledge sharing. Learning from successful initiatives implemented in other contexts can inspire innovative solutions and policy interventions.

By addressing economic disparities and promoting equal access to high school education, these potential solutions aim to create a more inclusive and equitable educational landscape. The shared goal is to ensure that economic conditions do not serve as insurmountable barriers to educational opportunities, fostering a global commitment to providing quality high school education for all.

Socio-economic Factors in Educational Success

The interplay between socio-economic factors and educational success is a complex and influential dynamic that significantly shapes the high school experiences of students worldwide. Socio-economic conditions encompass a range of elements, including income levels, parental education, access to resources, and community environments. This exploration delves into the nuanced ways in which socio-economic factors impact educational success in high school, examining the challenges faced by students and identifying potential strategies to mitigate disparities.

Global Overview: Socio-economic Disparities as Determinants of Educational Trajectories

At a global level, socio-economic disparities are pivotal determinants of educational trajectories, influencing students' access to resources and opportunities. The World Bank estimates that socio-economic factors account for a significant portion of the variation in educational outcomes globally. The correlation between family background and educational success is a recurring theme, with students from more affluent families often benefiting from enhanced learning environments, access to extracurricular activities, and additional academic support.

Socio-economic factors impact not only the ability to access high-quality education but also the trajectory of educational paths. Students from economically advantaged backgrounds may have greater access to higher education, potentially leading to increased opportunities for career advancement. In contrast, those facing socio-economic challenges may encounter barriers that limit their educational aspirations and future prospects.

Understanding the nuanced ways in which socio-economic factors intersect with high school education is crucial for developing targeted interventions and policies aimed at fostering greater equity and inclusivity within the educational landscape.

United States: Socio-economic Disparities in Academic Achievement

In the United States, socio-economic disparities play a profound role in shaping academic achievement in high school. Students from higher-income households often have access to resources such as private tutoring, educational enrichment programs, and a conducive home learning environment. These advantages contribute to higher academic performance and better preparation for standardized tests.

Conversely, students from lower-income families may face challenges related to inadequate access to learning resources, limited exposure to cultural and extracurricular activities, and potential socio-economic stressors that can impact their academic focus. The achievement gap between students from different socio-economic backgrounds is a persistent challenge within the U.S. education system.

Parental involvement, a key socio-economic factor, also influences educational success. Higher-income families often have the resources and time to actively engage in their children's education, participating in school activities, providing additional support at home, and fostering a conducive learning environment. This active involvement contributes to positive educational outcomes.

Efforts to address socio-economic disparities in the United States involve targeted interventions such as early childhood education programs, initiatives to reduce the digital divide, and policies that aim to create more equitable funding for schools in economically disadvantaged areas.

United Kingdom: Class-Based Influences on Educational Attainment

In the United Kingdom, class-based influences significantly impact educational attainment in high school. The historic association between social class and educational opportunities persists, with students from higher social classes often benefiting from a range of advantages that contribute to academic success.

Private education, predominantly accessed by students from higher-income families, can provide smaller class sizes, enhanced extracurricular activities, and a network of educational support. These factors contribute to higher academic achievement and greater access to prestigious universities.

Conversely, students from working-class backgrounds may face challenges related to limited access to educational resources, fewer opportunities for enrichment activities, and potential barriers to academic aspirations. Socio-economic factors intersect with cultural influences, creating a complex dynamic that shapes the educational experiences of students.

Government initiatives in the United Kingdom aim to address class-based disparities through policies such as affirmative action in university admissions, targeted funding for schools in economically deprived areas, and efforts to promote social mobility. However, the entrenched nature of socio-economic influences requires ongoing and comprehensive strategies to create a more level playing field in high school education.

Germany: Vocational Pathways and Socio-economic Backgrounds

In Germany, socio-economic backgrounds influence the choice of educational pathways, particularly in the context of vocational education. The German dual education system, which combines classroom learning with practical apprenticeships, reflects a cultural emphasis on vocational training as a viable and respected pathway.

Students from lower socio-economic backgrounds may opt for vocational training as a more accessible route that provides practical skills and direct entry into the workforce. This choice is often influenced by economic considerations, as vocational training allows students to earn while they learn, avoiding the financial burden associated with higher education.

Conversely, students from more affluent backgrounds may have the flexibility to pursue higher education, potentially leading to managerial or specialized roles. The socio-economic background can thus shape not only the educational trajectory but also the subsequent career paths of individuals.

Addressing socio-economic factors in the German context involves initiatives to ensure equal access to vocational opportunities, career guidance programs that challenge stereotypes, and efforts to reduce stigmas associated with vocational pathways. Fostering a culture that values diverse educational and career trajectories is crucial for mitigating socio-economic influences on high school students.

China: Urban-Rural Disparities and Educational Aspirations

In China, socio-economic factors are intricately tied to urban-rural disparities, significantly influencing educational aspirations and outcomes. Economic growth in urban centers has led to the development of well-equipped schools with access to advanced educational resources. Students in these areas may have greater exposure to cultural and extracurricular activities, contributing to broader educational experiences.

Conversely, students in rural areas may face challenges related to limited access to quality educational resources, fewer extracurricular opportunities, and potential socio-economic constraints that impact their aspirations. The socio-economic divide between urban and rural environments creates disparities in the quality of high school education.

Socio-economic factors also intersect with cultural expectations, influencing the perceived value of education and the types of careers students aspire to pursue. Students from higher socio-economic backgrounds may have greater access to information about diverse career paths, while those facing economic challenges may have more limited exposure.

Government initiatives in China often involve targeted policies aimed at improving educational infrastructure in rural areas, providing financial assistance to families, and implementing programs to raise awareness about the importance of education. These measures aim to address socio-economic disparities and create a more equitable educational landscape.

Japan: Socio-economic Influences on Educational Choices

In Japan, socio-economic influences play a crucial role in shaping educational choices and aspirations. While high school education in Japan is generally accessible, socio-economic conditions can impact the type of high school a student attends and the subsequent trajectory of their educational journey.

Students from higher-income families may have the means to choose private high schools that offer additional educational resources, smaller class sizes, and enhanced extracurricular activities. This choice can contribute to a more competitive academic environment and potentially impact university admissions.

Conversely, students from lower socio-economic backgrounds may attend public high schools, where class sizes may be larger, and resources may be more limited. Socio-economic factors can thus create disparities in the quality of high school education and subsequent opportunities for higher education.

Government initiatives in Japan often focus on making education more accessible through financial assistance programs, scholarships, and support for families facing economic challenges. However, addressing entrenched socio-economic influences requires ongoing efforts to create a more equitable high school education system.

South Korea: Socio-economic Pressures and Academic Performance

In South Korea, socio-economic factors contribute to intense academic pressures and disparities in educational outcomes. The prevalence of private education institutions, known as "hagwon," introduces socio-economic influences on the competitiveness of students within the high-stakes education system.

Families with greater financial resources may afford extensive private education for their children, potentially leading to advantages in academic performance and university admissions. Socio-economic conditions can thus influence the ability of students to access additional academic support and resources, contributing to disparities in academic achievement.

The socio-economic pressures on South Korean students are also linked to cultural expectations regarding academic success. Families may invest significant resources in private education to enhance their children's prospects, creating a competitive environment where socio-economic factors intersect with academic performance.

Government efforts in South Korea aim to address the influence of socio-economic factors on education by implementing regulations on hagwon fees, providing financial assistance programs for low-income families, and initiatives to ensure equal access to academic resources for all students.

India: Economic Barriers and Educational Inequities

In India, socio-economic factors contribute to significant educational inequities, particularly in rural and economically disadvantaged areas. While efforts have been made to improve primary education, socio-economic challenges persist at the secondary level.

Students from lower socio-economic backgrounds may face barriers such as the cost of education, lack of access to transportation, and limited availability of high schools in their vicinity. These challenges can result in higher dropout rates, especially among girls, perpetuating socio-economic disparities in educational attainment.

Government initiatives, including scholarship programs, the provision of free textbooks, and awareness campaigns, aim to alleviate socio-economic barriers and promote high school education. However, the complex intersection of socio-economic factors requires a comprehensive approach that considers infrastructure development, community engagement, and targeted support for families facing financial challenges.

Brazil: Socio-economic Inequality and Educational Resources

In Brazil, socio-economic conditions contribute to inequality in educational resources, impacting access to high school education. Economic disparities between urban and rural areas, as well as between affluent and impoverished neighborhoods, can create stark differences in the quality of schools and available educational resources.

Students from economically disadvantaged backgrounds may face challenges related to inadequate infrastructure, limited access to qualified teachers, and insufficient learning materials. Socio-economic factors can thus create barriers that hinder the educational experiences and outcomes of certain groups.

Government efforts in Brazil often involve policies aimed at reducing socio-economic disparities in education, including targeted investments in infrastructure, teacher training programs, and initiatives to improve the overall quality of education in underserved areas.

Comparative Analysis: Common Themes in Socio-economic Influences

A comparative analysis of the impact of socio-economic factors on high school education across diverse global contexts reveals common themes that transcend national boundaries. While the specific manifestations may vary, several shared challenges and potential solutions emerge.

Common Challenges:

1. Limited Access to Resources: Students from lower socio-economic backgrounds often have limited access to resources such as private tutoring, extracurricular activities, and educational materials, creating disparities in educational experiences.

2. Inequities in Parental Involvement: Socio-economic factors can influence the level of parental involvement in a child's education, with higher-income families often having more resources and time to actively engage in supporting their children's learning.

3. Impact on Academic Aspirations: Socio-economic conditions can shape students' aspirations, influencing the types of careers they consider and the level of educational attainment they strive for.

4. Cultural Expectations and Pressures: Socio-economic influences intersect with cultural expectations, contributing to academic pressures and influencing the perceived value of certain educational paths.

Potential Solutions:

1. Targeted Financial Assistance: Implementing scholarship programs, grants, and financial assistance initiatives can help alleviate economic barriers and ensure that students from all socio-economic backgrounds have equal access to educational opportunities.

2. Community Engagement Programs: Initiatives that engage communities and raise awareness about the importance of education can help overcome cultural and economic barriers, fostering a supportive environment for all students.

3. Equalizing Access to Resources: Policies that focus on equalizing access to educational resources, including extracurricular activities, tutoring, and educational materials, can help bridge socio-economic gaps in high school education.

4. Culturally Responsive Teaching: Recognizing and addressing the cultural influences on education, educators can adopt culturally responsive teaching practices that acknowledge and respect the diverse backgrounds of students.

5. Mentorship Programs: Establishing mentorship programs can provide additional support for students facing socio-economic challenges, offering guidance and encouragement to navigate educational pathways.

6. Policy Interventions: Governments can implement policy interventions that address systemic inequalities, including targeted funding for schools in economically disadvantaged areas, regulations on private education costs, and efforts to reduce the digital divide.

By acknowledging and addressing the common challenges arising from socio-economic influences, educational systems can work towards creating more inclusive and equitable high school environments. The shared goal is to ensure that socio-economic factors do not become insurmountable barriers to educational success, fostering a global commitment to providing quality high school education for all.

Impact of Income Inequality

Income inequality stands as a significant societal challenge with far-reaching implications, and its impact on high school education is a multifaceted and nuanced aspect of this broader issue. This exploration delves into the ways in which income inequality influences the educational landscape, shaping access to resources, opportunities, and the overall quality of high school education. From a global perspective to specific case studies, this section examines the intricate relationship between income inequality and high school education.

Global Overview: Income Inequality as a Determinant of Educational Opportunities

At a global level, income inequality is a critical determinant of educational opportunities, with profound implications for high school education. The World Economic Forum reports that income inequality remains a persistent challenge, contributing to disparities in access to education, educational outcomes, and future economic prospects.

Income Inequality and Access to High-Quality Education:

In many parts of the world, income inequality directly impacts access to high-quality education. Higher-income families often have the means to enroll their children in well-funded private schools, providing smaller class sizes, better facilities, and a broader range of extracurricular activities. This access to resources creates a significant advantage in terms of academic preparation and overall educational experience.

Conversely, lower-income families may face barriers to accessing quality education. Public schools in economically disadvantaged areas may experience underfunding, leading to larger class sizes, limited resources, and fewer enrichment opportunities. The impact of income inequality on educational access contributes to a cycle of disadvantage, where economic conditions directly influence the quality of education a student receives.

Educational Outcomes and Future Prospects:

The consequences of income inequality extend beyond high school education, influencing educational outcomes and future prospects. Students from higher-income backgrounds often have access to additional educational support, including private tutoring and test preparation resources. This advantage can contribute to higher academic achievement, better performance on standardized tests, and increased opportunities for higher education.

In contrast, students from lower-income backgrounds may face challenges related to limited access to academic resources, less exposure to cultural and extracurricular activities, and potential socio-economic stressors that impact their academic focus. The educational outcomes associated with income inequality can perpetuate disparities in employment opportunities, income levels, and overall economic mobility.

Case Studies: Income Inequality's Varied Impact on High School Education

United States: Persistent Gaps in Educational Resources:

In the United States, income inequality contributes to persistent gaps in educational resources and opportunities. The U.S. Department of Education reports that schools with higher percentages of students from low-income families often receive less funding than schools with more affluent student populations.

This funding disparity translates into differences in teacher quality, access to advanced coursework, and availability of extracurricular activities. Students in economically disadvantaged schools may face challenges related to outdated infrastructure, fewer educational materials, and a less supportive learning environment. The impact of income inequality on high school education in the U.S. is evident in the unequal distribution of resources, hindering the ability of students from lower-income backgrounds to compete on an equal footing.

Efforts to address the impact of income inequality on high school education in the United States involve initiatives to equalize funding for schools, increase support for teachers in economically disadvantaged areas, and implement policies that promote equity in access to educational resources. Despite these efforts, income inequality continues to pose challenges to achieving educational equity.

Brazil: Disparities in Educational Quality Between Urban and Rural Areas:

In Brazil, income inequality contributes to disparities in educational quality between urban and rural areas. The World Bank highlights the challenges faced by students in rural schools, where economic conditions often result in limited access to qualified teachers, inadequate infrastructure, and insufficient learning materials.

Students in urban areas, particularly those from higher-income families, may benefit from better-funded schools with more experienced teachers and a wider range of educational resources. The impact of income inequality on high school education in Brazil is reflected in the divergent experiences of students based on their geographical and socio-economic contexts.

Government efforts in Brazil include policies aimed at reducing income inequality, such as targeted investments in rural education, teacher training programs, and initiatives to improve the overall quality of schools in economically disadvantaged regions. However, addressing the impact of income inequality on high school education requires sustained efforts to bridge the urban-rural divide.

South Africa: Legacy of Apartheid and Educational Inequities:

In South Africa, the historical legacy of apartheid has left a lasting impact on income inequality and educational inequities. The apartheid era systematically marginalized certain racial groups, resulting in economic disparities that continue to influence educational opportunities.

Students from historically disadvantaged communities, often characterized by lower income levels, face challenges related to inadequate infrastructure, a shortage of qualified teachers, and limited access to educational resources. The impact of income inequality on high school education in South Africa is intertwined with historical injustices, creating barriers that persist despite post-apartheid efforts to promote equality.

Government initiatives in South Africa involve affirmative action policies, targeted funding for schools in historically disadvantaged areas, and efforts to address systemic inequities. However, the deeply entrenched nature of income inequality requires comprehensive strategies to create a more inclusive and equitable high school education system.

China: Urban-Rural Disparities and Educational Access:

In China, income inequality manifests in urban-rural disparities, significantly influencing educational access and opportunities. The rapid economic growth in urban centers has led to the development of well-equipped schools with access to advanced educational resources. Students in urban areas, particularly those from higher-income families, may benefit from a more competitive learning environment.

Conversely, students in rural areas may face challenges related to limited access to quality educational resources, fewer extracurricular opportunities, and potential socio-economic constraints that impact their ability to pursue high school education. The impact of income inequality on high school education in China is closely tied to geographical disparities, creating a divide in educational experiences based on urbanization and economic development.

Government initiatives in China include targeted policies aimed at improving educational infrastructure in rural areas, providing financial assistance to families, and implementing programs to raise awareness about the importance of education. These measures aim to address income inequality and create a more equitable educational landscape by bridging the urban-rural gap.

India: Socio-economic Barriers and Educational Inequities:

In India, income inequality contributes to significant educational inequities, particularly in rural and economically disadvantaged areas. The challenges faced by students in these regions include the cost of education, lack of access to transportation, and limited availability of high schools.

Students from lower-income backgrounds may encounter barriers that hinder their ability to pursue high school education, perpetuating a cycle of socio-economic disparities in educational attainment. The impact of income inequality on high school education in India is evident in the uneven distribution of resources and opportunities, creating challenges for students striving to overcome economic constraints.

Government initiatives in India include scholarship programs, the provision of free textbooks, and awareness campaigns to promote high school education. However, addressing the impact of income inequality requires a comprehensive approach that considers infrastructure development, community engagement, and targeted support for families facing financial challenges.

Comparative Analysis: Common Threads in the Impact of Income Inequality

A comparative analysis of the impact of income inequality on high school education across diverse global contexts reveals common threads that underscore the universality of certain challenges and potential solutions.

Common Challenges:

1. Resource Disparities: Income inequality consistently results in disparities in educational resources, with higher-income individuals having greater access to well-funded schools, experienced teachers, and a broader range of extracurricular activities.

2. Geographical Divides: The impact of income inequality often manifests in geographical divides, creating disparities in educational experiences between urban and rural areas.

3. Historical Legacies: In regions with a history of systemic inequalities, such as apartheid in South Africa, the impact of income inequality is intertwined with historical legacies that continue to shape educational opportunities.

4. Cost of Education: The cost of education emerges as a common barrier, with students from lower-income backgrounds facing challenges related to affordability and access to financial resources.

Potential Solutions:

1. Equitable Funding: Policies that promote equitable funding for schools, irrespective of socio-economic conditions, can help bridge resource disparities and create a more level playing field.

2. Geographical Equity: Initiatives aimed at reducing urban-rural disparities, including targeted investments in rural

education and efforts to improve infrastructure, can address the impact of income inequality on high school education.

3. Historical Redress: Acknowledging and addressing historical injustices, as seen in post-apartheid South Africa, involves policies that seek to redress systemic inequalities and promote educational equity.

4. Financial Assistance Programs: Implementing financial assistance programs, including scholarships and grants, can help alleviate the cost barriers associated with high school education.

5. Community Engagement: Initiatives that engage communities and raise awareness about the importance of education can foster a supportive environment and overcome cultural and economic barriers.

6. Policy Interventions: Governments can implement policy interventions that target income inequality at its roots, addressing systemic issues and promoting economic inclusivity.

By recognizing the common challenges and potential solutions that emerge from the impact of income inequality on high school education, educational systems can work towards creating more inclusive and equitable environments. The shared goal is to ensure that income inequality does not become a barrier to educational success, fostering a global commitment to providing quality high school education for all.

Government Initiatives to Address Economic Disparities

As the impact of economic disparities on high school education becomes increasingly evident, governments worldwide are recognizing the urgency of implementing targeted initiatives to address these disparities and promote educational equity. This exploration delves into various government interventions designed to mitigate economic inequalities and ensure that all students have equal access to quality high school education. From financial assistance programs to policy frameworks, this section examines the multifaceted approaches governments are employing to bridge the gap in educational opportunities.

Global Overview: A Collective Call to Action

On the global stage, there is a collective acknowledgment of the need to address economic disparities in education. International organizations, such as UNESCO and the World Bank, advocate for inclusive policies that prioritize access to education, irrespective of socio-economic conditions. The United Nations Sustainable Development Goals (SDGs) specifically highlight the importance of achieving quality education for all, emphasizing the role of governments in creating an equitable educational landscape.

Financial Assistance Programs: Empowering Students Across Economies

One of the primary tools governments employ to address economic disparities in high school education is the implementation of financial assistance programs. These programs aim to alleviate the financial burden on families, making education more accessible to students from economically disadvantaged backgrounds.

Scholarships and Grants:

Governments often establish scholarship and grant programs to provide financial support to students pursuing high school education. These initiatives may be merit-based, need-based, or a combination of both, ensuring that talented students with limited financial means can access quality education. Scholarships may cover tuition fees, textbooks, and other educational expenses, allowing students to focus on their studies without the burden of excessive costs.

Examples from Around the Globe:

- United States: The U.S. federal government, along with state governments, offers various scholarship and grant programs to support students in accessing higher education. Programs like Pell Grants target low-income students, providing financial aid based on need.

- India: The National Scholarship Portal in India centralizes scholarship schemes offered by different government departments. These scholarships cover a range of educational levels, including high school, and aim to support students from economically weaker sections.

- Brazil: The Brazilian government's Bolsa Família program includes educational grants to encourage school attendance among children from low-income families. This initiative contributes to reducing economic barriers to education.

Subsidized Education: Making Quality Education Affordable

Governments also implement subsidized education programs to reduce the overall cost of high school education for all students. By providing financial assistance to educational institutions, governments can ensure that tuition fees remain affordable, making education more accessible to a broader spectrum of society.

Examples from Around the Globe:

- Germany: The German education system, known for its emphasis on free or low-cost higher education, extends this philosophy to high school education. Public high schools are generally funded by the government, minimizing the financial burden on students and their families.

- South Korea: South Korea has implemented policies to reduce the financial burden on families, including offering free high school education in public schools. This initiative aims to ensure that economic considerations do not hinder students' access to quality education.

- Nordic Countries: Countries like Sweden, Denmark, and Norway have a tradition of providing free education at all levels, including high school. This approach is rooted in the belief that education is a public good and should be accessible to all, regardless of economic status.

Policy Frameworks Globally: A Holistic Approach to Inclusivity

Governments adopt comprehensive policy frameworks to create an inclusive educational environment that addresses economic disparities. These frameworks encompass a range of initiatives, from funding allocation strategies to targeted interventions aimed at specific socio-economic groups.

Examples from Around the Globe:

- Finland: Finland's education system is often lauded for its inclusivity. The country's policies focus on minimizing socio-economic disparities by ensuring that all schools, regardless of location or economic standing, receive adequate funding. This contributes to a more equitable distribution of resources and opportunities.

- Canada: Canada's commitment to inclusivity is reflected in its policies that address the unique needs of Indigenous communities. Initiatives such as the First Nations Education Act aim to provide culturally relevant and equitable education, acknowledging the historical economic disparities faced by Indigenous populations.

- Singapore: Singapore's policies prioritize equal access to education for all students. The government emphasizes early intervention programs to support students from lower-income families, providing additional resources and guidance to ensure a level playing field.

Community Engagement Programs: Fostering Supportive Environments

In addition to financial assistance and policy frameworks, governments recognize the importance of community engagement programs to create a supportive educational environment. These programs involve collaboration between schools, families, and communities to address not only economic disparities but also the broader social factors that may affect educational outcomes.

Examples from Around the Globe:

- Australia: Australia's Indigenous Education Strategy involves community engagement initiatives to improve educational outcomes for Indigenous students. These programs aim to bridge cultural and economic gaps, recognizing the interconnected nature of these disparities.

- Japan: Japan's community-based support programs involve local governments and educational institutions working together to identify and address the needs of economically disadvantaged students. These initiatives focus on creating a holistic support system that extends beyond financial aid.

- United Kingdom: Community-based mentoring programs in the United Kingdom connect students with mentors who provide guidance and support. These initiatives are particularly beneficial for students from economically disadvantaged backgrounds, offering them personalized assistance in navigating educational challenges.

Innovative Approaches: Leveraging Technology to Bridge Gaps

Governments are increasingly leveraging technology to bridge economic gaps in education. By integrating digital tools and online resources into high school education, authorities aim to provide equal access to educational content, irrespective of students' economic backgrounds.

Examples from Around the Globe:

- Kenya: The Kenyan government's Digital Literacy Program equips primary school students with tablets, aiming to enhance their learning experience. By introducing technology at an early stage, the government seeks to create a more level playing field in accessing educational resources.

- Uruguay: Uruguay's One Laptop per Child initiative provides laptops to students in public schools, emphasizing the importance of digital literacy. This program is designed to ensure that all students, regardless of economic status, have access to educational technology.

- India: Initiatives like the National Digital Library of India aim to provide free access to a vast repository of educational resources, including textbooks, journals, and multimedia content. This digital platform helps bridge economic gaps by offering a wealth of information to students across the country.

Challenges in Implementation: Navigating Complex Realities

While governments strive to address economic disparities in high school education, the implementation of these initiatives is not without challenges. Navigating complex economic, social, and cultural landscapes requires careful planning, continuous evaluation, and adaptability to evolving circumstances.

1. Resource Allocation Challenges:

Ensuring equitable resource allocation remains a persistent challenge. Limited financial resources, coupled with competing demands in areas such as healthcare and infrastructure, can constrain the funding available for education. Governments must prioritize education as a key investment for societal development.

2. Cultural Sensitivity and Inclusivity:

Developing policies and programs that are culturally sensitive and inclusive is essential. Recognizing the diverse cultural contexts within a country and tailoring initiatives to address specific socio-economic challenges faced by different communities is crucial for the success of government interventions.

3. Accessibility to Remote and Marginalized Areas:

Ensuring that educational opportunities reach remote and marginalized areas poses logistical challenges. In regions with limited infrastructure, providing access to quality high school education may require innovative solutions, such as mobile classrooms or virtual learning platforms.

4. Long-Term Impact Assessment:

Assessing the long-term impact of government initiatives on economic disparities and educational outcomes requires sustained efforts. Rigorous evaluation mechanisms are essential to determine the effectiveness of policies and identify areas for improvement.

Conclusion: A Continued Commitment to Educational Equity

Governments play a pivotal role in shaping the educational landscape and addressing economic disparities in high school education. Through a combination of financial assistance programs, policy frameworks, community engagement, and innovative approaches, authorities worldwide are working towards creating a more inclusive and equitable educational environment.

As we navigate the complexities of economic disparities, it is imperative to recognize that achieving educational equity is an ongoing process. Governments must remain committed to refining and expanding their initiatives, adapting to emerging challenges, and fostering a collective sense of responsibility for the well-being and educational success of all students. By prioritizing inclusive education, governments contribute not only to individual empowerment but also to the broader goal of building a society where every student has the opportunity to reach their full potential, irrespective of economic circumstances.

Chapter 5: Government Policies and High School Education

Policy Frameworks Globally: Navigating the Educational Landscape

Government policies play a pivotal role in shaping the high school education landscape globally. These policies are crafted to address diverse challenges, ranging from economic disparities to cultural influences, and are designed to create an environment conducive to learning and development. This exploration delves into policy frameworks adopted by governments worldwide, analyzing their key components, successes, and challenges. From overarching education policies to targeted interventions, this section examines the dynamic and evolving nature of government strategies in the realm of high school education.

Global Overview: Diverse Approaches to Educational Governance

As high school education is a cornerstone of individual development and societal progress, governments across the globe formulate policy frameworks to guide the functioning of educational systems. While the specific details of these policies vary significantly based on cultural, economic, and historical contexts, certain overarching themes and principles underpin many policy frameworks globally.

1. Universal Access to Education:

A common thread in policy frameworks worldwide is the commitment to achieving universal access to high school education. Governments recognize the transformative power of education and aim to ensure that all students, irrespective of socio-economic background or geographical location, have the opportunity to attend and complete high school.

2. Quality and Relevance of Education:

Beyond mere access, policy frameworks emphasize the importance of delivering high-quality and relevant education. Governments strive to equip students with the skills and knowledge needed to navigate an increasingly complex global landscape. This includes updating curricula, incorporating technology, and fostering critical thinking and problem-solving skills.

3. Inclusivity and Diversity:

In recognition of diverse student populations, policy frameworks often emphasize inclusivity and diversity. Governments aim to create an educational environment that respects and accommodates various cultural, linguistic, and socio-economic backgrounds. Inclusive policies also extend to students with disabilities, ensuring equal opportunities for all.

4. Lifelong Learning and Continuous Education:

Acknowledging the rapid pace of change in the modern world, policy frameworks increasingly emphasize the importance of lifelong learning. High school education is seen as a stepping stone in a broader educational journey, with policies encouraging continuous education and skill development throughout individuals' lives.

5. Global Competence and Citizenship:

In an interconnected world, governments recognize the need to cultivate global competence among high school students. Policy frameworks often incorporate elements that foster an understanding of global issues, intercultural communication skills, and a sense of global citizenship.

6. Collaboration and Stakeholder Engagement:

Effective education policies involve collaboration among various stakeholders, including educators, parents, communities, and businesses. Governments seek to engage these stakeholders in the policymaking process to ensure that diverse perspectives are considered and that policies are effectively implemented.

Examples from Around the Globe:

- Finland: Finland's education system is often lauded for its comprehensive and inclusive policies. The Finnish National Core Curriculum emphasizes holistic development, individualized learning paths, and a reduced emphasis on standardized testing. The overarching goal is to provide a high-quality, equitable education for all students.

- Singapore: Singapore's policy framework prioritizes educational excellence and global competitiveness. The government's emphasis on a meritocratic system, a strong focus on science and mathematics education, and continuous curriculum updates align with the country's goal of preparing students for the challenges of a knowledge-based economy.

- Canada: Canada's education policies reflect a commitment to inclusivity and cultural diversity. Efforts to incorporate Indigenous perspectives in curricula, bilingual education in regions with significant linguistic diversity, and targeted programs for marginalized communities contribute to a more inclusive high school education system.

- South Korea: South Korea's policies highlight the country's dedication to academic achievement and global competitiveness. The emphasis on rigorous standardized testing, after-school tutoring programs, and initiatives to promote science and technology education reflects the government's commitment to excellence in high school education.

- New Zealand: New Zealand's policy framework emphasizes a holistic approach to education. The incorporation of Maori cultural perspectives, a focus on student well-being, and an inclusive curriculum that recognizes diverse learning needs contribute to a balanced and comprehensive high school education system.

Addressing Regional Disparities: Tailoring Policies to Diverse Contexts

The global educational landscape is characterized by significant regional disparities, and governments tailor their policy frameworks to address the unique challenges and opportunities present in different regions.

1. Urban-Rural Divide:

In many countries, the urban-rural divide is a notable factor influencing educational access and outcomes. Policies are designed to bridge this gap, ensuring that students in rural areas have equitable access to high-quality education. Initiatives may include investments in rural infrastructure, incentives for educators to work in rural schools, and the use of technology to deliver educational content.

Examples from Around the Globe:

- China: China's policies recognize the urban-rural disparities in educational resources. Initiatives such as the Rural Teacher Support Program aim to attract and retain qualified teachers in rural areas, addressing the imbalance in educational opportunities between urban and rural schools.

- India: India's Sarva Shiksha Abhiyan (Education for All) program focuses on improving the quality of education in rural areas. The program includes provisions for infrastructure development, teacher training, and community involvement to enhance educational outcomes in remote and underserved regions.

2. Indigenous Education:

Governments in regions with Indigenous populations often develop specific policies to address the unique needs and challenges faced by Indigenous students. These policies aim to incorporate Indigenous perspectives into curricula, provide culturally relevant education, and address historical injustices.

Examples from Around the Globe:

- Australia: Australia's Closing the Gap initiative focuses on improving educational outcomes for Indigenous students. The initiative includes measures to increase school attendance, enhance cultural responsiveness in education, and provide targeted support for Indigenous students.

- Canada: Canada's commitment to Indigenous education is reflected in policies such as the First Nations Education Act. The act aims to empower Indigenous communities in overseeing their education systems, incorporating Indigenous languages and cultures, and addressing historical inequities.

3. Socio-Economic Disparities:

Policies addressing socio-economic disparities in education often focus on providing additional support to students from economically disadvantaged backgrounds. Financial assistance programs, subsidized education, and targeted interventions aim to level the playing field and ensure that economic circumstances do not limit educational opportunities.

Examples from Around the Globe:

- Brazil: Brazil's Bolsa Família program includes components that incentivize school attendance and academic performance among children from low-income families. The program's educational grants contribute to reducing socio-economic barriers to high school education.

- United States: In the United States, federal programs such as Title I aim to provide financial assistance to schools with a high percentage of students from low-income families. These funds support initiatives to improve educational outcomes and opportunities for economically disadvantaged students.

4. Cultural Sensitivity:

Recognizing the diversity of cultural contexts within a country, some governments develop policies that promote cultural sensitivity in education. These policies aim to create an inclusive curriculum that reflects the cultural heritage of students and fosters a positive learning environment.

Examples from Around the Globe:

- Japan: Japan's policies emphasize the importance of education that is sensitive to local cultural contexts. Efforts are made to incorporate regional perspectives into curricula, ensuring that students' cultural identities are respected and valued in the educational process.

- South Africa: South Africa's policies reflect the country's commitment to multicultural education. Initiatives focus on promoting the use of multiple languages in education, acknowledging the diverse cultural backgrounds of students, and creating an inclusive educational environment.

Innovative Approaches: Adapting to a Changing Educational Landscape

In response to the rapid evolution of technology and the shifting demands of the job market, governments are incorporating innovative approaches into their policy frameworks. These approaches aim to prepare students for the challenges of the future by integrating technology, fostering critical thinking skills, and promoting creativity.

1. Technology Integration:

The integration of technology in education is a common feature of modern policy frameworks. Governments recognize the potential of digital tools to enhance learning experiences, provide access to diverse educational resources, and prepare students for a technology-driven world.

Examples from Around the Globe:

- Estonia: Estonia's policies highlight the country's commitment to digital education. Initiatives include providing students with digital devices, promoting e-learning platforms, and incorporating coding into the curriculum. These efforts aim to equip students with the digital skills necessary for the 21st-century workforce.

- United Arab Emirates: The UAE's Smart Learning Initiative focuses on integrating technology into all aspects of education. Policies promote the use of e-learning resources, interactive platforms, and digital assessments to enhance the quality and accessibility of high school education.

2. Project-Based Learning and Skills Development:

As the nature of work evolves, policies increasingly emphasize the development of practical skills through project-based learning. Governments aim to equip students with problem-solving abilities, creativity, and adaptability, preparing them for a dynamic and competitive job market.

Examples from Around the Globe:

- Singapore: Singapore's SkillsFuture initiative focuses on skills development and lifelong learning. The policy encourages students to explore diverse learning pathways, including vocational education and apprenticeships, to acquire practical skills aligned with industry needs.

- Germany: Germany's dual education system combines classroom learning with practical apprenticeships. The policy framework emphasizes the importance of hands-on experience, ensuring that students develop both theoretical knowledge and practical skills that are directly applicable in the workforce.

3. Flexible Learning Pathways:

Recognizing the diverse talents and interests of students, some governments implement policies that offer flexible learning pathways. These policies provide alternatives to traditional academic routes, allowing students to pursue vocational education, arts, or other specialized fields.

Examples from Around the Globe:

- Netherlands: The Netherlands' policies support a diverse range of learning pathways. The Dutch education system allows students to choose between academic and vocational tracks, providing flexibility to pursue careers in fields such as technology, healthcare, or the arts.

- Australia: Australia's policies emphasize the importance of flexible and personalized learning. Initiatives such as the Australian Curriculum aim to provide a broad education foundation while allowing students to tailor their learning experiences to align with their interests and career goals.

Challenges in Implementation: Navigating Complex Realities

While policy frameworks are designed to address the multifaceted challenges of high school education, the implementation of these policies often encounters various obstacles. Navigating the complex realities of educational systems requires governments to be adaptive, responsive, and mindful of the diverse contexts in which policies are enacted.

1. Resource Allocation Challenges:

Effective policy implementation relies on adequate resource allocation. However, limited financial resources, competing priorities, and bureaucratic hurdles can pose challenges. Governments must strike a balance between ambitious policy goals and the practicalities of funding and resource availability.

2. Curriculum Relevance and Adaptability:

Developing a curriculum that remains relevant and adaptable to changing societal needs is an ongoing challenge. Policymakers face the task of ensuring that educational content reflects emerging knowledge, technological advancements, and evolving global trends.

3. Teacher Training and Professional Development:

The success of policy frameworks depends significantly on the capacity of educators to implement changes in the classroom. Teacher training and ongoing professional development are crucial aspects of successful policy implementation, requiring continuous investment and support.

4. Cultural Sensitivity and Local Contexts:

Policies that aim to be culturally sensitive and inclusive must navigate the diverse cultural contexts within a country. The challenge lies in developing policies that are applicable across various cultural landscapes while acknowledging and respecting the unique identities of different communities.

5. Technological Infrastructure and Accessibility:

The integration of technology in education faces challenges related to technological infrastructure and accessibility. In regions with limited access to digital resources, ensuring that all students can benefit from technology-driven educational initiatives requires strategic planning and investment.

Conclusion: A Dynamic Path Forward

As we explore the policy frameworks shaping high school education globally, it becomes evident that the educational landscape is dynamic and continually evolving. Governments play a critical role in steering this evolution, responding to challenges, embracing innovation, and prioritizing the educational needs of diverse student populations.

The success of policy frameworks lies not only in their formulation but also in their adaptability to changing circumstances. Governments must remain agile, continuously reassessing policies, and engaging with stakeholders to address emerging challenges. By fostering a collaborative approach, respecting cultural diversity, and incorporating innovative strategies, policymakers can contribute to the creation of high school education systems that empower students to thrive in the complexities of the 21st century.

In the chapters that follow, we will delve deeper into specific aspects of high school education, examining the impact of cultural influences, economic disparities, technology integration, and global assessments. Each facet contributes to the intricate tapestry of learning, and understanding the policies that underpin these elements is crucial for comprehending the challenges and opportunities inherent in high school education on a global scale.

Educational Reforms: Transforming High School Education Globally

Educational reforms represent a dynamic and essential component of government policies aimed at shaping high school education globally. These reforms are driven by the recognition of evolving societal needs, technological advancements, and the imperative to prepare students for a rapidly changing world. In this exploration, we delve into the multifaceted realm of educational reforms, examining their objectives, implementation challenges, and transformative impact on the high school education landscape.

Introduction to Educational Reforms: A Catalyst for Change

Educational reforms encompass deliberate and systematic changes to the structure, curriculum, and methodologies of high school education. These reforms are typically driven by a combination of factors, including shifts in the job market, advancements in pedagogical understanding, and the need to address emerging challenges in the educational landscape. Governments worldwide recognize the importance of staying ahead of these changes to ensure that high school education remains relevant, effective, and inclusive.

Key Objectives of Educational Reforms:

- Enhancing Relevance: Reforms aim to align high school education with the evolving needs of society and the job market. This includes updating curricula to reflect current knowledge, fostering critical thinking skills, and incorporating real-world applications into learning experiences.

- Promoting Inclusivity: Educational reforms often prioritize inclusivity by addressing disparities in access and outcomes. This involves designing policies that cater to diverse student populations, accommodating various learning styles, and ensuring that educational opportunities are accessible to all.

- Integrating Technology: Recognizing the role of technology in modern life, reforms focus on integrating digital tools into high school education. This includes leveraging educational technology for enhanced learning experiences, expanding access to resources, and preparing students for a technology-driven future.

- Emphasizing Lifelong Learning: Educational reforms promote a shift towards a lifelong learning mindset. This involves instilling in students the importance of continuous skill development, adaptability, and a readiness to embrace learning opportunities throughout their lives.

- Improving Assessment Practices: Reforms often reevaluate assessment methods to ensure they align with educational goals. This includes exploring alternative assessment methods, moving beyond traditional standardized testing, and adopting approaches that provide a more comprehensive view of students' capabilities.

Global Trends in Educational Reforms:

While educational reforms are context-specific, certain global trends highlight shared challenges and priorities across countries.

- Competency-Based Education: Many reforms are centered around a shift from time-based education to competency-based education. This approach focuses on students mastering specific skills and knowledge, allowing for more personalized learning paths.

- Project-Based Learning: Emphasizing practical application, project-based learning is gaining prominence in educational reforms. This method engages students in real-world projects, fostering critical thinking, collaboration, and problem-solving skills.

- Social-Emotional Learning (SEL): Acknowledging the importance of emotional intelligence, SEL is becoming integral to educational reforms. This includes initiatives to develop students' social and emotional skills, such as self-awareness, empathy, and interpersonal communication.

- Global Citizenship Education: Educational reforms increasingly emphasize the importance of preparing students to be global citizens. This involves incorporating global perspectives into curricula, promoting cultural awareness, and encouraging a sense of responsibility towards global challenges.

Implementation Challenges in Educational Reforms:

Despite the transformative potential of educational reforms, their successful implementation is often fraught with challenges.

- Resistance to Change: Stakeholders, including educators, parents, and administrators, may resist changes to established educational practices. Overcoming resistance requires effective communication, professional development, and a clear understanding of the benefits of the proposed reforms.

- Resource Constraints: Implementing reforms often requires significant financial and human resources. Budgetary constraints, inadequate infrastructure, and a lack of trained personnel can hinder the successful execution of ambitious reform initiatives.

- Policy Consistency and Long-Term Commitment: Consistency in policy across political transitions is crucial for the sustained success of educational reforms. Frequent changes in policy direction or a lack of long-term commitment can impede progress and create uncertainty.

- Assessment Challenges: Shifting assessment practices is a complex undertaking. Designing and implementing new assessment methods that effectively measure the desired outcomes of reforms while avoiding unintended consequences is a persistent challenge.

- Equity Concerns: Reforms may inadvertently exacerbate existing inequalities in educational access and outcomes. Policymakers must carefully consider the potential impact of reforms on different socio-economic groups to ensure equity.

Case Studies in Educational Reforms:

- Finland's Holistic Approach: Finland's education system is often lauded for its holistic approach and student-centric reforms. The emphasis on reduced standardized testing, minimal homework, and a focus on well-rounded education contributes to Finland's success in educational outcomes.

- Singapore's SkillsFuture Initiative: Singapore's SkillsFuture initiative exemplifies a forward-looking approach to education. The initiative emphasizes skills development, continuous learning, and the importance of preparing students for the demands of a rapidly changing economy.

- Canada's Inclusive Education Policies: Canada's commitment to inclusivity is reflected in its education policies. Efforts to integrate Indigenous perspectives, accommodate linguistic diversity, and address the unique needs of various communities contribute to a more inclusive high school education system.

- South Korea's Technological Integration: South Korea's education system has undergone significant technological integration. The government's commitment to digital learning, smart classrooms, and technology-driven pedagogies reflects a proactive stance toward preparing students for a digital future.

- New Zealand's Cultural Inclusivity: New Zealand's education reforms emphasize cultural inclusivity. Incorporating Maori cultural perspectives, recognizing diverse learning needs, and fostering a sense of cultural identity contribute to a more inclusive high school education experience.

Opportunities and Innovations in Educational Reforms:

- Personalized Learning Platforms: Advances in technology allow for personalized learning platforms that cater to individual student needs. These platforms leverage artificial intelligence and data analytics to provide adaptive learning experiences tailored to students' strengths and weaknesses.

- Global Collaborations in Education: Educational reforms present opportunities for global collaboration. Sharing best practices, collaborating on research, and establishing international partnerships contribute to a more interconnected and mutually beneficial global education landscape.

- Community Engagement: Involving communities in the reform process enhances the chances of success. Engaging parents, local organizations, and community leaders fosters a sense of shared responsibility for education and can lead to more effective implementation of reforms.

- Teacher Professional Development: Investing in the professional development of teachers is critical for successful reforms. Providing training, resources, and support enables educators to effectively implement new methodologies and adapt to evolving educational landscapes.

- Interdisciplinary Approaches: Reforms that promote interdisciplinary approaches to education prepare students for the complexity of real-world challenges. Integrating subjects, fostering collaboration between disciplines, and encouraging creative problem-solving contribute to a more holistic educational experience.

Conclusion: Charting the Future of High School Education

Educational reforms are pivotal in shaping the future of high school education on a global scale. As we navigate the complexities of a rapidly changing world, governments must remain proactive in adapting educational systems to meet the evolving needs of students and society.

The success of reforms hinges on thoughtful planning, collaboration among stakeholders, and a commitment to equity and inclusivity. By leveraging innovative approaches, learning from successful case studies, and addressing implementation challenges, governments can transform high school education into a dynamic and responsive force for individual empowerment and societal progress.

In the subsequent chapters, we will delve deeper into specific aspects of high school education, exploring the impact of cultural influences, economic disparities, technology integration, and global assessments. Each exploration contributes to the overarching narrative of unveiling the tapestry of learning in high school classrooms globally, emphasizing the role of educational reforms in shaping this intricate landscape.

Effectiveness of Government Initiatives: Navigating Impact and Outcomes

As governments worldwide engage in comprehensive high school education policies, assessing the effectiveness of these initiatives becomes paramount. This exploration delves into the intricate landscape of government interventions, scrutinizing the impact of policies on various facets of high school education. From access and quality to inclusivity and equity, understanding the effectiveness of government initiatives provides critical insights into the successes and challenges shaping the global educational narrative.

Introduction: Evaluating the Educational Landscape

The effectiveness of government initiatives in high school education is a multifaceted inquiry that requires careful consideration of diverse factors. Governments implement policies with the overarching goal of enhancing educational outcomes, ensuring inclusivity, and preparing students for the complexities of the modern world. Evaluating the impact of these initiatives involves assessing changes in access, quality, and the overall educational experience of students.

Access to High School Education: Bridging Gaps and Removing Barriers

- Improving Enrollment Rates: Government initiatives often focus on increasing enrollment rates, ensuring that a higher percentage of students have access to high school education. Strategies may include targeted outreach programs, financial assistance, and policies that mandate compulsory education.

- Reducing Dropout Rates: Addressing factors that contribute to dropout rates is a key aspect of effectiveness. Initiatives may target socio-economic challenges, provide additional support for struggling students, and implement interventions to keep students engaged in their educational journey.

- Bridging Urban-Rural Disparities: Government initiatives aim to bridge the gap between urban and rural educational opportunities. This involves investing in rural infrastructure, providing incentives for educators in remote areas, and leveraging technology to deliver education where traditional infrastructure is lacking.

- Inclusivity for Marginalized Communities: Assessing the effectiveness of government initiatives requires a focus on inclusivity. Policies should aim to reduce disparities among various socio-economic, ethnic, and cultural groups, ensuring that marginalized communities have equal access to quality high school education.

Quality of High School Education: Nurturing Academic Excellence

- Curricular Enhancements: Governments often implement changes in curricula to enhance the quality of education. Evaluating effectiveness involves assessing whether these changes align with evolving societal needs, foster critical thinking, and prepare students for higher education and the workforce.

- Teacher Training and Professional Development: The impact of initiatives on the quality of education is closely tied to the professional development of educators. Effective policies prioritize ongoing training, support innovative teaching methodologies, and ensure that educators are equipped to meet the evolving needs of students.

- Technology Integration: Assessing the effectiveness of government initiatives includes an evaluation of technology integration in education. Initiatives that successfully leverage technology contribute to a more dynamic and engaging learning environment, preparing students for the digital age.

- Global Competence: Governments aim to cultivate global competence among students. Initiatives that effectively incorporate global perspectives, encourage intercultural understanding, and foster collaboration contribute to the development of well-rounded and globally aware individuals.

Equity in High School Education: Addressing Disparities

- Socio-Economic Equity: Government initiatives seek to address socio-economic disparities in high school education. Assessing effectiveness involves examining the impact of financial assistance programs, targeted interventions, and policies aimed at leveling the playing field for students from economically disadvantaged backgrounds.

- Inclusive Policies for Diverse Learners: Evaluating effectiveness requires an examination of policies that cater to diverse learners. Inclusive education initiatives should address the needs of students with disabilities, accommodate various learning styles, and create an environment where every student feels valued and supported.

- Cultural Sensitivity: Assessing the effectiveness of government initiatives involves considering their impact on cultural sensitivity. Policies that promote cultural inclusivity, incorporate diverse perspectives into curricula, and address cultural barriers contribute to an equitable educational experience.

- Gender Equity: Government initiatives should strive to achieve gender equity in high school education. Evaluating effectiveness involves examining policies that ensure equal opportunities for male and female students, address gender-based discrimination, and promote a supportive environment for all.

Technology Integration in High School Education: Navigating the Digital Landscape

- Access to Technology: Evaluating the effectiveness of technology integration initiatives requires assessing access to technology. Policies should aim to bridge the digital divide, ensuring that all students, regardless of socio-economic background, have access to the necessary tools for learning.

- Innovations in EdTech: Effective initiatives go beyond providing access and explore innovations in educational technology. Evaluating impact involves assessing the integration of virtual classrooms, interactive learning platforms, and other cutting-edge technologies that enhance the educational experience.

- Digital Literacy Skills: Government initiatives should contribute to the development of digital literacy skills among students. Evaluating effectiveness includes examining policies that equip students with the ability to critically assess information, navigate digital platforms responsibly, and utilize technology for learning.

- Challenges and Opportunities: Assessing the effectiveness of technology integration initiatives involves understanding challenges such as the digital divide and cybersecurity concerns. Governments should address these challenges while maximizing the opportunities that technology presents for enhancing education.

Transition to Higher Education: Navigating Pathways for Success

- Challenges in Transitioning: Government initiatives often focus on addressing challenges in transitioning from high school to higher education. Evaluating effectiveness involves assessing the success of programs that provide guidance, counseling, and resources to ease the transition for students.

- Vocational Education and Training: Effective initiatives recognize the importance of vocational education and training pathways. Evaluating impact involves examining policies that offer diverse career options, integrate vocational education into high school curricula, and provide support for students pursuing non-traditional paths.

- Role of High School Education in Career Paths: Assessing the effectiveness of initiatives requires understanding their impact on students' career paths. Government policies should align with workforce needs, prepare students for diverse career options, and provide resources for career exploration and planning.

- Global Trends in Higher Education Admission: Initiatives aimed at facilitating higher education admission must align with global trends. Evaluating effectiveness involves understanding the impact of policies on students' readiness for higher education in an international context.

Success Stories and Innovations in Education: Learning from Best Practices

- Educational Initiatives Making a Difference: Evaluating the effectiveness of government initiatives involves highlighting success stories. By showcasing educational initiatives that have made a positive impact, policymakers can learn from best practices and identify strategies that can be replicated or adapted.

- Innovative Approaches to Educational Challenges: Effective initiatives often involve innovative approaches to addressing educational challenges. Evaluating impact includes examining how policies encourage experimentation, foster creativity, and support the development of novel solutions to complex problems.

- Lessons Learned from Success Stories: Learning from success stories is integral to assessing effectiveness. Governments should identify lessons learned from initiatives that have achieved positive outcomes, incorporating these insights into future policy development.

- Scalability and Replicability: Evaluating the effectiveness of initiatives involves considering their scalability and replicability. Successful policies should be scalable to accommodate larger populations and replicable in different contexts to ensure widespread positive impact.

Global Assessments in High School Education: Benchmarking Performance

- Overview of International Assessments: Governments often participate in international assessments to benchmark their educational performance. Evaluating effectiveness involves analyzing the results of assessments such as PISA (Programme for International Student Assessment) and TIMSS (Trends in International Mathematics and Science Study) to gauge the standing of a country's high school education system.

- Role of PISA and TIMSS: Understanding the impact of government initiatives requires assessing the role of international assessments. Policymakers should consider how participation in PISA and TIMSS influences educational policies, shapes curriculum priorities, and informs strategies for improvement.

- Standardized Testing Practices Globally: Effective initiatives should align with global standards in standardized testing. Evaluating impact involves examining how policies reflect best practices in assessment methods and contribute to the overall competitiveness of a country's high school graduates.

- Alternative Assessment Methods: Recognizing the limitations of standardized testing, effective initiatives explore alternative assessment methods. Policymakers should consider how policies encourage the development and implementation of assessments that provide a more comprehensive view of students' capabilities.

Standardized Testing: Pros and Cons - Balancing Assessment Practices

- Advantages of Standardized Testing: Evaluating the effectiveness of policies involves considering the advantages of standardized testing. Policymakers should assess how standardized tests contribute to accountability, provide a standardized benchmark, and offer a quantifiable measure of student performance.

- Limitations and Criticisms: Effective initiatives acknowledge the limitations and criticisms of standardized testing. Policymakers should address concerns related to bias, the narrowing of curriculum focus, and the potential negative impact on teaching practices.

- Impact on Educational Policy: Evaluating the effectiveness of initiatives includes understanding how standardized testing influences educational policy. Policymakers should consider how test results inform decisions on curriculum development, resource allocation, and overall educational priorities.

- Evolving Trends in Standardized Testing: Effective policies respond to evolving trends in standardized testing. Policymakers should be proactive in adapting assessment practices to align with emerging educational philosophies, technological advancements, and a deeper understanding of effective evaluation methods.

Quality Indicators in Education: Navigating Measures of Success

- Key Indicators of Educational Quality: Evaluating the effectiveness of government initiatives involves defining key indicators of educational quality. Policymakers should identify measures that encompass academic achievement, student well-being, teacher effectiveness, and overall system performance.

- Correlation with Academic Success: Effective initiatives should demonstrate a positive correlation between implemented measures and academic success. Policymakers should assess how selected quality indicators contribute to improved educational outcomes and student achievement.

- Infrastructure, Spending, and Educational Outcomes: Evaluating the impact of initiatives includes examining the correlation between infrastructure, spending, and educational outcomes. Policymakers should consider how resource allocation and investments in educational infrastructure contribute to improved quality.

- Challenges in Implementing Quality Indicators: Recognizing challenges in implementing quality indicators is crucial for evaluating effectiveness. Policymakers should address obstacles related to data collection, measurement accuracy, and the diverse factors influencing educational quality.

Global Educational Rankings: Understanding the Metrics

- Overview of Ranking Systems: Governments often seek to improve their standing in global educational rankings. Evaluating the effectiveness of initiatives involves understanding the metrics used in ranking systems and aligning policies with areas that contribute to positive rankings.

- Criteria Used in Educational Rankings: Effective initiatives should address the criteria used in educational rankings. Policymakers should align policies with metrics such as academic performance, innovation, inclusivity, and preparation for future challenges to improve global standings.

- Implications for Educational Policy: Evaluating effectiveness includes considering the implications of rankings on educational policy. Policymakers should assess how rankings influence resource allocation, curriculum development, and overall strategic priorities in high school education.

- Criticisms and Alternatives to Ranking Systems: Effective initiatives respond to criticisms of ranking systems and explore alternatives. Policymakers should address concerns related to the oversimplification of complex educational landscapes and explore alternative methods that provide a more nuanced understanding of educational quality.

Emerging Trends and Future Prospects: Shaping the Educational Landscape

- Evolving Landscape of High School Education: Evaluating the effectiveness of initiatives requires an understanding of the evolving landscape of high school education. Policymakers should consider how emerging trends, including advancements in technology, societal shifts, and changes in the job market, influence policy priorities.

- Anticipated Changes and Challenges: Effective initiatives anticipate changes and challenges on the educational horizon. Policymakers should be proactive in identifying potential disruptions, understanding societal shifts, and preparing the education system to adapt to emerging trends.

- Opportunities for Global Collaboration: Evaluating effectiveness involves exploring opportunities for global collaboration. Policymakers should consider how initiatives can benefit from international partnerships, knowledge exchange, and collaborative efforts to address shared challenges in high school education.

- Vision for the Future of High School Education: Effective initiatives articulate a vision for the future of high school education. Policymakers should outline a clear vision that encompasses inclusivity, innovation, global competence, and responsiveness to the evolving needs of students and society.

Conclusion: Towards Informed Policy and Educational Transformation

As governments grapple with the complexities of high school education, the effectiveness of their initiatives becomes a critical focal point. Navigating impact and outcomes requires a comprehensive understanding of diverse factors, ranging from access and quality to equity and global competitiveness. Policymakers must engage in continuous evaluation, learning from successes and challenges, and adapting strategies to ensure that high school education remains a dynamic force for individual empowerment and societal progress.

In the subsequent chapters, we will delve deeper into specific aspects of high school education, examining the impact of cultural influences, economic disparities, technology integration, and global assessments. Each exploration contributes to the overarching narrative of unveiling the tapestry of learning in high school classrooms globally, emphasizing the role of informed policy in shaping this intricate landscape.

Challenges in Policy Implementation: Navigating the Complexities of Educational Reform

The effectiveness of government policies in high school education is contingent on successful implementation. However, the path from policy formulation to tangible impact is riddled with challenges that policymakers must navigate. In this exploration, we delve into the intricacies of policy implementation, identifying and analyzing the hurdles that governments face in their efforts to transform high school education on a global scale.

Introduction: The Crucial Link Between Policy and Implementation

The development of robust policies in high school education is only the first step in a complex journey. The true measure of success lies in how well these policies are implemented to bring about positive change. The challenges in policy implementation are diverse and multifaceted, often requiring a nuanced understanding of local contexts, stakeholder dynamics, and the ever-evolving nature of education.

Alignment with Stakeholder Interests: A Delicate Balancing Act

- Teacher Engagement and Resistance: Teachers play a pivotal role in the implementation of educational policies. However, achieving alignment with their interests and overcoming potential resistance can be challenging. Teachers may resist changes perceived as additional workload or deviations from familiar practices. Effective strategies involve comprehensive communication, professional development opportunities, and involving teachers in the policy development process.

- Parental Involvement and Expectations: Engaging parents in the implementation process is crucial for success.

Challenges may arise when parental expectations differ from the intended outcomes of policies. Establishing clear communication channels, addressing concerns, and involving parents in decision-making forums contribute to building a supportive network for policy implementation.

- Student Perspectives and Buy-In: The success of policy implementation hinges on student buy-in. Challenges emerge when students perceive policies as irrelevant or when their perspectives are not adequately considered. Integrating student input, fostering open communication, and creating a positive narrative around policy changes are essential strategies.

- Collaboration with Educational Institutions: Educational institutions are key stakeholders in policy implementation. Challenges may arise when institutions resist changes due to resource constraints, organizational inertia, or a lack of understanding of the policy objectives. Collaboration, providing support mechanisms, and acknowledging institutional constraints are vital for successful implementation.

Resource Allocation and Budgetary Constraints: Navigating Financial Realities

- Insufficient Funding for Implementation: One of the primary challenges in policy implementation is the allocation of adequate financial resources. Insufficient funding can hinder the execution of planned initiatives, limiting the scope and scale of intended reforms. Policymakers must carefully assess resource needs, advocate for budget allocations, and explore innovative funding mechanisms.

- Equitable Resource Distribution: Ensuring equitable distribution of resources presents another challenge. Disparities in resource allocation among urban and rural areas or affluent and economically disadvantaged communities can perpetuate existing inequalities. Policies must incorporate mechanisms to address these disparities and prioritize resource allocation based on need.

- Long-Term Funding Sustainability: The sustainability of policy initiatives over the long term is a critical consideration. Many reforms require sustained financial support, and challenges arise when funding is subject to political changes or economic uncertainties. Policymakers must strategize for long-term funding sustainability and explore avenues for stable financial backing.

- Prioritization Amidst Competing Needs: Education competes with various sectors for government funding. Policymakers face challenges in prioritizing education amidst competing needs such as healthcare, infrastructure, and defense. Clear advocacy, demonstrating the long-term societal benefits of education, and building alliances with other sectors can help address these challenges.

Policy Consistency and Stability: Overcoming the Pitfalls of Transition

- Political Transitions and Policy Instability: Changes in political leadership can lead to shifts in educational priorities and policy directions. The challenge lies in maintaining policy consistency and stability across political transitions. Establishing bipartisan support for key educational objectives, enshrining policies in legislation, and fostering a culture of long-term commitment to education are essential strategies.

- Alignment with Societal Values and Norms: Policies that do not align with societal values and norms may face resistance. Challenges arise when policies challenge cultural traditions, religious beliefs, or deeply ingrained educational philosophies. Ensuring inclusive policy development processes that consider diverse perspectives and engage stakeholders from various backgrounds helps mitigate these challenges.

- Adaptability to Evolving Educational Needs: The dynamic nature of education demands policies that can adapt to evolving needs. Challenges emerge when policies become outdated or fail to address emerging issues. Policymakers must build flexibility into policy frameworks, regularly review their relevance, and be willing to make adjustments based on evolving educational landscapes.

- Consistency Across Administrative Levels: Achieving consistency in policy implementation across different administrative levels presents a challenge. Variations in interpretation and implementation at the local, regional, and national levels can lead to disparities in outcomes. Clear communication channels, standardized guidelines, and regular monitoring mechanisms are vital for ensuring consistency.

Capacity Building and Professional Development: Nurturing Competence

- Educator Training and Skill Development: The successful implementation of educational policies relies on the competence of educators. Challenges arise when policies require skills that educators have not been adequately trained for. Investing in comprehensive educator training programs, aligning professional development with policy objectives, and creating opportunities for continuous learning are essential strategies.

- Administrative Competence: School administrators and policymakers must possess the necessary administrative skills to implement reforms effectively. Challenges emerge when there is a lack of administrative capacity or understanding of the intricacies of policy execution. Building administrative competence through targeted training and mentorship programs is crucial.

- Technological Proficiency: Policies that involve technology integration may face challenges if educators lack technological proficiency. Addressing the digital divide, providing access to training programs, and fostering a culture of technological innovation in education are essential for successful implementation.

- Community Engagement Competence: Engaging communities in the implementation process requires specific competencies. Challenges may arise when there is a lack of community involvement or when engagement strategies are not culturally sensitive. Capacity-building initiatives that empower communities, provide relevant information, and facilitate dialogue contribute to successful engagement.

Monitoring and Evaluation: Ensuring Accountability and Effectiveness

- Lack of Monitoring Mechanisms: Challenges in policy implementation often stem from a lack of robust monitoring mechanisms. In the absence of effective monitoring, policymakers may struggle to assess progress, identify challenges, and make data-driven adjustments. Implementing comprehensive monitoring systems, leveraging technology, and establishing regular reporting protocols are crucial.

- Data Quality and Availability: Reliable data is indispensable for effective monitoring and evaluation. Challenges arise when data quality is compromised, or relevant data is not readily available. Policymakers must invest in data infrastructure, ensure the accuracy of information, and address gaps in data collection and reporting.

- Evaluation Bias and Objectivity: Ensuring objectivity in policy evaluation is essential for accurate assessments. Challenges may arise when evaluations are influenced by biases, political considerations, or external pressures. Establishing independent evaluation bodies, transparent evaluation criteria, and incorporating diverse perspectives contribute to impartial assessments.

- Balancing Accountability and Innovation: The pursuit of accountability must be balanced with fostering innovation. Challenges emerge when stringent accountability measures stifle experimentation and creativity. Policymakers must strike a balance between accountability and flexibility, encouraging a culture that values both compliance and continuous improvement.

Community and Stakeholder Engagement: Building Inclusive Partnerships

- Ineffective Communication Strategies: Successful policy implementation relies on effective communication with stakeholders. Challenges arise when communication strategies are ineffective, leading to misunderstandings, misinformation, or resistance. Employing diverse communication channels, ensuring language accessibility, and incorporating feedback mechanisms enhance engagement.

- Inadequate Community Involvement: Policies that lack community involvement may encounter challenges in gaining local support. Communities may resist changes perceived as externally imposed. Establishing collaborative decision-making processes, involving community representatives, and recognizing the unique needs of different communities foster inclusive partnerships.

- Stakeholder Conflict of Interest: Conflicting interests among stakeholders can impede implementation. Challenges arise when different groups have divergent views on policy objectives. Mediation, transparent decision-making processes, and finding common ground among stakeholders are crucial for navigating conflicts of interest.

- Cultural Sensitivity and Inclusivity: Policies that are not culturally sensitive may face challenges in diverse educational contexts. A lack of inclusivity can perpetuate inequalities. Policymakers must prioritize cultural sensitivity, engage with diverse communities, and incorporate varied cultural perspectives into policy development and implementation.

Conclusion: Navigating the Complexities Towards Transformative Change

The challenges in policy implementation underscore the intricate nature of educational reform. Navigating these complexities requires a holistic and adaptive approach, recognizing the diversity of educational contexts, stakeholder interests, and the dynamic nature of the education landscape.

In the subsequent chapters, we will delve into specific aspects of high school education, exploring the impact of cultural influences, economic disparities, technology integration, and global assessments. Each exploration contributes to the overarching narrative of unveiling the tapestry of learning in high school classrooms globally, emphasizing the need for strategic and informed policy implementation in shaping this intricate landscape.

Chapter 6: Technology Integration in High School Education

Global Perspectives on Educational Technology: A Window into the Digital Classroom

In the ever-evolving landscape of high school education, technology integration has emerged as a transformative force. This exploration delves into global perspectives on educational technology, uncovering the diverse ways in which nations are leveraging digital tools to enhance teaching and learning experiences in high schools worldwide.

Introduction: The Digital Revolution in High School Classrooms

The integration of technology in high school education represents a paradigm shift, ushering in new possibilities and challenges. Understanding global perspectives on educational technology requires an exploration of the motivations, strategies, and outcomes as nations navigate the digital revolution in their high school classrooms.

The Digital Divide: Disparities in Access and Connectivity

Access to technology remains a critical factor in shaping global perspectives on educational technology. Disparities in access create a digital divide that can exacerbate existing inequalities in educational opportunities. Nations grapple with addressing these disparities to ensure that all students have equitable access to the tools that can enrich their learning experiences.

Global Trends in Technology Adoption: A Comparative Analysis

- Ubiquitous Presence of Devices: In examining global trends, a common thread is the ubiquitous presence of devices in high school classrooms. From laptops and tablets to smartphones, nations are adopting various devices to facilitate learning. Understanding the prevalence of these devices provides insights into the level of technological immersion in high school education.

- Emergence of Learning Management Systems: Learning Management Systems (LMS) have become central to educational technology strategies globally. These platforms facilitate content delivery, student engagement, and assessment. The adoption and customization of LMS showcase how nations are integrating digital platforms to streamline educational processes.

- Blended Learning Models: Blended learning, combining traditional classroom methods with online components, has gained traction worldwide. Examining how nations implement blended learning models sheds light on their approach to balancing technology with face-to-face instruction, catering to diverse learning styles and preferences.

- Virtual Reality (VR) and Augmented Reality (AR): The incorporation of VR and AR technologies into high school education is a growing trend. Nations embracing these immersive technologies aim to provide students with interactive and experiential learning opportunities. A comparative analysis reveals the extent to which VR and AR are influencing pedagogical approaches globally.

- Adaptive Learning Platforms: Adaptive learning platforms, leveraging artificial intelligence to personalize learning experiences, are on the rise. Nations employing these platforms seek to tailor education to individual student needs. Understanding the prevalence and impact of adaptive learning platforms offers insights into the commitment to personalized education.

Policy Approaches to Technology Integration: Strategies and Considerations

- National Technology Integration Policies: Nations differ in their approach to crafting policies that guide technology integration in high school education. Examining these policies reveals the overarching vision and goals, such as fostering digital literacy, preparing students for the future workforce, and enhancing overall educational quality.

- Government Investments in EdTech: The level of government investment in educational technology varies globally. Nations prioritizing substantial investments aim to create a robust technological infrastructure, provide training for educators, and ensure widespread access to digital resources. Analyzing these investments provides insights into the commitment to leveraging technology for educational improvement.

- Public-Private Partnerships: Collaboration between public institutions and private enterprises is a noteworthy strategy in some nations. Public-private partnerships in educational technology initiatives showcase innovative solutions, resource-sharing, and the synergy between government and industry. Understanding these collaborations illuminates the role of diverse stakeholders in shaping the digital landscape.

- Inclusive Approaches to Digital Inequality: Addressing the digital divide requires inclusive policies that ensure all students, regardless of socio-economic background, have access to technology. Nations employing targeted initiatives, such as providing subsidized devices, internet connectivity, and digital literacy programs, showcase a commitment to reducing disparities in technology access.

Challenges in Technology Integration: Lessons from Global Experiences

- Teacher Training and Professional Development: Across nations, a common challenge in technology integration is ensuring that educators are proficient in leveraging digital tools. The approaches taken to address this challenge, such as comprehensive training programs, ongoing professional development, and incentives for tech-savvy educators, offer valuable lessons for overcoming barriers to implementation.

- Resistance to Change: Resistance to technological change exists in various educational contexts. Examining global perspectives on overcoming resistance provides insights into strategies such as effective communication, involving educators in decision-making, and fostering a culture of adaptability and innovation.

- Data Privacy and Security Concerns: Protecting student data and ensuring privacy are paramount in educational technology. Nations grapple with developing robust frameworks for data privacy and security. Analyzing how different nations address these concerns offers lessons in establishing ethical and secure practices in technology integration.

- Sustainability of Technology Initiatives: Sustaining technology integration initiatives over the long term is a shared challenge. Nations that implement successful strategies for sustainability, such as aligning initiatives with broader educational goals, regularly assessing impact, and incorporating feedback loops, provide valuable insights for fostering lasting change.

Innovations in EdTech: Showcasing Success Stories

- Emerging Educational Technologies: Exploring global perspectives on emerging technologies reveals innovative approaches that transcend traditional boundaries. Nations at the forefront of adopting emerging technologies, such as blockchain in credentialing, artificial intelligence for personalized learning, and gamification, showcase the potential for transformative innovations.

- Tech-driven Pedagogical Innovations: High school education is witnessing pedagogical innovations driven by technology. Nations embracing student-centric approaches, project-based learning, and collaborative online platforms illustrate the power of technology to redefine teaching and learning methodologies.

- Inclusive EdTech for Diverse Learners: Inclusive educational technology that caters to diverse learners, including those with special needs, is a hallmark of successful initiatives. Nations adopting inclusive technologies, such as adaptive learning apps and assistive devices, highlight the importance of accessibility and equity in the digital age.

- Global Collaborations in EdTech: Collaborations between nations in the realm of educational technology showcase the potential for collective innovation. Understanding how global partnerships contribute to the sharing of best practices, joint research endeavors, and the development of universally applicable technologies provides a blueprint for fostering collaborative advancements.

Challenges and Opportunities in Technology Integration: A Holistic Perspective

- Addressing Socio-economic Disparities: Nations face the challenge of ensuring that technology integration does not exacerbate existing socio-economic disparities. Strategies that focus on targeted interventions, community engagement, and policy frameworks promoting equitable access provide insights into addressing this critical challenge.

- Balancing Screen Time and Well-being: The impact of increased screen time on student well-being is a global concern. Nations addressing this challenge through strategies like incorporating digital wellness education, promoting mindful technology use, and integrating well-being into educational technology policies offer valuable lessons in achieving a balanced approach.

- Preparing Students for the Future Workforce: The intersection of technology integration and workforce preparation is a key consideration. Nations aligning educational technology initiatives with the skills demanded by the future workforce provide insights into effective strategies for preparing students for a rapidly evolving job market.

- Fostering Critical Digital Literacy: With the proliferation of information online, fostering critical digital literacy is imperative. Nations incorporating digital literacy education into their high school curricula and employing strategies to empower students as discerning consumers of digital information contribute to a global perspective on addressing this challenge.

Conclusion: Crafting a Digital Future for High School Education

Global perspectives on educational technology underscore the transformative potential and challenges associated with integrating digital tools into high school classrooms. As nations navigate this digital frontier, the lessons learned from diverse experiences contribute to a collective understanding of how technology can shape the future of education.

In the subsequent chapters, we will continue our exploration, delving into challenges and innovations related to the transition to higher education, success stories, global assessments, and the broader landscape of high school education. Each facet adds another layer to the tapestry of learning, emphasizing the need for informed strategies to harness the power of technology in shaping the educational journey.

Digital Divide and Its Implications: Bridging Gaps in Access and Opportunity

In the era of technology-driven education, the digital divide has become a pivotal challenge with profound implications for high school students globally. This exploration delves into the complexities of the digital divide, examining its origins, manifestations, and the far-reaching consequences it poses for equitable access to educational opportunities.

Introduction: Unveiling the Digital Divide in High School Education

The digital divide, a term coined to describe disparities in access to information and communication technologies, has evolved into a multifaceted challenge in the context of high school education. Understanding the roots of this divide and its implications is essential for crafting inclusive strategies that ensure all students have equal access to the benefits of educational technology.

Defining the Digital Divide: Dimensions of Disparity

- Access to Hardware and Devices: One of the primary dimensions of the digital divide is the uneven access to hardware and devices. Students in affluent areas or well-funded schools may have ready access to personal laptops, tablets, or other devices, while those in economically disadvantaged communities may lack such resources.

- Internet Connectivity: The availability and quality of internet connectivity are critical factors in the digital divide. Disparities in reliable high-speed internet access create barriers to online learning, collaborative projects, and access to a wealth of educational resources available on the web.

- Digital Literacy and Skills: Beyond physical access, the divide extends to digital literacy and skills. Students who are familiar with technology and possess digital literacy skills have a distinct advantage over their peers who lack such knowledge, impacting their ability to navigate digital learning environments effectively.

- Educational Software and Resources: Disparities also exist in access to educational software and online resources. Schools with ample resources can afford to invest in a variety of digital tools, interactive software, and online libraries, providing their students with a richer learning experience compared to those in schools with limited resources.

Origins of the Digital Divide: Unraveling Root Causes

- Socio-economic Disparities: The digital divide is intricately linked to socio-economic disparities. Students from affluent families often have greater access to personal devices, reliable internet, and a supportive home environment conducive to digital learning. In contrast, economically disadvantaged students face barriers stemming from a lack of resources and infrastructure.

- Rural vs. Urban Disparities: Geographic location plays a crucial role in the digital divide. Rural areas may lack the necessary infrastructure for high-speed internet, making it challenging for students in these regions to access online educational resources on par with their urban counterparts.

- Global Disparities: The digital divide is not confined to individual countries; it extends globally. Developing nations may face more significant challenges due to infrastructural limitations, economic constraints, and disparities in educational policies, impacting the ability of students to participate in the digital learning landscape.

- Cultural and Linguistic Barriers: Cultural and linguistic factors contribute to the divide. Educational technology often relies on content presented in specific languages, and disparities in language proficiency can hinder students from fully engaging with digital resources.

Implications of the Digital Divide: Unequal Educational Landscapes

- Academic Performance Disparities: The digital divide correlates with disparities in academic performance. Students with limited access to technology may struggle to keep pace with their digitally literate peers, leading to gaps in academic achievement.

- Inequitable Access to Educational Opportunities: The digital divide exacerbates existing inequalities in access to educational opportunities. Students without access to technology may miss out on online courses, collaborative projects, and exposure to a broader range of educational materials.

- Impact on Career Readiness: The ability to navigate digital tools is increasingly critical for career readiness. The digital divide can impede students' preparedness for the modern workforce, limiting their exposure to essential skills in technology-driven industries.

- Reinforcement of Socio-economic Disparities: The digital divide has the potential to reinforce socio-economic disparities. Students from economically disadvantaged backgrounds face hurdles in accessing the same educational resources and opportunities as their more affluent peers, perpetuating existing social inequalities.

Addressing the Digital Divide: Strategies for Inclusive Access

- Infrastructure Development: Closing the digital divide requires robust infrastructure development. Governments and educational institutions must invest in expanding high-speed internet access to underserved areas, particularly in rural and economically disadvantaged regions.

- One-to-One Device Programs: Implementing one-to-one device programs, where each student is provided with a personal device, can contribute to equalizing access. Such initiatives aim to ensure that all students have the necessary tools for digital learning.

- Community Wi-Fi Initiatives: Extending internet access beyond school premises through community Wi-Fi initiatives can enhance connectivity for students in areas with limited internet infrastructure. These programs focus on creating a broader network that benefits the entire community.

- Digital Literacy Programs: Integrating digital literacy programs into the curriculum is essential for addressing the skills gap associated with the digital divide. These programs should equip students with the knowledge and skills needed to navigate digital environments effectively.

- Public-Private Partnerships: Collaboration between public institutions and private enterprises is a viable strategy. Public-private partnerships can facilitate the provision of devices, internet connectivity, and educational software, ensuring a more comprehensive and sustainable approach to addressing the digital divide.

Innovative Solutions: Leveraging Technology to Bridge Gaps

- Mobile Learning Initiatives: Leveraging the widespread use of smartphones, mobile learning initiatives offer an innovative solution. Educational content delivered through mobile apps can reach students even in areas with limited access to traditional computing devices.

- Offline Learning Solutions: To address connectivity challenges, offline learning solutions are gaining traction. Educational content that can be downloaded and accessed without an internet connection ensures that students can continue learning even in areas with limited connectivity.

- Community Technology Centers: Establishing community technology centers provides access to technology beyond school hours. These centers, equipped with computers and internet access, serve as hubs for students and community members to engage in digital learning activities.

- Customized Learning Paths: Personalized and customized learning paths can accommodate diverse learning needs. Technology can be leveraged to tailor educational content to individual students, allowing for a more inclusive approach that considers different learning styles and paces.

Global Initiatives: Collaborative Efforts to Bridge Divides

- International Collaborations for Technology Access: Collaborative efforts between countries and international organizations play a vital role. Initiatives focused on providing technology access to underserved regions, sharing best practices, and fostering global partnerships contribute to a more inclusive educational landscape.

- Global Funding for Educational Technology: Global funding mechanisms dedicated to bridging the digital divide in education support initiatives in developing nations. These funds aim to address infrastructure challenges, provide devices, and enhance digital literacy on a broader scale.

- Knowledge Sharing Platforms: Creating platforms for knowledge sharing allows nations to learn from each other's experiences and successes in addressing the digital divide. Such platforms foster a collaborative approach, enabling countries to adopt effective strategies and adapt them to their unique contexts.

Conclusion: A Call for Inclusive Technological Transformation

The digital divide poses profound challenges to the goal of providing equitable access to high-quality education for all students. Addressing this divide requires a concerted effort from governments, educational institutions, and the global community. By understanding the origins and implications of the digital divide, and by implementing inclusive strategies, we can strive towards a future where technology acts as a bridge, not a barrier, to educational opportunities.

In the subsequent chapters, we will continue our exploration of technology integration in high school education, examining innovations, challenges, and global perspectives that contribute to shaping the digital landscape of learning. Each facet adds another layer to the tapestry of education, emphasizing the need for comprehensive strategies to harness the potential of technology for the benefit of every student.

Innovations in EdTech: Transforming Learning Landscapes

The integration of technology in high school education has ushered in a wave of innovations, reshaping traditional teaching and learning paradigms. This exploration delves into the dynamic landscape of educational technology (EdTech) innovations, showcasing initiatives that have demonstrated transformative potential and promising avenues for the future.

Introduction: The Evolution of EdTech Innovations

As technology continues to advance at an unprecedented pace, the realm of high school education is witnessing a surge in innovative solutions designed to enhance the learning experience. From interactive platforms to artificial intelligence-driven tools, EdTech innovations are catalyzing a shift towards more personalized, engaging, and effective educational practices.

Emerging Educational Technologies: A Glimpse into the Future

- Blockchain in Credentialing: The application of blockchain technology in credentialing and certification is gaining traction. Blockchain ensures secure, transparent, and tamper-resistant verification of academic credentials, offering a decentralized approach to validating educational achievements.

- Artificial Intelligence (AI) for Personalized Learning: AI-driven systems are revolutionizing personalized learning experiences. These technologies analyze individual learning patterns, adapting content and pacing to match students' strengths and weaknesses, fostering a more tailored approach to education.

- Gamification in Education: Gamification leverages elements of game design in non-game contexts, including education. Integrating gamified elements into learning modules enhances student engagement, motivation, and collaboration, making the learning process more enjoyable and effective.

- Virtual Reality (VR) and Augmented Reality (AR): The immersive experiences facilitated by VR and AR technologies are transforming how students interact with educational content. From virtual field trips to simulated experiments, these technologies provide experiential learning opportunities, enhancing comprehension and retention.

Tech-driven Pedagogical Innovations: Redefining Teaching Methods

- Student-centric Approaches: EdTech innovations support student-centric teaching methods, emphasizing active participation, collaboration, and critical thinking. Platforms that facilitate project-based learning, group activities, and interactive assessments empower students to take ownership of their learning journeys.

- Flipped Classroom Models: The flipped classroom model reverses traditional teaching methods, with students accessing instructional content online before class and using class time for discussions and collaborative activities. EdTech tools enable educators to create and share multimedia content, fostering a more interactive and engaging learning environment.

- Collaborative Online Platforms: Online platforms that facilitate collaboration among students, teachers, and even global communities are reshaping the dynamics of education. Real-time collaboration tools, discussion forums, and virtual classrooms promote interactive learning experiences beyond physical boundaries.

- Adaptive Learning Platforms: EdTech solutions employing adaptive learning algorithms tailor educational content to individual student needs. These platforms adjust the difficulty and pace of lessons based on a student's progress, ensuring a personalized and efficient learning experience.

Inclusive EdTech for Diverse Learners: Addressing Unique Needs

- Assistive Technologies: Innovations in assistive technologies cater to the needs of students with diverse learning abilities. Text-to-speech software, screen readers, and voice recognition tools empower students with disabilities, ensuring they have equal access to educational materials.

- Multimodal Learning Resources: Providing multimodal learning resources, such as videos, podcasts, and interactive simulations, accommodates diverse learning styles. EdTech innovations that offer content in various formats ensure that students can engage with materials in ways that suit their individual preferences.

- Language Learning Apps: Language learning apps leverage technology to make language acquisition more accessible and enjoyable. These apps often incorporate gamified elements, real-time feedback, and interactive exercises, enhancing the language-learning experience for students of varying proficiency levels.

- Adaptive Assessment Tools: Adaptive assessment tools use technology to tailor assessments to the individual abilities of students. These tools go beyond traditional exams, offering dynamic assessments that adjust based on a student's responses, providing a more accurate measure of their understanding.

Global Collaborations in EdTech: Sharing Best Practices

- Cross-cultural Learning Platforms: EdTech platforms that facilitate cross-cultural learning experiences contribute to a globalized perspective. Students can collaborate with peers from different countries, share insights, and gain exposure to diverse perspectives, fostering a more inclusive and interconnected educational community.

- Joint Research Endeavors: Collaborative research initiatives between educational institutions globally leverage technology to address common challenges and explore innovative solutions. Sharing research findings and best practices enhances the collective knowledge base, driving continuous improvement in EdTech.

- Universal Design for Learning (UDL): Embracing the principles of Universal Design for Learning, EdTech innovations aim to create inclusive learning environments for all students. Platforms designed with UDL in mind provide flexibility and multiple means of engagement, representation, and expression to accommodate diverse learners.

- Open Educational Resources (OER): The open sharing of educational content and resources transcends geographical boundaries. OER platforms enable educators to access a wealth of materials, fostering collaboration and the exchange of ideas on a global scale.

Challenges in EdTech Innovation: Navigating Complexities

- Accessibility and Equity: Ensuring that EdTech innovations are accessible to all students, regardless of socio-economic background or geographical location, remains a challenge. Addressing issues of accessibility and equity requires concerted efforts to bridge digital divides and eliminate barriers to technology access.

- Teacher Training and Professional Development: The successful integration of EdTech relies on educators' proficiency in leveraging these tools. Adequate training and ongoing professional development are essential to equip teachers with the skills needed to effectively incorporate technology into their teaching practices.

- Data Privacy and Security Concerns: EdTech innovations often involve the collection and storage of student data. Safeguarding this data against privacy breaches and ensuring compliance with data protection regulations present ongoing challenges that require robust security measures and ethical practices.

- Balancing Screen Time and Well-being: The increasing reliance on digital tools raises concerns about the impact of extended screen time on students' physical and mental well-being. Striking a balance between technology use and promoting overall well-being is a complex consideration in the era of EdTech integration.

Success Stories: Inspirational Tales of EdTech Impact

- Project-Based Learning Platforms: Platforms that facilitate project-based learning have empowered students to take on real-world challenges. Success stories highlight how students, through collaborative projects and hands-on experiences, develop critical skills, such as problem-solving, creativity, and teamwork.

- Global Online Learning Initiatives: Online learning initiatives with a global reach have enabled students to access high-quality education from anywhere in the world. Success stories underscore the transformative impact of breaking down geographical barriers and providing equal educational opportunities to diverse learners.

- Innovative Assessment Practices: EdTech innovations in assessment have yielded success stories in moving beyond traditional exams. Adaptive assessments, real-time feedback mechanisms, and alternative evaluation methods showcase how technology can enhance the assessment process, providing a more accurate reflection of student understanding.

- Digital Inclusion Initiatives: Success stories in digital inclusion highlight initiatives that have effectively bridged gaps in technology access. Programs providing devices, internet connectivity, and digital literacy training to underserved communities demonstrate the positive outcomes of focused efforts to promote digital equity.

Scalability and Replicability: Lessons for the Future

- Scalable EdTech Solutions: Innovations that demonstrate scalability offer insights into their potential to be implemented on a broader scale. Understanding the factors that contribute to the scalability of EdTech solutions provides valuable lessons for designing initiatives with widespread impact.

- Replicability Across Contexts: EdTech success stories that can be replicated across different educational contexts underscore the adaptability and universality of certain innovations. Identifying key elements that contribute to replicability informs the development of initiatives that can be tailored to diverse cultural, economic, and educational settings.

Conclusion: Charting the Future of EdTech

The landscape of EdTech innovations is dynamic, with ongoing advancements shaping the future of high school education. As we navigate the complexities, challenges, and successes within this realm, the chapters that follow will continue our exploration, delving into global perspectives on technology integration, assessments, quality indicators, rankings, and emerging trends. Each facet contributes to the unfolding tapestry of learning, emphasizing the need for continuous innovation and thoughtful consideration of the impact of technology on education.

Challenges and Opportunities in Technology Integration: Navigating the Digital Frontier

The integration of technology in high school education brings forth a spectrum of challenges and opportunities that educators, policymakers, and students must navigate. This exploration delves into the complexities of technology integration, examining the hurdles faced and the potential for transformative impact on the educational landscape.

Introduction: The Pivotal Role of Technology in Education

The infusion of technology into high school education has been hailed as a transformative force, promising to enhance learning outcomes, engagement, and the overall educational experience. However, this integration is not without its challenges. Understanding the nuances of both obstacles and opportunities is crucial for maximizing the benefits of technology in the classroom.

Challenges in Technology Integration: Navigating the Complexities

- Digital Divide and Access Disparities: One of the foremost challenges in technology integration is the existence of a digital divide. Disparities in access to devices, high-speed internet, and digital literacy skills create inequities among students. Bridging this divide is essential to ensure that all students have equal access to the benefits of educational technology.

- Resistance to Change: Resistance to change among educators, administrators, and even students can impede the successful integration of technology. Overcoming entrenched traditional practices and fostering a mindset open to innovation is a continual challenge in the dynamic landscape of education.

- Insufficient Teacher Training: Effective technology integration relies heavily on the proficiency of educators in utilizing digital tools. Insufficient training and professional development opportunities for teachers hinder their ability to harness the full potential of technology, leading to underutilization or misuse of available resources.

- Data Privacy and Security Concerns: The collection, storage, and use of student data raise significant privacy and security concerns. Safeguarding sensitive information and ensuring compliance with privacy regulations are ongoing challenges that require robust policies, practices, and awareness among educational stakeholders.

- Balancing Screen Time and Well-being: The increased reliance on digital devices in the classroom raises concerns about the impact of extended screen time on students' physical and mental well-being. Striking a balance between utilizing technology for educational purposes and safeguarding students' overall health poses a complex challenge for educators and parents alike.

- Funding Limitations: Adequate funding is paramount for successful technology integration. Many educational institutions, particularly those in economically disadvantaged areas, face limitations in securing the necessary resources for acquiring devices, maintaining infrastructure, and providing ongoing support for technology initiatives.

Opportunities in Technology Integration: Unlocking Educational Potential

- Personalized Learning Experiences: Technology enables the creation of personalized learning experiences tailored to individual student needs. Adaptive learning platforms, interactive content, and data analytics empower educators to cater to diverse learning styles, fostering a more inclusive and effective educational environment.

- Enhanced Collaboration and Communication: Digital tools facilitate seamless collaboration and communication among students, teachers, and even global communities. Virtual classrooms, collaborative platforms, and communication tools break down geographical barriers, creating a more interconnected and globally aware educational community.

- Innovative Pedagogical Approaches: Technology integration opens avenues for innovative pedagogical approaches. Flipped classrooms, project-based learning, and gamified lessons leverage technology to engage students actively, encouraging critical thinking, creativity, and problem-solving skills.

- Global Perspectives on Learning: Technology provides access to a wealth of information and diverse perspectives from around the world. Virtual field trips, online resources, and collaborative projects connect students with global issues, fostering a broader understanding of different cultures, societies, and viewpoints.

- Preparation for the Future Workforce: Integrating technology into high school education prepares students for the demands of the modern workforce. Exposure to digital tools, coding, and technological literacy equips students with essential skills for success in fields driven by technology and innovation.

- Inclusive Education for Diverse Learners: Technology has the potential to enhance inclusivity in education. Assistive technologies, customizable learning paths, and online resources cater to the needs of diverse learners, ensuring that every student, regardless of ability, has equal access to educational opportunities.

Strategies to Address Challenges and Maximize Opportunities

- Comprehensive Digital Literacy Programs: Implementing comprehensive digital literacy programs is essential to address challenges related to the digital divide and insufficient teacher training. These programs should encompass not only students but also educators, parents, and administrators, fostering a holistic understanding of digital tools and responsible usage.

- Equitable Access Initiatives: Initiatives focused on bridging the digital divide, such as providing devices, internet connectivity, and digital resources to underserved communities, are crucial. Equitable access initiatives contribute to creating a level playing field for all students, irrespective of their socio-economic background.

- Professional Development for Educators: Ongoing professional development opportunities for educators are key to overcoming resistance to change and ensuring effective technology integration. Training programs should cover not only the technical aspects of using digital tools but also pedagogical strategies for incorporating technology into teaching practices.

- Robust Data Privacy Policies: Establishing and enforcing robust data privacy policies is essential to address concerns related to the security of student information. Educational institutions must prioritize the protection of sensitive data, implement secure systems, and educate stakeholders about privacy best practices.

- Collaborative Funding Models: Collaborative funding models that involve partnerships between educational institutions, government entities, and private enterprises can help overcome funding limitations. Shared resources and financial support from multiple stakeholders contribute to the sustainability of technology integration initiatives.

- Balanced Technology Use Policies: Implementing balanced technology use policies that address concerns about screen time and well-being is crucial. These policies should consider age-appropriate guidelines, incorporate breaks from screen-based activities, and emphasize the importance of a holistic approach to student well-being.

Case Studies: Learning from Successful Implementations

- Singapore's Smart Nation Initiative: Singapore's Smart Nation initiative exemplifies a holistic approach to technology integration. With a focus on digital literacy, extensive teacher training, and collaborative partnerships, Singapore has successfully transformed its education system, preparing students for a tech-driven future.

- Uruguay's One Laptop per Child (OLPC) Program: Uruguay's OLPC program is a pioneering initiative that provided laptops to every primary school student in the country. The program focused on equity, ensuring that students from all socio-economic backgrounds had access to digital tools, ultimately enhancing learning outcomes.

- Canada's Coding Education Initiatives: Canada's emphasis on coding education illustrates the importance of preparing students for the digital age. Nationwide initiatives to introduce coding in primary and secondary schools empower students with essential skills for a future where technology plays a central role in various industries.

Conclusion: Navigating the Future of Education

The challenges and opportunities in technology integration underscore the dynamic nature of high school education in the digital era. As we navigate this ever-evolving landscape, the subsequent chapters will delve into specific aspects of global perspectives, assessments, quality indicators, rankings, and emerging trends. Each exploration contributes to the overarching narrative of how technology shapes and transforms the educational journey, emphasizing the need for informed strategies and collaborative efforts to harness its full potential.

Chapter 7: Transition to Higher Education

Challenges in Transitioning to Universities: Navigating the Bridge to Higher Learning

The transition from high school to higher education is a critical juncture in a student's academic journey, marked by significant challenges and adjustments. This exploration delves into the multifaceted challenges students encounter during this pivotal transition, shedding light on the complexities and potential strategies for facilitating a smoother bridge to university life.

Introduction: The Crucial Bridge Between High School and Higher Education

The transition from high school to university represents a transformative period, where students navigate academic, social, and personal changes. Recognizing and understanding the challenges inherent in this transition is essential for educators, policymakers, and students themselves. This chapter explores the multifaceted challenges students face as they embark on their higher education journey.

Academic Challenges in the Transition Phase

- Differences in Learning Environment: One of the primary academic challenges in transitioning to university life is the shift in the learning environment. Unlike high school, universities often emphasize independent learning, critical thinking, and self-motivation. Students accustomed to structured high school curricula may find it challenging to adapt to the more autonomous and research-oriented nature of university education.

- Increased Academic Rigor: University courses tend to be more rigorous and demanding than high school curricula. The depth of subject matter, the pace of instruction, and the expectations for independent research and analysis can be overwhelming for students who may not be adequately prepared for the heightened academic demands.

- Shift in Assessment Methods: The transition to university often comes with a shift in assessment methods. While high school assessments may rely heavily on standardized tests and continuous evaluation, university assessments frequently include research papers, presentations, and in-depth examinations. Students may struggle to adjust to these new evaluation formats.

- Time Management Challenges: Effective time management becomes crucial in university, where students are responsible for organizing their schedules and balancing multiple courses and assignments. The lack of structured class periods and the need for self-directed study can pose challenges for students accustomed to more regimented high school schedules.

Social and Personal Adjustment Challenges

- Diversity in Student Population: Universities typically have more diverse student populations than high schools. Interacting with peers from various cultural, socioeconomic, and academic backgrounds can be enriching but may also present challenges in terms of forming social connections and adapting to a diverse community.

- Independence and Personal Responsibility: University life requires a higher degree of independence and personal responsibility. Students must manage their finances, make academic and career decisions, and navigate the complexities of adulthood. The newfound independence can be liberating but may also lead to feelings of uncertainty and stress.

- Social Integration: Forming new social connections and establishing a sense of belonging can be challenging in the university setting. Students may grapple with feelings of isolation, homesickness, or anxiety about fitting in. Building a supportive social network is crucial for overall well-being during the university transition.

- Mental Health and Stress: The increased academic demands, coupled with the pressures of personal and social adjustments, can contribute to heightened stress levels and mental health challenges. Recognizing and addressing the mental health needs of students during this transition is essential for their overall well-being.

Navigating Cultural and Environmental Shifts

- Cultural Adjustment: For international students, the transition to a new country and cultural environment adds an extra layer of complexity. Adapting to a different education system, language, and social norms requires resilience and a willingness to embrace cultural diversity.

- Financial Strain: University education often comes with financial burdens, including tuition fees, accommodation costs, and living expenses. Students may face challenges in managing their finances and adapting to a more independent financial lifestyle.

- Access to Support Services: Recognizing and accessing support services is critical during the transition phase. Many students may be unaware of the available resources for academic, personal, and mental health support. Improving awareness and accessibility of these services is vital for student success.

Strategies to Address Transition Challenges

- Pre-University Preparation Programs: Implementing pre-university preparation programs can help students acclimate to the academic expectations and learning environment of universities. These programs may include workshops on study skills, time management, and academic writing.

- Mentorship Programs: Establishing mentorship programs where incoming students are paired with more experienced peers or faculty members can provide valuable guidance and support. Mentors can share insights, offer advice, and help newcomers navigate the challenges of university life.

- Enhanced Guidance Counseling: High schools can play a crucial role in preparing students for the transition by enhancing guidance counseling services. This includes providing information on university expectations, offering career counseling, and addressing mental health awareness.

- Orientation Programs: Comprehensive orientation programs can ease the social and cultural transition. These programs should cover not only academic aspects but also introduce students to campus resources, support services, and opportunities for social integration.

- Holistic Student Support Services: Universities should invest in holistic student support services that address academic, personal, and mental health needs. This includes counseling services, academic tutoring, and initiatives promoting overall well-being.

Case Studies: Successful Transition Initiatives

- Transition Programs at the University of California, Berkeley: The University of California, Berkeley, offers a range of transition programs designed to support incoming students. These programs include academic workshops, mentorship opportunities, and orientation sessions, contributing to a smoother transition experience.

- Peer Support Networks at Australian Universities: Many Australian universities have implemented peer support networks where experienced students mentor and guide new arrivals. These networks foster a sense of community, provide practical advice, and enhance social integration.

- First-Year Experience Initiatives at Harvard University: Harvard University's First-Year Experience initiatives aim to ease the academic and social transition for incoming students. These initiatives include dedicated courses, workshops, and support services tailored to the unique needs of first-year students.

Conclusion: Nurturing Success in the University Transition

The challenges in transitioning to universities are diverse and multifaceted, requiring a comprehensive and collaborative approach from educational institutions, policymakers, and students themselves. As we delve further into the chapters exploring global trends in higher education, vocational training, and admission practices, the insights gained from understanding the challenges of the transition phase will inform our exploration of creating a more supportive and inclusive higher education landscape.

Vocational Education and Training: Forging Alternative Paths to Success

The journey from high school to higher education encompasses diverse pathways, and vocational education and training (VET) represent a vital avenue for students seeking practical skills and immediate entry into the workforce. This exploration delves into the significance of vocational education, its evolving landscape, and the role it plays in providing students with tangible skills and career readiness.

Introduction: The Evolution of Vocational Education and Training

Vocational education and training (VET) have emerged as a dynamic and integral component of the educational landscape, offering students a pragmatic and hands-on approach to learning. This chapter examines the evolution of vocational education, its relevance in the context of transitioning from high school to higher education, and the societal importance of cultivating a skilled and adaptable workforce.

Understanding Vocational Education and Training

Vocational education and training (VET) encompass a range of educational programs designed to equip students with specific skills, knowledge, and competencies related to particular trades, industries, or professions. Unlike traditional academic pathways, VET programs emphasize practical, hands-on learning and are tailored to meet the demands of the workforce.

Key Characteristics of Vocational Education and Training

- Practical Skill Development: VET programs focus on cultivating practical skills that directly align with the requirements of specific occupations. Whether in healthcare, construction, information technology, or other fields, students engage in hands-on learning experiences that mirror real-world job scenarios.

- Industry-Relevant Curriculum: VET curricula are developed in collaboration with industry stakeholders, ensuring that the content remains current and aligned with the latest industry practices. This close partnership between education providers and industries helps bridge the gap between education and employment.

- Structured Apprenticeships and Internships: Many VET programs incorporate apprenticeships or internships, providing students with opportunities to gain real-world experience in their chosen fields. This hands-on exposure enhances their employability and allows them to apply theoretical knowledge in practical settings.

- Flexibility and Customization: VET programs often offer flexibility in terms of duration and scheduling. Students can choose from a variety of courses that cater to their specific interests and career goals. The customizable nature of VET allows individuals to tailor their education to suit their unique aspirations.

- Dual-Pathway Opportunities: Some VET programs offer dual-pathway options, allowing students to earn academic credentials while simultaneously gaining practical skills. This integrated approach provides a holistic education that combines theoretical knowledge with hands-on experience.

The Role of VET in the Transition from High School to Higher Education

- Immediate Employability: One of the primary advantages of VET is its focus on immediate employability. Graduates of VET programs often enter the workforce with a skill set that makes them well-suited for specific roles, reducing the time between education and employment.

- Alternative to Traditional Higher Education: VET serves as a valuable alternative to traditional higher education pathways. For students who prefer a more practical and vocational approach to learning, VET offers a direct route to acquiring industry-relevant skills without the extended duration of traditional degree programs.

- Meeting Labor Market Needs: VET programs play a crucial role in addressing the skills gap in various industries. By aligning curriculum with the needs of the labor market, VET institutions contribute to the development of a skilled workforce that meets the demands of evolving industries.

- Fostering Entrepreneurship: VET programs often instill entrepreneurial skills by emphasizing practical problem-solving and critical thinking. Graduates with vocational training may choose to start their own businesses, contributing to economic growth and innovation.

Challenges in Vocational Education and Training

- Perceived Stigma: Despite the practical benefits of VET, there can be a perceived stigma associated with non-traditional educational paths. Some individuals may view vocational training as inferior to a university degree, leading to misconceptions about the value and potential of VET qualifications.

- Resource Allocation: Adequate funding and resources are essential for the success of VET programs. Insufficient investment in vocational education can result in outdated facilities, limited access to modern technology, and challenges in maintaining high-quality training environments.

- Changing Nature of Work: The rapid evolution of technology and changes in the nature of work pose challenges for VET programs to remain relevant. Continuous adaptation of curricula to incorporate emerging technologies and industry trends is crucial for ensuring graduates are prepared for the contemporary workforce.

- Coordination Between Education and Industry: Effective collaboration between education providers and industries is vital for the success of VET programs. Challenges may arise when there is a lack of alignment between educational curricula and the evolving needs of industries.

Opportunities and Innovations in Vocational Education and Training

- Digital Transformation in VET: Embracing digital technologies, such as virtual reality (VR), augmented reality (AR), and online simulations, enhances the learning experience in VET programs. These technologies provide immersive training environments, allowing students to practice skills in a safe and controlled setting.

- Integration of Soft Skills: Recognizing the importance of soft skills, such as communication, teamwork, and problem-solving, VET programs are increasingly integrating these skills into their curricula. Developing a well-rounded set of competencies enhances graduates' adaptability in the workplace.

- Global Collaboration in VET: Collaborative initiatives between VET institutions globally offer opportunities for sharing best practices, exchanging expertise, and addressing common challenges. This global perspective contributes to the continuous improvement of VET programs on an international scale.

- Recognition of Prior Learning: Acknowledging and accrediting prior learning experiences is gaining prominence in VET. This approach values the skills and knowledge individuals bring from their prior work or life experiences, allowing for more flexible and personalized learning pathways.

Case Studies: Exemplary VET Programs

- Germany's Dual Education System: Germany's dual education system is often cited as a model for successful VET. The system combines classroom learning with on-the-job training, allowing students to earn while they learn. This approach has contributed to Germany's highly skilled workforce and low youth unemployment rates.

- Singapore's SkillsFuture Initiative: Singapore's SkillsFuture initiative is a comprehensive national effort to promote lifelong learning and skills development. The initiative includes various measures such as SkillsFuture Credit, which provides individuals with funds to pursue skills-related courses and certifications.

- Switzerland's Apprenticeship Model: Switzerland's apprenticeship model emphasizes a close collaboration between schools and employers. Students engage in vocational training while attending school, resulting in a seamless integration of theoretical knowledge and practical skills.

Conclusion: Nurturing Practical Skills for Future Success

Vocational education and training (VET) stand as a cornerstone in the diverse landscape of educational pathways, offering students a direct route to practical skills and immediate employability. As we delve further into the chapters exploring global trends in higher education admission, success stories, assessments, and emerging prospects, the insights gained from understanding the role of VET will contribute to a comprehensive view of the multifaceted journey from high school to higher education.

Role of High School Education in Career Paths: Charting Futures through Academic Foundations

High school education serves as the bedrock for students' academic and personal development, playing a pivotal role in shaping their future career paths. This chapter explores the multifaceted influence of high school education on career trajectories, examining how academic foundations, extracurricular activities, and guidance shape students' vocational aspirations.

Introduction: The Crucial Link Between High School and Careers

The journey from high school to career is a transformative period where students make crucial decisions that impact their professional futures. High school education serves as the foundation, imparting not only academic knowledge but also essential skills, values, and a sense of direction that guide students as they navigate their career paths.

Academic Foundations: Nurturing Skills and Knowledge

High school education lays the groundwork for academic proficiency and intellectual growth. The curriculum, spanning various subjects, provides students with a broad knowledge base, enabling them to explore diverse fields before committing to a specific career path. Key aspects of academic foundations influencing career trajectories include:

- Core Subjects and Interdisciplinary Learning: The core subjects of high school, including mathematics, science, literature, and social sciences, offer students a well-rounded education. Interdisciplinary learning experiences expose students to connections between different fields, fostering critical thinking and a holistic understanding of the world.

- Advanced Placement (AP) and Honors Courses: High schools often offer advanced courses, such as AP and honors classes, providing students with opportunities to delve deeper into specific subjects. These advanced courses not only challenge students academically but also allow them to explore potential areas of interest at a more advanced level.

   - Career-oriented Electives: Some high schools offer career-oriented electives, allowing students to gain practical skills and insights into specific professions. Courses in areas like computer programming, healthcare, or business can shape students' career aspirations by providing hands-on experiences in relevant fields.

   - Extracurricular Activities and Leadership: Beyond the formal curriculum, extracurricular activities play a crucial role in shaping students' characters and career goals. Participation in clubs, sports, student government, and community service can enhance leadership skills, teamwork, and communication abilities – attributes highly valued in the professional world.

Guidance and Counseling: Navigating Career Choices

High school guidance and counseling services play a vital role in helping students navigate the complex landscape of career choices. Counselors offer personalized support, assist in career assessments, and provide valuable information about different professions and educational pathways. Key components of guidance and counseling in shaping career paths include:

   - Career Assessments and Aptitude Testing: High school counselors often administer career assessments and aptitude tests to help students identify their strengths, interests, and potential career matches. These tools provide valuable insights that aid students in making informed decisions about their academic and professional pursuits.

   - College and Career Planning: Guidance counselors work closely with students on college and career planning. They provide information about different academic pathways, assist with college applications, and offer insights into various career options. This guidance helps students align their educational choices with their long-term career goals.

- Internship and Job Shadowing Opportunities: Some high schools facilitate internship programs or job shadowing opportunities, allowing students to gain firsthand experience in professional environments. Exposure to real-world work settings helps students refine their career goals and make more informed decisions about their future paths.

- Individualized Career Counseling: Recognizing the diverse needs of students, individualized career counseling sessions provide a platform for students to discuss their aspirations, concerns, and questions about potential career paths. These one-on-one interactions foster a supportive environment for personalized guidance.

Extracurricular and Leadership Activities: Shaping Professional Skills

Extracurricular activities play a significant role in developing skills that are transferable to the professional realm. Beyond academic knowledge, these activities contribute to the cultivation of leadership, teamwork, communication, and resilience – qualities highly valued by employers. Key aspects of extracurricular activities shaping professional skills include:

- Leadership Roles in Clubs and Organizations: High school students often have the opportunity to take on leadership roles in clubs, student government, or other organizations. Serving as a club president, team captain, or event organizer helps students develop leadership skills, organizational abilities, and a sense of responsibility.

- Sports and Team Activities: Participation in sports fosters teamwork, discipline, and perseverance. Team sports, in particular, provide students with experiences in collaboration, strategic thinking, and effective communication – skills that are transferable to professional settings.

- Community Service and Volunteer Work: Engaging in community service and volunteer work instills a sense of social responsibility and empathy. These experiences contribute to the development of interpersonal skills, cultural awareness, and a commitment to making a positive impact – qualities that resonate in professional environments.

- Creative Arts and Performances: Involvement in creative arts, such as music, drama, or visual arts, nurtures creativity, expression, and resilience in the face of challenges. These artistic endeavors contribute to a well-rounded skill set that is valuable in both creative and analytical professions.

Challenges in Career Decision-Making: Navigating Uncertainty

Despite the guidance and support available, high school students often face challenges in making career decisions. Factors such as uncertainty about future trends, familial expectations, and external pressures can create complexity in the decision-making process. Key challenges in career decision-making include:

- Uncertainty About Future Trends: Rapid changes in technology, industries, and global dynamics can create uncertainty about the future job market. Students may struggle to align their career aspirations with emerging trends, leading to apprehension about the relevance and stability of their chosen paths.

- Family Expectations and Influences: Family expectations and influences can significantly impact students' career choices. Cultural, societal, or familial expectations may shape students' decisions, sometimes steering them toward specific professions or industries that align with family traditions or perceived prestige.

- External Pressures and Peer Comparisons: External pressures, including peer comparisons and societal expectations, can influence students' perceptions of success and fulfillment. The desire to conform to societal norms or match the achievements of peers may lead students to pursue careers that may not align with their true interests or passions.

- Limited Exposure to Diverse Professions: Some students may have limited exposure to a diverse range of professions. Lack of information about various career options can hinder students' ability to make informed decisions, as they may not be aware of the breadth of opportunities available to them.

Navigating Global Trends in Career Paths

Understanding global trends in career paths is essential for high school students as they prepare for the evolving job market. Exploration of emerging sectors, demand for specific skills, and the impact of technology on various industries can help students align their academic and career choices with the changing landscape. Key global trends influencing career paths include:

- Rise of Technology and Digital Skills: The increasing reliance on technology across industries highlights the importance of digital skills. Professions related to cybersecurity, data analytics, artificial intelligence, and digital marketing are experiencing high demand, emphasizing the need for students to develop technological proficiency.

- Focus on Sustainability and Environmental Careers: Growing concerns about climate change and environmental sustainability have led to increased demand for careers in renewable energy, environmental science, and sustainable development. Students interested in making a positive impact on the environment may find opportunities in these burgeoning fields.

- Healthcare and Biotechnology Advancements: Advances in healthcare and biotechnology are shaping the landscape of medical and life sciences careers. The COVID-19 pandemic has underscored the critical importance of healthcare professionals and researchers, making these fields attractive for those interested in contributing to public health and scientific advancements.

- Remote Work and Flexible Employment: The rise of remote work and flexible employment arrangements has transformed the traditional work landscape. Students may consider careers that offer flexibility in terms of remote work options, as this trend is likely to continue influencing the professional world.

Success Stories: Nurturing Dreams into Achievements

Exploring success stories of individuals who navigated their career paths from high school to professional success provides inspiration and insights for current students. These stories highlight the diverse trajectories individuals have taken, emphasizing the importance of perseverance, adaptability, and a passion for one's chosen path.

- Entrepreneurial Journeys: Success stories of entrepreneurs who started their ventures straight out of high school underscore the potential for innovative and entrepreneurial pursuits. These individuals often showcase the significance of creativity, determination, and resilience in building successful businesses.

- Career Pivot Stories: Individuals who have successfully navigated career pivots share valuable insights into the importance of adaptability and continuous learning. These stories demonstrate that it's never too late to change career paths, and high school education can serve as a foundation for diverse professional journeys.

- STEM Achievements: Success stories in the fields of science, technology, engineering, and mathematics (STEM) highlight the impact of high school education on nurturing the skills required for success in these dynamic and rapidly evolving sectors. These stories inspire students to pursue STEM careers and contribute to technological advancements.

Conclusion: Charting Futures, Embracing Possibilities

The role of high school education in shaping career paths is a dynamic and multifaceted journey, encompassing academic foundations, guidance and counseling, extracurricular activities, and the navigation of global trends. As we delve further into the chapters exploring global assessments, standardized testing, educational rankings, and emerging trends, the insights gained from understanding the intersection of high school education and career paths will contribute to a comprehensive view of the intricate landscape of education and professional development.

Global Trends in Higher Education Admission: Navigating the Evolving Landscape of College Entrances

The transition from high school to higher education is a critical juncture that reflects not only individual aspirations but also broader global trends in admissions. This chapter delves into the multifaceted landscape of higher education admissions, exploring evolving criteria, shifts in application processes, and the impact of global trends on students' journeys to college.

Introduction: The Changing Dynamics of Higher Education Admissions

The process of gaining admission to higher education institutions has undergone significant transformations in response to shifting societal needs, technological advancements, and an increasingly interconnected world. This section provides an overview of the key factors influencing global trends in higher education admission.

Diversity and Inclusion: A Paradigm Shift in Admissions Criteria

In recent years, there has been a noticeable shift towards fostering diversity and inclusion within higher education institutions. Admissions criteria are expanding beyond traditional metrics, such as grades and standardized test scores, to consider a more holistic view of applicants. This trend is driven by the recognition that a diverse student body enhances the learning experience and prepares graduates for an interconnected global society.

- Holistic Admissions Approaches: Many universities now embrace holistic admissions approaches, considering not only academic achievements but also personal qualities, extracurricular activities, and unique life experiences. This broader perspective aims to identify candidates who bring diverse perspectives and contribute to a rich campus community.

- Inclusive Recruitment Strategies: Higher education institutions are actively implementing inclusive recruitment strategies to attract a wide range of applicants. Outreach efforts target underrepresented groups, including minorities, first-generation college students, and individuals from socioeconomically disadvantaged backgrounds, fostering a more equitable representation in admissions.

- Commitment to Equity: Admissions offices are placing a greater emphasis on equity in their evaluation processes. Recognizing the impact of systemic inequalities, institutions are implementing policies and practices that level the playing field for all applicants, ensuring that socio-economic background or educational disparities do not unduly influence admission decisions.

Technology and Digitalization: Transforming Application Processes

Advancements in technology have revolutionized the higher education admissions process, making it more accessible, efficient, and globally connected. From application submission to virtual campus tours, technology plays a central role in shaping how students engage with and navigate the admissions landscape.

- Online Application Platforms: The traditional paper-based application processes are increasingly being replaced by online application platforms. This not only streamlines the submission process for applicants but also allows institutions to manage and review applications more efficiently.

- Virtual Campus Tours and Information Sessions: Technology enables prospective students to explore campuses virtually through online tours and information sessions. This not only broadens access for international applicants but also provides a more immersive and inclusive experience for all prospective students.

- Digital Portfolios and Multimedia Submissions: Some institutions now allow applicants to submit digital portfolios or multimedia presentations as part of their application. This innovation provides students with the opportunity to showcase their talents, creativity, and accomplishments in a more dynamic and personalized manner.

- Use of Artificial Intelligence (AI) in Admissions: AI is being increasingly employed in the admissions process to analyze large volumes of applications and identify patterns that may inform decision-making. While AI can enhance efficiency, there are ongoing discussions about ensuring fairness, transparency, and ethical use in admissions.

Globalization of Higher Education: Navigating International Admissions

As higher education becomes increasingly globalized, students are exploring opportunities beyond their home countries. International admissions processes are evolving to accommodate the diverse needs and aspirations of a global student population.

- Rise of International Student Exchanges: Collaborative programs and international student exchanges are on the rise. Institutions are fostering partnerships with universities worldwide, allowing students to seamlessly transition between campuses and gain a broader perspective on their chosen fields of study.

- Recognition of International Qualifications: Many universities are expanding their recognition of international qualifications. This includes acknowledging a wider range of grading systems, standardized tests, and alternative credentials, facilitating a more inclusive approach to admitting students from diverse educational backgrounds.

- Language Proficiency Requirements: With the increasing number of non-native English speakers pursuing higher education globally, language proficiency requirements have gained prominence. Standardized tests such as the TOEFL (Test of English as a Foreign Language) and IELTS (International English Language Testing System) play a crucial role in assessing applicants' language skills.

- Cultural Competency and Global Citizenship: Admissions criteria often include an emphasis on cultural competency and global citizenship. Institutions seek students who demonstrate an awareness of diverse cultures, perspectives, and a commitment to contributing positively to a global community.

Emphasis on Skills and Competencies: Beyond Academic Achievements

In response to the changing demands of the job market and the recognition that traditional academic metrics may not fully capture an individual's potential, there is a growing emphasis on assessing applicants' skills, competencies, and real-world readiness.

- Shift Towards Skills-Based Assessments: Some institutions are incorporating skills-based assessments into their admissions processes. These assessments may evaluate critical thinking, communication, problem-solving, and other skills essential for success in higher education and the professional world.

- Portfolio and Project-Based Submissions: Applicants are increasingly encouraged to submit portfolios or engage in project-based submissions to showcase their practical skills and accomplishments. This approach allows individuals with diverse talents, including those in the arts, humanities, and applied sciences, to present a more comprehensive picture of their abilities.

- Focus on Leadership and Extracurricular Engagement: Admissions committees often look for evidence of leadership qualities and extracurricular engagement. Participation in clubs, community service, sports, or other activities that demonstrate leadership, teamwork, and a commitment to community involvement can positively influence admission decisions.

- Adaptability and Lifelong Learning: The ability to adapt to change and demonstrate a commitment to lifelong learning is increasingly valued. Admissions committees are interested in applicants who exhibit a growth mindset, resilience, and a willingness to embrace new challenges and opportunities.

Challenges and Controversies: Navigating the Complexities of Admissions

While higher education institutions strive for fairness and inclusivity in their admissions processes, challenges and controversies persist. These issues range from debates about standardized testing to concerns about favoring certain demographics.

- Debates on Standardized Testing: The role of standardized testing in admissions remains a subject of debate. Critics argue that standardized tests may not accurately measure an individual's potential and may perpetuate inequalities. Some institutions have moved towards test-optional policies, while others continue to use standardized tests as part of their evaluation process.

- Economic Disparities and Access: Economic disparities can create barriers to access higher education. Affordability of application fees, test preparation resources, and other associated costs may disproportionately affect applicants from lower-income backgrounds, raising concerns about equitable access to higher education.

- Affirmative Action and Diversity Policies: Affirmative action and diversity policies in admissions have faced legal challenges and debates. While these policies aim to address historical inequalities and promote diversity, controversies often arise around questions of fairness, meritocracy, and potential reverse discrimination.

- Ethical Concerns in AI Use: The use of AI in admissions processes raises ethical concerns related to bias, privacy, and transparency. Ensuring that AI algorithms are fair, unbiased, and do not perpetuate existing inequalities is an ongoing challenge for institutions embracing technology in their admissions procedures.

Future Trends and Prospects: Shaping the Admissions Landscape

As higher education continues to evolve, several trends and prospects are shaping the future of admissions. These include advancements in technology, the integration of innovative assessment methods, and a continued focus on fostering diverse and inclusive learning environments.

- Blockchain Technology in Credential Verification: The use of blockchain technology for credential verification is gaining traction. This innovation provides a secure and transparent way to verify academic credentials, reducing the risk of fraud and simplifying the admissions process.

- Gamification of Admissions Processes: Some institutions are exploring the gamification of admissions processes to make the experience more engaging for applicants. Gamification may include interactive elements, challenges, and simulations that assess applicants' problem-solving abilities and creativity.

- Personalized Admissions Experiences: Admissions processes are becoming more personalized. Institutions are leveraging data analytics and AI to tailor the admissions experience for individual applicants, providing relevant information and guidance based on their unique profiles and preferences.

- Continued Emphasis on Soft Skills: Soft skills, including communication, collaboration, and adaptability, will likely continue to be a focal point in admissions criteria. As the importance of interpersonal and emotional intelligence grows in professional settings, institutions may place greater emphasis on assessing these skills.

Conclusion: Navigating the Pathways to Higher Education

The journey from high school to higher education is a transformative period influenced by global trends, technological innovations, and societal shifts. As we explore further in the chapters on success stories, educational innovations, global assessments, and emerging trends, understanding the complexities and dynamics of higher education admissions contributes to a comprehensive view of the intricate tapestry of global high school education.

Chapter 8: Success Stories and Innovations in Education

Educational Initiatives Making a Difference: Transformative Pathways to Learning Excellence

In the ever-evolving landscape of education, success stories and innovative initiatives stand as beacons of inspiration and progress. This chapter delves into educational initiatives worldwide that have made a significant impact, showcasing how these endeavors have transformed learning experiences, enhanced accessibility, and propelled positive change in diverse educational settings.

Introduction: The Power of Educational Initiatives

Educational initiatives play a crucial role in shaping the future of learning. Whether driven by grassroots movements, institutional innovations, or government-led reforms, these initiatives have the potential to address challenges, unlock potential, and pave the way for a more inclusive and effective education system. This section introduces the diverse range of educational initiatives explored in the chapter, emphasizing their collective impact on the global educational landscape.

Inclusive Education: Breaking Barriers, Empowering Learners

Inclusive education initiatives aim to create learning environments that accommodate the diverse needs and abilities of all students, regardless of background or circumstance. By focusing on accessibility, equity, and individualized support, these initiatives foster a sense of belonging and empowerment among learners.

- The Inclusive Education Model in Finland: Finland's education system is renowned for its commitment to inclusivity. The country's emphasis on providing individualized support and minimizing segregation of students with special needs has resulted in a more inclusive learning environment.

Teachers receive training to address diverse learning styles, ensuring that every student has the opportunity to thrive.

- Universal Design for Learning (UDL): UDL is an educational framework that guides the design of instructional materials, assessments, and activities to accommodate diverse learning needs. By considering the variability of all learners, UDL aims to create flexible learning environments that support individualized learning paths. Initiatives incorporating UDL principles have demonstrated success in promoting accessibility and inclusivity.

- Project-Based Learning for Inclusion: Project-based learning (PBL) has emerged as an inclusive educational approach, engaging students in collaborative, hands-on projects. This initiative not only enhances academic learning but also fosters teamwork, communication, and problem-solving skills. PBL can be adapted to accommodate diverse learning styles, making it an effective tool for inclusive education.

Digital Literacy Initiatives: Navigating the Digital Frontier

In an increasingly digital world, digital literacy initiatives are essential to equip students with the skills needed to thrive in the 21st century. From basic digital literacy to advanced coding and programming skills, these initiatives empower learners to navigate the digital landscape and contribute meaningfully to the global knowledge economy.

- Estonia's E-Government and Digital Literacy: Estonia has been a pioneer in digital literacy, implementing e-government initiatives that streamline public services and promote digital engagement. Digital literacy is integrated into the national curriculum, ensuring that students develop essential skills for navigating online platforms, understanding data privacy, and using digital tools for learning and communication.

- Coding and Computational Thinking Programs: Initiatives promoting coding and computational thinking have gained momentum globally. Programs such as Code.org and Scratch provide students with interactive platforms to learn coding in a fun and accessible way. These initiatives aim to bridge the digital divide, fostering an early interest in computer science and technology.

- Online Safety and Cybersecurity Education: As digital connectivity expands, the importance of online safety and cybersecurity education becomes paramount. Initiatives focusing on educating students about responsible online behavior, data privacy, and cybersecurity measures contribute to creating a safer digital learning environment.

Community Engagement: Building Bridges for Educational Success

Educational initiatives that prioritize community engagement recognize the pivotal role communities play in supporting and enhancing the learning experience. By fostering collaboration between schools, families, and local organizations, these initiatives create a holistic and supportive educational ecosystem.

- Community Schools in the United States: The community schools model in the United States emphasizes collaboration between schools and community resources to address students' academic, social, and health needs. By providing services such as healthcare, counseling, and afterschool programs within the school setting, this initiative aims to create a comprehensive support system for students.

- Parental Involvement Programs: Initiatives promoting parental involvement in education have a significant impact on student success. Programs that encourage parents to actively participate in their children's education, attend school events, and collaborate with teachers contribute to a positive and supportive learning environment.

- Partnerships with Local Businesses: Collaborations between schools and local businesses create opportunities for students to gain real-world experience and explore potential career paths. Initiatives that establish internships, mentorship programs, and apprenticeships enhance the relevance of education and strengthen the ties between education and the local workforce.

Environmental Education: Nurturing Stewardship for the Planet

As environmental challenges become more prominent, initiatives focusing on environmental education aim to instill a sense of responsibility and stewardship for the planet. These initiatives integrate sustainability principles into the curriculum, promoting awareness, and encouraging students to become environmentally conscious citizens.

- The Green Schools Movement: The Green Schools movement advocates for sustainable practices in school infrastructure, operations, and curriculum. Initiatives under this movement focus on reducing environmental impact, promoting energy efficiency, and incorporating environmental education into the curriculum. Students actively participate in eco-friendly initiatives, fostering a sense of environmental responsibility.

- Outdoor and Nature-Based Education: Programs that embrace outdoor and nature-based education provide students with hands-on experiences in natural environments. These initiatives not only enhance academic learning but also promote a connection to nature, fostering environmental awareness and a sense of ecological responsibility.

- Global Environmental Education Initiatives: Collaborative efforts at the global level, such as the United Nations Decade of Education for Sustainable Development (2005-2014), have aimed to integrate sustainability principles into education worldwide. These initiatives underscore the importance of preparing students to address global environmental challenges through informed decision-making and responsible actions.

Innovations in Assessment: Beyond Traditional Testing

Initiatives that explore innovative approaches to assessment recognize the limitations of traditional testing methods and seek to measure a broader range of skills and competencies. By incorporating alternative assessment methods, these initiatives aim to provide a more comprehensive understanding of students' abilities.

- Competency-Based Education (CBE): CBE is an initiative that shifts the focus from time-based learning to mastery of competencies. Students progress through the curriculum at their own pace, demonstrating mastery of skills before moving on to the next level. CBE fosters personalized learning and ensures that students acquire a deep understanding of content.

- Portfolios and Project-Based Assessments: Instead of relying solely on standardized testing, initiatives incorporating portfolios and project-based assessments provide a more holistic view of students' abilities. These assessments allow students to showcase their practical skills, creativity, and critical thinking in real-world scenarios.

- Formative Assessment Strategies: Formative assessment strategies, such as peer assessments, self-assessments, and classroom discussions, provide ongoing feedback to both students and teachers. These initiatives focus on the continuous improvement of learning outcomes, emphasizing the importance of reflection and collaboration in the learning process.

Conclusion: Inspiring Change through Educational Initiatives

The educational initiatives highlighted in this chapter represent a tapestry of transformative efforts that have enriched learning experiences, empowered learners, and paved the way for positive change in education. As we move forward in exploring global assessments, standardized testing, quality indicators, and educational rankings, the insights gained from these initiatives contribute to a comprehensive understanding of the dynamic landscape of global high school education.

Innovative Approaches to Educational Challenges: Pioneering Solutions for 21st-Century Learning

In the complex landscape of education, innovative approaches have emerged as powerful solutions to address diverse challenges. This chapter explores success stories and initiatives that have pioneered transformative pathways, offering insights into how innovative thinking can reshape educational paradigms and meet the evolving needs of students and educators.

Introduction: The Imperative of Innovation in Education

Innovation in education is essential to navigate the rapidly changing landscape of the 21st century. From adapting to technological advancements to fostering inclusive learning environments, innovative approaches offer dynamic solutions to the multifaceted challenges faced by educators, institutions, and learners. This section sets the stage for exploring success stories and initiatives that exemplify the power of innovation in education.

Technology-Enhanced Learning: Revolutionizing the Classroom Experience

In the digital age, technology-enhanced learning initiatives have redefined the traditional classroom experience, providing dynamic tools and platforms that engage students, personalize learning, and prepare them for the skills required in a tech-driven world.

- Flipped Classroom Models: Flipped classroom models invert traditional teaching methods, with students accessing instructional content online before class and engaging in collaborative activities during class time. This approach, embraced by initiatives like the Khan Academy, fosters active learning, student participation, and a deeper understanding of concepts.

- Virtual Reality (VR) in Education: Virtual reality has introduced immersive learning experiences, allowing students to explore historical events, scientific phenomena, and cultural landmarks in a virtual environment. Initiatives leveraging VR, such as Google Expeditions, enhance experiential learning, making complex subjects more accessible and engaging.

- Adaptive Learning Platforms: Adaptive learning platforms use data and artificial intelligence to tailor instruction to individual students' needs. These platforms, exemplified by initiatives like DreamBox and Knewton, provide personalized learning pathways, adapting content based on students' progress and learning styles.

Open Educational Resources (OER): Democratizing Access to Knowledge

The open educational resources movement seeks to make high-quality educational materials freely available to learners worldwide. By leveraging digital platforms, OER initiatives democratize access to knowledge, promote collaboration among educators, and alleviate barriers to educational resources.

- MIT OpenCourseWare (OCW): MIT's OpenCourseWare initiative makes course materials for thousands of MIT's courses available online for free. This pioneering effort has inspired similar initiatives globally, enabling learners to access university-level content across a range of disciplines.

- OER Commons: OER Commons serves as a digital library of open educational resources, offering educators a platform to discover, share, and adapt resources for diverse educational settings. This initiative facilitates collaboration among educators and supports the development of a rich repository of freely accessible learning materials.

- Collaborative Textbook Creation: Initiatives encouraging collaborative textbook creation, such as the CK-12 Foundation, enable educators and students to co-author textbooks. This approach not only reduces the financial burden of textbooks but also allows for the customization of content to align with specific curricular needs.

Project-Based Learning (PBL): Fostering Critical Thinking and Collaboration

Project-based learning initiatives immerse students in real-world projects, fostering critical thinking, problem-solving skills, and collaboration. By connecting classroom learning to practical applications, PBL transforms education into a dynamic and engaging experience.

- High Tech High Model: High Tech High, a network of project-based learning schools, emphasizes interdisciplinary projects that integrate subjects and address real-world problems. This initiative showcases the power of PBL to prepare students for the complexities of the modern workforce.

- Global Collaboration Projects: Initiatives that facilitate global collaboration, such as the Global Virtual Classroom project, connect students from different parts of the world to work together on projects. This not only broadens students' perspectives but also develops cross-cultural communication skills.

- Design Thinking in Education: Design thinking, an iterative problem-solving approach, has been incorporated into education initiatives like the Stanford d.school's K12 Lab Network. This method empowers students to identify and solve complex challenges through empathy, experimentation, and collaboration.

Personalized Learning Pathways: Tailoring Education to Individual Needs

Recognizing the diversity of learning styles and paces, personalized learning initiatives aim to tailor education to individual needs, fostering a more student-centric approach that empowers learners to take ownership of their educational journeys.

- AltSchool Model: AltSchool, founded by former Google executive Max Ventilla, utilizes technology to create personalized learning plans for each student. This initiative emphasizes small class sizes, individualized instruction, and a flexible curriculum that adapts to students' strengths and interests.

- Competency-Based Education (CBE): Competency-based education initiatives, such as the New Hampshire Department of Education's efforts, focus on students mastering specific skills before progressing to the next level. This approach allows for flexibility in pacing and ensures that students acquire a deep understanding of content.

- Adaptive Learning Platforms for Skill Development: Initiatives like Duolingo, which offers personalized language learning experiences, showcase the effectiveness of adaptive learning platforms in tailoring content to learners' proficiency levels and providing instant feedback to enhance skill development.

Social and Emotional Learning (SEL): Nurturing Holistic Development

Recognizing the importance of social and emotional skills in academic success and life, initiatives focused on social and emotional learning aim to cultivate students' emotional intelligence, resilience, and interpersonal skills.

- CASEL's Collaborative for Academic, Social, and Emotional Learning: CASEL's approach to SEL is widely recognized for its comprehensive framework that integrates social and emotional development into educational practices.

Initiatives aligned with CASEL's framework emphasize the importance of fostering self-awareness, social awareness, relationship skills, and responsible decision-making.

- Mindfulness Programs in Schools: Initiatives introducing mindfulness practices in schools, like the Inner Kids program, provide students with tools to manage stress, enhance focus, and cultivate emotional well-being. Incorporating mindfulness into education supports a positive school climate and contributes to students' overall mental health.

- Restorative Justice Practices: Restorative justice practices in education, such as those implemented by Oakland Unified School District, focus on building positive relationships and resolving conflicts through dialogue and understanding. These initiatives contribute to a supportive and inclusive school culture.

Conclusion: Embracing a Future of Educational Innovation

The success stories and innovations explored in this chapter showcase the transformative power of innovative approaches in addressing educational challenges. As we delve into global assessments, standardized testing, quality indicators, and educational rankings, these initiatives serve as beacons of inspiration, guiding us toward an educational landscape that embraces change, fosters creativity, and prepares students for the complexities of the future.

Lessons Learned from Success Stories: Guiding Principles for Educational Transformation

Success stories in education offer valuable insights into the strategies, approaches, and initiatives that have yielded positive outcomes. This chapter explores the lessons learned from various success stories, distilling key principles that can guide educational transformation on local, national, and global scales.

Introduction: Unpacking the Wisdom of Educational Success

Success in education is not a monolithic achievement but a tapestry woven with diverse threads of innovation, perseverance, and adaptability. This section introduces the overarching theme of the chapter—learning from success stories—and highlights the significance of distilling actionable lessons to inform future educational endeavors.

1. The Power of Inclusivity: Embracing Diversity for Enhanced Learning

Success Story: The Inclusive Education Model in Finland

Finland's commitment to inclusivity serves as a beacon for educational systems worldwide. The lesson learned from this success story is the transformative impact of embracing diversity in all its forms. By fostering an inclusive environment, educators can unlock the full potential of every student, recognizing and accommodating individual learning styles, abilities, and backgrounds.

Key Lessons:

- Individualized Support: Tailoring education to the unique needs of each student promotes a sense of belonging and ensures that no learner is left behind.

- Professional Development: Providing ongoing training for educators on inclusive practices is essential to creating an inclusive culture within schools.

- Community Engagement: Inclusivity extends beyond the classroom, involving parents, communities, and various stakeholders in the educational journey.

2. Democratizing Access to Knowledge: Open Educational Resources (OER)

Success Story: MIT OpenCourseWare (OCW) and OER Commons

The success of open educational resources underscores the importance of democratizing access to knowledge. The lesson learned here is that freely available, high-quality educational materials have the potential to level the playing field, providing learners globally with access to resources previously limited to privileged institutions.

Key Lessons:

- Global Collaboration: Creating and sharing open educational resources fosters a global community of educators and learners, encouraging collaboration and knowledge exchange.

- Adaptability: OER allows for the adaptation of materials to suit diverse cultural contexts, languages, and educational needs.

- Sustainability: The sustainability of OER initiatives depends on ongoing support, community engagement, and continuous updates to ensure relevance.

3. Project-Based Learning (PBL): Bridging Theory and Real-World Application

Success Story: High Tech High Model

The success of High Tech High's project-based learning model emphasizes the importance of bridging theory and real-world application in education. The lesson learned is that project-based learning not only enhances academic understanding but also cultivates critical thinking, problem-solving, and collaboration skills essential for success in the modern world.

Key Lessons:

- Interdisciplinary Approach: Integrating subjects in project-based learning promotes a holistic understanding of concepts and their real-world applications.

- Authentic Assessment: Projects provide opportunities for authentic assessment, allowing students to showcase their skills in practical, real-world scenarios.

- Student Engagement: Project-based learning engages students by making education relevant to their lives and fostering a sense of curiosity and creativity.

4. Personalized Learning: Tailoring Education to Individual Needs

Success Story: AltSchool Model and Competency-Based Education (CBE)

The success stories of AltSchool's personalized learning model and competency-based education highlight the transformative potential of tailoring education to individual needs. The lesson learned is that acknowledging and accommodating diverse learning styles, paces, and interests can lead to more meaningful and personalized learning experiences.

Key Lessons:

- Flexible Curriculum: Personalized learning thrives on a flexible curriculum that adapts to students' strengths, interests, and learning preferences.

- Student Agency: Empowering students to take ownership of their learning journey enhances motivation, autonomy, and a sense of responsibility.

- Data-Informed Instruction: Using data to inform instructional decisions helps educators tailor interventions and support to meet individual student needs.

5. Technology-Enhanced Learning: Navigating the Digital Frontier

Success Story: Adaptive Learning Platforms and Virtual Reality in Education

The success stories of adaptive learning platforms and virtual reality in education underscore the transformative role of technology. The lesson learned is that judicious integration of technology can enhance engagement, accessibility, and personalized learning experiences for students.

Key Lessons:

- Balancing Technology and Pedagogy: Technology should complement effective pedagogical practices, enhancing, not replacing, the role of educators.
- Accessibility: Technology can bridge gaps in access to education, providing resources and learning opportunities to students globally.
- Innovation and Iteration: Embracing a culture of innovation and continuous improvement ensures that technology in education remains dynamic and effective.

6. Social and Emotional Learning (SEL): Nurturing Holistic Development

Success Story: CASEL's Collaborative for Academic, Social, and Emotional Learning

The success of CASEL's approach to social and emotional learning emphasizes the importance of nurturing holistic development in students. The lesson learned is that prioritizing emotional intelligence, resilience, and interpersonal skills contributes to a positive school climate and prepares students for success beyond academics.

Key Lessons:

- Teacher Training: Educators play a crucial role in fostering social and emotional learning, necessitating ongoing training and professional development.

- Integration into Curriculum: SEL is most effective when seamlessly integrated into the curriculum, creating a cohesive approach to academic and social-emotional development.

- Community Involvement: Involving parents and communities in social and emotional learning initiatives creates a holistic support system for students.

Conclusion: Guiding Principles for Educational Transformation

The lessons learned from these success stories serve as guiding principles for educational transformation. By embracing inclusivity, democratizing access to knowledge, incorporating innovative pedagogies, and prioritizing holistic development, educators and policymakers can create a foundation for an educational landscape that prepares students for the challenges and opportunities of the future. As we navigate global assessments, standardized testing, quality indicators, and educational rankings, these lessons provide a roadmap for fostering excellence, equity, and innovation in education.

Scalability and Replicability of Educational Innovations: Unlocking Global Potential

Success stories in education not only inspire but also hold the potential to drive systemic change. This chapter explores the scalability and replicability of various educational innovations, examining how successful models and initiatives can be expanded and adapted to diverse contexts, ultimately unlocking global potential.

Introduction: The Challenge of Scaling Educational Innovations

Scaling educational innovations presents a unique set of challenges and opportunities. While success stories offer valuable insights, ensuring that innovative practices reach a broader audience requires careful consideration of cultural, contextual, and logistical factors. This section introduces the overarching theme of the chapter—scaling and replicating educational innovations—and underscores its significance in fostering widespread positive impact.

1. Inclusive Education: Scaling Access and Equity

Success Story: The Inclusive Education Model in Finland

Finland's inclusive education model has garnered international acclaim for its success in promoting equity and access. The scalability and replicability of this model depend on recognizing the core principles that make it effective and adapting them to diverse educational contexts.

Key Considerations:

- Teacher Training Programs: Developing comprehensive teacher training programs that emphasize inclusive practices is crucial for scaling the model.

- Policy Alignment: Aligning national education policies with the principles of inclusivity is essential to create a supportive framework for scaling.

- Community Engagement: Involving local communities in the process ensures that inclusive education reflects and respects diverse cultural contexts.

2. Democratizing Access to Knowledge: The Global Reach of Open Educational Resources (OER)

Success Story: MIT OpenCourseWare (OCW) and OER Commons

The success of open educational resources lies in their potential to reach learners globally. Scalability in this context involves expanding the availability of high-quality educational materials beyond their original context while considering linguistic, cultural, and pedagogical adaptations.

Key Considerations:

- Multilingual Platforms: Developing multilingual platforms ensures that OER can be accessed and utilized by learners from diverse linguistic backgrounds.

- Localization Strategies: Adapting content to local contexts and educational frameworks enhances the relevance and effectiveness of OER initiatives.

- Global Collaboration Networks: Establishing networks for global collaboration enables educators to share best practices and collectively improve the quality of open educational resources.

3. Project-Based Learning (PBL): Scaling Impact through Interdisciplinary Integration

Success Story: High Tech High Model

Scaling project-based learning involves not only replicating successful models but also adapting them to various subjects and disciplines. The High Tech High model offers insights into how interdisciplinary integration can enhance the scalability of PBL.

Key Considerations:

- Cross-Disciplinary Training: Providing educators with cross-disciplinary training ensures they can effectively implement PBL in various subjects.

- Flexible Curriculum Design: Creating adaptable curriculum frameworks allows schools to customize PBL initiatives based on the unique needs of their students.

- Networks of Collaboration: Establishing networks of collaboration between schools and educators facilitates the sharing of PBL best practices and resources.

4. Personalized Learning: Tailoring Education at Scale

Success Story: AltSchool Model and Competency-Based Education (CBE)

Scaling personalized learning requires a balance between customization and standardization. The AltSchool model and competency-based education offer insights into how individualized learning can be extended to a broader audience.

Key Considerations:

- Technology Integration: Leveraging technology for personalized learning platforms can enhance scalability, allowing students to access tailored content.

- Teacher Professional Development: Ongoing teacher training ensures that educators can effectively implement personalized learning strategies.

- Adaptable Assessment Methods: Developing adaptable assessment methods allows for a nuanced understanding of individual student progress.

5. Technology-Enhanced Learning: Adapting to Diverse Contexts

Success Story: Adaptive Learning Platforms and Virtual Reality in Education

The scalability of technology-enhanced learning depends on the adaptability of digital tools to diverse contexts. While certain platforms may have achieved success in specific regions, replicating this success globally requires strategic planning.

Key Considerations:

- Infrastructure Readiness: Ensuring that educational institutions have the necessary infrastructure for technology integration is critical for scalability.

- Cultural Sensitivity: Adapting digital content to align with cultural sensitivities and preferences is essential for global applicability.

- Professional Development for Educators: Training educators to effectively utilize technology in teaching is crucial for successful implementation at scale.

6. Social and Emotional Learning (SEL): Scaling Empathy and Resilience

Success Story: CASEL's Collaborative for Academic, Social, and Emotional Learning

Scaling social and emotional learning initiatives involves embedding these principles into the broader educational landscape. The CASEL framework provides insights into how SEL can be integrated at scale.

Key Considerations:

- Integration into National Curricula: Embedding SEL principles into national curricula ensures widespread adoption and scalability.

- Teacher Training Programs: Equipping educators with the skills to incorporate SEL into their teaching practices is fundamental for successful scaling.

- Parent and Community Involvement: Engaging parents and communities in SEL initiatives creates a supportive environment that extends beyond the classroom.

Conclusion: A Blueprint for Global Educational Transformation

The scalability and replicability of educational innovations are critical considerations as we strive for global educational transformation. By distilling key lessons from success stories and applying thoughtful strategies for scaling, educators, policymakers, and stakeholders can contribute to the creation of a more inclusive, equitable, and innovative educational landscape worldwide. As we navigate global assessments, standardized testing, quality indicators, and educational rankings, the ability to scale successful innovations becomes a powerful tool for addressing the challenges and opportunities of 21st-century education.

Chapter 9: Global Assessments in High School Education

Overview of International Assessments: Benchmarking Educational Excellence

International assessments play a crucial role in benchmarking educational excellence on a global scale. This chapter provides a comprehensive overview of various international assessments, exploring their purposes, methodologies, and implications for high school education worldwide. Examining the landscape of global assessments sets the stage for understanding how educational systems compare and compete in the pursuit of excellence.

Introduction: The Significance of Global Assessments

Global assessments have become integral tools for evaluating the effectiveness of high school education systems. These assessments provide valuable insights into the strengths and weaknesses of educational practices, allowing policymakers, educators, and stakeholders to make informed decisions. This section introduces the importance of global assessments in shaping educational policies and practices on an international scale.

Defining International Assessments

International assessments are standardized evaluations conducted across multiple countries, aiming to measure the performance of students, educational systems, and the effectiveness of various teaching methodologies. These assessments are designed to provide a comparative analysis of educational outcomes, offering a nuanced understanding of how different nations approach and achieve educational goals.

Purposes of International Assessments

Comparative Analysis of Educational Systems:

One primary purpose of international assessments is to facilitate a comparative analysis of educational systems. By evaluating the academic performance of students across different countries, these assessments highlight disparities and similarities in teaching methods, curriculum structures, and overall educational approaches.

Informing Educational Policy and Reform:

International assessments serve as crucial tools for informing educational policy and driving reform initiatives. The data and insights generated from these assessments empower policymakers to identify areas of improvement, implement targeted interventions, and align educational practices with global standards.

Promoting Best Practices and Innovation:

Successful educational systems highlighted in international assessments often serve as sources of inspiration for innovation and best practices. By showcasing effective teaching methodologies and policies, these assessments contribute to a global dialogue on educational excellence and improvement.

Types of International Assessments

Programme for International Student Assessment (PISA):

PISA is a widely recognized international assessment administered by the Organisation for Economic Co-operation and Development (OECD). It evaluates 15-year-old students' performance in reading, mathematics, and science, providing insights into their preparedness for real-life challenges.

Trends in International Mathematics and Science Study (TIMSS):

TIMSS assesses the mathematics and science knowledge of students in grades four and eight. Conducted by the International Association for the Evaluation of Educational Achievement (IEA), TIMSS offers a comparative analysis of students' achievements in these key subjects.

Progress in International Reading Literacy Study (PIRLS):

PIRLS focuses on assessing the reading literacy of fourth-grade students. It provides valuable information about students' reading comprehension skills and the factors influencing their reading abilities.

International Baccalaureate (IB) Examinations:

The IB program offers a globally recognized diploma that includes assessments in six subject areas, including languages, sciences, and humanities. The IB examinations assess students' understanding and application of knowledge across a broad spectrum of disciplines.

Methodologies of International Assessments

Standardized Testing:

Many international assessments rely on standardized testing methodologies to ensure consistency and comparability across diverse educational systems. Standardized tests present a set of uniform questions to all participants, allowing for an objective evaluation of their knowledge and skills.

Performance-Based Assessments:

Some international assessments incorporate performance-based assessments, which require students to demonstrate their abilities in practical applications, critical thinking, and problem-solving. These assessments aim to evaluate not only knowledge but also the application of that knowledge in real-world scenarios.

Surveys and Questionnaires:

In addition to traditional testing, international assessments often include surveys and questionnaires to gather qualitative data. These instruments may explore students' attitudes toward learning, their perceptions of their educational experiences, and the influence of socio-cultural factors on their academic performance.

Challenges and Criticisms of International Assessments

Cultural Bias and Contextual Differences:

One of the primary criticisms of international assessments is the potential for cultural bias. Standardized tests may not adequately account for cultural nuances and differences in educational contexts, potentially disadvantaging students from certain cultural backgrounds.

Limited Scope of Assessment:

Critics argue that standardized tests may have a limited scope, focusing primarily on cognitive skills and neglecting other essential aspects of education, such as creativity, social-emotional development, and practical skills relevant to real-world challenges.

Pressure and Stress on Students:

The high stakes associated with international assessments, especially when used for ranking and comparison, can create undue pressure and stress on students. This pressure may impact their mental well-being and skew the results of the assessments.

Implications for High School Education

Informed Educational Policies:

International assessments provide policymakers with valuable data to inform the development and adjustment of educational policies. By understanding the strengths and weaknesses of their educational systems in comparison to others, policymakers can implement targeted reforms to enhance overall effectiveness.

Identification of Best Practices:

High-performing countries in international assessments often serve as sources of inspiration for best practices. The identification of successful strategies and methodologies can inform educational leaders and practitioners seeking to improve their own systems.

Global Collaboration and Benchmarking:

International assessments create opportunities for global collaboration and benchmarking. Educators and policymakers can engage in cross-cultural dialogue, sharing insights and strategies to address common challenges and improve overall educational quality.

Conclusion: Shaping the Future of High School Education

The landscape of international assessments shapes the future of high school education by providing a comprehensive understanding of global educational trends, challenges, and successes. As we delve into the subsequent chapters exploring standardized testing, alternative assessment methods, quality indicators, and educational rankings, the insights gained from international assessments serve as a foundation for informed discussions on advancing high school education worldwide.

Role of PISA and TIMSS: Unveiling Educational Landscapes

International assessments, particularly the Programme for International Student Assessment (PISA) and the Trends in International Mathematics and Science Study (TIMSS), play pivotal roles in shaping our understanding of educational landscapes. This section delves into the unique contributions, methodologies, and impacts of PISA and TIMSS, unraveling their roles in benchmarking educational achievements and influencing policy decisions globally.

Introduction: PISA and TIMSS as Pillars of Global Education Evaluation

PISA and TIMSS stand as pillars of global education evaluation, providing invaluable insights into the performance of students and educational systems. These assessments serve as benchmarks, offering a comparative analysis of achievements in key subjects and contributing to the ongoing discourse on educational excellence and improvement.

Programme for International Student Assessment (PISA): Shaping Educational Policies Globally

Purpose and Objectives:

PISA, developed by the Organisation for Economic Co-operation and Development (OECD), aims to assess the extent to which 15-year-old students, nearing the end of their compulsory education, can apply their knowledge and skills to real-life situations. The primary focus is on reading, mathematics, and science literacy, with an additional emphasis on evaluating students' abilities to think critically and solve problems.

Methodology:

PISA employs a unique approach that distinguishes it from traditional assessments. Instead of focusing solely on assessing students' mastery of curriculum content, PISA evaluates their ability to apply knowledge in novel and practical contexts. This methodological shift emphasizes the importance of equipping students with skills relevant to the challenges they will encounter in adulthood.

Three-Year Assessment Cycle:

PISA operates on a three-year assessment cycle, enabling the continuous monitoring of educational trends globally. Each cycle assesses different domains of knowledge and skills, ensuring a comprehensive and evolving understanding of educational effectiveness. The cyclical nature of PISA allows for the adaptation of assessments to the changing needs of the education landscape.

Global Participation:

One of the defining features of PISA is its global reach. Over 80 countries and economies participate in the assessment, providing a diverse and representative sample of educational systems worldwide. The wide participation ensures that the insights derived from PISA reflect the global context and contribute to a nuanced understanding of educational achievements.

Impacts of PISA on Education Policy and Practice

Informed Policymaking:

PISA results have a significant impact on education policymaking globally. Policymakers use the insights gained from PISA to identify areas of improvement, implement reforms, and align their educational systems with best practices observed in high-performing countries. The data generated by PISA acts as a guide for evidence-based decision-making.

Identification of Educational Disparities:

PISA highlights educational disparities, shedding light on factors contributing to variations in student performance. This identification of disparities allows policymakers to address issues related to equity, access, and the quality of education. It serves as a catalyst for interventions aimed at reducing gaps in educational outcomes.

Promotion of Innovation and Best Practices:

High-performing countries in PISA become sources of inspiration for innovation and best practices. Policymakers and educators look to these countries to understand the strategies and methodologies that contribute to success. PISA fosters a culture of learning from global exemplars, promoting the adoption of effective educational approaches.

Public Awareness and Accountability:

PISA results often garner public attention, leading to increased awareness and scrutiny of educational systems. The transparency provided by PISA encourages accountability at both the national and international levels. The public dissemination of results fosters dialogue and engagement, driving a collective commitment to improving educational outcomes.

Trends in International Mathematics and Science Study (TIMSS): Gauging Proficiency in STEM Education

Purpose and Objectives:

TIMSS, conducted by the International Association for the Evaluation of Educational Achievement (IEA), focuses specifically on assessing students' proficiency in mathematics and science. The study aims to provide a comparative analysis of students' achievements in these critical STEM subjects, offering insights into the effectiveness of educational systems in preparing students for careers in science, technology, engineering, and mathematics.

Assessment Framework:

TIMSS employs a detailed assessment framework that outlines the content areas and cognitive domains covered in the tests. The framework ensures a comprehensive evaluation of students' knowledge and skills in mathematics and science. The cyclical nature of TIMSS allows for the monitoring of trends and changes in educational outcomes over time.

Grade Levels and Participation:

TIMSS assesses students at various grade levels, providing a longitudinal perspective on their educational development. The assessment includes both fourth and eighth-grade levels, allowing for the examination of foundational knowledge as well as more advanced competencies. Similar to PISA, TIMSS involves a broad spectrum of countries, ensuring a diverse and representative sample.

Contextual Questionnaires:

In addition to subject-specific assessments, TIMSS includes contextual questionnaires that gather information about students' educational experiences, instructional practices, and school environments. These questionnaires provide a richer context for interpreting the results, offering insights into the factors influencing educational outcomes.

Impacts of TIMSS on STEM Education and Policy

Global Benchmarking in STEM:

TIMSS serves as a global benchmark for proficiency in STEM education. The results provide a comparative analysis of how well educational systems prepare students in mathematics and science, offering countries the opportunity to gauge their strengths and areas needing improvement in these critical subjects.

Influencing Curriculum and Instructional Practices:

The insights derived from TIMSS influence curriculum development and instructional practices in participating countries. Policymakers and educators use the data to identify effective teaching methods, adjust curricula to align with global standards, and implement evidence-based strategies to enhance students' STEM proficiency.

Informing STEM Education Policies:

TIMSS results play a vital role in shaping STEM education policies globally. Policymakers utilize the data to make informed decisions about resource allocation, teacher training programs, and initiatives aimed at fostering STEM interest and proficiency. The study's cyclical nature allows for ongoing adjustments to policies based on emerging trends.

Addressing Gender Disparities in STEM:

TIMSS provides a lens through which gender disparities in STEM education can be examined. By disaggregating results based on gender, the study contributes to a deeper understanding of how educational systems can address inequities and create more inclusive environments for students pursuing STEM subjects.

Comparative Analysis of PISA and TIMSS:

Subject Focus:

While both PISA and TIMSS contribute to the global understanding of education, they differ in their subject focus. PISA assesses a broader range of skills, including reading, mathematics, and science literacy, with an emphasis on real-world application. In contrast, TIMSS specializes in assessing proficiency in mathematics and science.

Age Group:

PISA primarily targets 15-year-old students, representing a stage nearing the end of compulsory education. This age group allows for an evaluation of students' preparedness for real-life challenges. TIMSS assesses students at both fourth and eighth-grade levels, providing insights into foundational and more advanced competencies in mathematics and science.

Methodological Approach:

The methodological approaches of PISA and TIMSS differ significantly. PISA focuses on assessing students' ability to apply knowledge in practical contexts, emphasizing critical thinking and problem-solving. TIMSS, on the other hand, employs a more traditional approach, evaluating students' proficiency in specific content areas through standardized testing.

Cycle Frequency:

PISA operates on a three-year assessment cycle, allowing for continuous monitoring and adaptation to evolving educational trends. TIMSS also follows a cycle, typically conducted every four years. Both assessment cycles contribute to a comprehensive understanding of global education by capturing a range of data points over time.

Conclusion: PISA, TIMSS, and the Global Educational Tapestry

PISA and TIMSS stand as beacons in the realm of global assessments, illuminating the diverse landscapes of education across nations. As we traverse the subsequent chapters exploring standardized testing, alternative assessment methods, quality indicators, and educational rankings, the insights derived from PISA and TIMSS serve as guiding lights, influencing our understanding of educational excellence and shaping the path toward improved high school education worldwide.

Standardized Testing Practices Globally: Navigating Assessment Landscapes

Standardized testing is a ubiquitous element in global education, providing a systematic way to evaluate student performance and educational effectiveness. This section explores the practices, purposes, and impacts of standardized testing on high school education worldwide. From the design of assessments to the implications for policy and pedagogy, we unravel the intricate tapestry of standardized testing in diverse educational contexts.

Introduction: The Ubiquity of Standardized Testing

Standardized testing has become a cornerstone of educational assessment, offering a methodical and structured approach to measure student knowledge and skills. This introduction sets the stage for understanding the prevalence of standardized testing practices globally, emphasizing their role in shaping educational policies and informing decision-making at various levels of the education system.

Defining Standardized Testing

Standardized testing refers to the administration of assessments in a consistent manner, under uniform conditions, and with a set of predetermined instructions for scoring. The goal is to ensure fairness and comparability in evaluating students' academic achievements, allowing for objective assessments across diverse populations.

Purposes of Standardized Testing

Assessing Student Proficiency:

One of the primary purposes of standardized testing is to assess students' proficiency in specific subjects. These assessments are designed to measure the extent to which students have acquired the knowledge and skills expected at their grade level.

Evaluating Educational Effectiveness:

Standardized testing serves as a tool for evaluating the effectiveness of educational systems. By analyzing aggregate test results, policymakers and educators can gauge the overall performance of schools, districts, and even entire national education systems.

Informing Instructional Strategies:

Individual student test results provide valuable insights into areas of strength and weakness. Teachers can use this information to tailor their instructional strategies, addressing the specific needs of students and fostering a more personalized learning experience.

Facilitating Accountability and Transparency:

Standardized testing contributes to educational accountability by providing a measurable metric for student and school performance. The results are often used to inform accountability systems, allowing stakeholders to assess the effectiveness of educational institutions.

Design and Administration of Standardized Tests

Test Construction and Validation:

The process of creating standardized tests involves careful construction and validation to ensure reliability and validity. Experts in educational measurement design test items that align with curriculum standards and undergo rigorous validation processes to ensure fairness and accuracy.

Uniform Testing Conditions:

To maintain consistency and fairness, standardized tests are administered under uniform conditions. This includes using standardized testing environments, clear instructions, and standardized time limits for all test-takers.

Scoring and Analysis:

Standardized tests typically employ a scoring system that allows for the comparison of results across a broad population. The use of statistical analysis ensures that scores accurately reflect students' relative proficiency in the assessed subject.

Reporting and Feedback:

Test results are communicated to various stakeholders, including students, parents, educators, and policymakers. Clear and comprehensive reporting helps interpret the results and provides feedback for improvement at the individual and systemic levels.

Types of Standardized Tests

Summative Assessments:

Summative assessments are conducted at the end of an instructional period to evaluate overall learning outcomes. High-stakes exams, such as high school exit exams or college entrance exams, often fall into this category.

Formative Assessments:

Formative assessments occur during the learning process to provide ongoing feedback. While not always traditional standardized tests, formative assessments contribute to the overall understanding of student progress.

Adaptive Testing:

Adaptive testing adjusts the difficulty of test items based on a student's performance. This personalized approach aims to more accurately measure a student's proficiency by tailoring the test to their abilities.

Global Variations in Standardized Testing Practices

High School Exit Exams:

Many countries employ high school exit exams, which students must pass to receive a diploma. These exams serve as a gatekeeper, ensuring that students have attained a minimum level of proficiency before completing their high school education.

College Entrance Exams:

College entrance exams, such as the SAT (Scholastic Assessment Test) and ACT (American College Testing), are widely used in the United States and some other countries. These exams assess students' readiness for college and are often considered during the college admissions process.

National Assessments:

Some countries conduct national assessments to evaluate the overall effectiveness of their education systems. These assessments may cover a range of subjects and serve as a benchmark for educational policies and reforms.

Challenges and Criticisms of Standardized Testing

Cultural Bias and Fairness:

Critics argue that standardized tests may exhibit cultural bias, favoring certain groups over others. The use of language, context, and cultural references in test items may disadvantage students from diverse backgrounds.

Narrowing of Curriculum:

The focus on test preparation and the alignment of curriculum with test content can lead to a narrowing of the educational experience. Teachers may feel pressured to prioritize test-related topics at the expense of a more holistic and diverse curriculum.

Stress and Well-being:

High-stakes nature and societal importance attached to standardized tests can create significant stress for students. The pressure to perform well can impact students' mental and emotional well-being, potentially affecting their overall learning experience.

Impacts of Standardized Testing on Educational Policy and Practice

Accountability Measures:

Standardized testing often forms the basis for accountability measures in education. Schools and educators may be held accountable for their students' performance on these tests, influencing decisions related to funding, interventions, and school improvement efforts.

Policy Reforms:

Test results can prompt educational policymakers to implement reforms aimed at addressing identified weaknesses. These reforms may include changes to curriculum, teacher training programs, or interventions targeting specific student populations.

Teacher and School Evaluations:

Standardized test results are frequently used to evaluate teacher and school performance. This evaluation can influence professional development opportunities, compensation structures, and even employment decisions.

Resource Allocation:

Governments and educational authorities may allocate resources based on standardized test results. Schools with higher performance may receive additional resources, while those with lower performance may face interventions or resource limitations.

Innovations and Evolving Trends in Standardized Testing

Technology-Enhanced Testing:

Advancements in technology have led to the development of technology-enhanced testing formats. These may include interactive items, simulations, and adaptive testing platforms that offer a more dynamic and engaging assessment experience.

Competency-Based Assessment:

Competency-based assessment focuses on evaluating students' mastery of specific skills or competencies rather than their performance on a standardized test. This approach aligns with a shift towards personalized and competency-driven education.

Portfolio Assessments:

Some educational systems incorporate portfolio assessments, where students compile a collection of their work to demonstrate their learning and achievements. This more holistic approach provides a comprehensive view of a student's abilities.

Conclusion: Navigating the Complex Landscape of Standardized Testing

Standardized testing practices, despite their widespread use, remain a subject of debate and scrutiny. As we progress through the subsequent chapters exploring quality indicators, educational rankings, and alternative assessment methods, the insights gained from standardized testing practices globally serve as a foundation for understanding the multifaceted nature of educational assessments and their impact on high school education worldwide.

Alternative Assessment Methods: Beyond Standardized Testing

In the evolving landscape of high school education, the limitations and criticisms associated with traditional standardized testing have prompted educators and policymakers to explore alternative assessment methods. This section delves into innovative approaches that aim to provide a more comprehensive and nuanced understanding of student learning, moving beyond the constraints of conventional testing.

Introduction: Rethinking Assessment in High School Education

The introduction sets the stage for a paradigm shift in assessment practices, acknowledging the shortcomings of traditional standardized testing and the need for alternative methods. It emphasizes the importance of embracing diverse assessment approaches that align with the complexities and individualities of high school education.

Understanding Alternative Assessment Methods

Defining Alternative Assessment:

Alternative assessment refers to a diverse set of methods and approaches that deviate from the traditional model of standardized testing. These methods aim to capture a more authentic and holistic understanding of student learning, taking into account individual strengths, skills, and real-world applications.

The Spectrum of Alternative Assessment:

Alternative assessment methods span a broad spectrum, encompassing various strategies that focus on different aspects of student performance. From project-based assessments and portfolios to performance tasks and collaborative projects, these methods offer a richer and more varied picture of students' capabilities.

Types of Alternative Assessment Methods

Project-Based Assessments:

Project-based assessments involve the completion of extended projects that require students to apply their knowledge and skills in real-world scenarios. These projects often involve research, problem-solving, and the creation of tangible artifacts, fostering critical thinking and creativity.

Portfolios:

Portfolios are collections of students' work over time, showcasing their progress, achievements, and reflections. This method allows for a longitudinal view of student development and provides evidence of their ability to apply knowledge in diverse contexts.

Performance Tasks:

Performance tasks require students to demonstrate specific skills or competencies through hands-on activities or simulations. These tasks may include experiments, presentations, or other practical demonstrations that go beyond traditional written exams.

Authentic Assessments:

Authentic assessments mirror real-world situations, assessing students' abilities in contexts that closely resemble the challenges they may encounter outside the classroom. This approach emphasizes the application of knowledge to practical, authentic scenarios.

Collaborative Projects:

Collaborative projects involve group work, encouraging students to collaborate, communicate, and contribute to a collective goal. This approach not only assesses individual contributions but also evaluates teamwork and interpersonal skills.

Self-Assessment and Reflection:

Self-assessment and reflection empower students to evaluate their own learning, set goals, and reflect on their progress. This metacognitive approach enhances students' awareness of their strengths and areas for improvement.

Benefits of Alternative Assessment Methods

Diverse Skill Evaluation:

Alternative assessment methods allow for the evaluation of a broader range of skills and competencies beyond what traditional tests measure. This includes critical thinking, problem-solving, creativity, communication, and collaboration—skills essential for success in the 21st century.

Individualized Learning Paths:

By considering students' strengths, interests, and learning styles, alternative assessments support individualized learning paths. This personalized approach recognizes the unique qualities of each learner and fosters a more student-centered educational experience.

Real-World Relevance:

Alternative assessments often mirror real-world scenarios, emphasizing the practical application of knowledge. This connection to real-world relevance enhances the transferability of skills and knowledge gained in the classroom to future endeavors.

Holistic Understanding of Student Growth:

The longitudinal nature of alternative assessments, such as portfolios, provides a more holistic understanding of student growth over time. Educators can track progress, identify patterns, and tailor instruction to meet individual needs.

Challenges and Considerations in Implementing Alternative Assessment

Assessment Bias:

While alternative assessments aim to minimize biases associated with traditional testing, they may introduce new forms of bias. Educators must be mindful of potential biases related to cultural background, socioeconomic status, or individual learning styles.

Scalability and Consistency:

Implementing alternative assessments on a large scale can pose challenges related to scalability and consistency. Ensuring that assessments maintain reliability and comparability across diverse contexts requires careful planning and standardization.

Resource and Time Constraints:

Alternative assessments often demand more resources and time compared to traditional testing methods. Educators may face challenges in terms of workload, infrastructure, and access to materials, particularly in resource-constrained settings.

Assessment Literacy:

Effective implementation of alternative assessments requires a level of assessment literacy among educators. Providing professional development and support to ensure educators are well-equipped to design, administer, and evaluate alternative assessments is crucial.

Innovative Approaches to Alternative Assessment

Digital Portfolios and E-Portfolios:

Digital portfolios, or e-portfolios, leverage technology to create multimedia-rich collections of students' work. This approach not only provides a convenient platform for storing and presenting artifacts but also allows for interactive and dynamic representations of learning.

Gamified Assessments:

Gamified assessments incorporate elements of game design into the assessment process. By creating engaging and interactive scenarios, gamified assessments can capture students' attention and motivation, offering a novel approach to evaluating skills and knowledge.

Open-Ended Tasks and Inquiry-Based Assessment:

Open-ended tasks and inquiry-based assessment encourage students to explore topics independently, fostering curiosity and self-directed learning. These approaches focus on the process of inquiry and discovery rather than just the final product.

Adaptive Learning Platforms:

Adaptive learning platforms use technology to tailor assessments to individual learning needs. These platforms adjust the difficulty and content of assessments based on students' performance, providing personalized and targeted feedback.

Implementing Alternative Assessments: Considerations and Best Practices

Clear Learning Objectives:

Clearly defined learning objectives are essential for designing effective alternative assessments. Aligning assessments with specific educational goals ensures that they measure the desired skills and competencies.

Student Involvement and Engagement:

Involving students in the assessment process and explaining the purpose of alternative assessments fosters a sense of ownership and engagement. When students understand the relevance and benefits, they are more likely to approach assessments with a positive mindset.

Training for Educators:

Providing professional development opportunities for educators is crucial for successful implementation. Training should cover the design, administration, and evaluation of alternative assessments, addressing any challenges or concerns.

Continuous Feedback and Reflection:

Establishing a system of continuous feedback and reflection enhances the effectiveness of alternative assessments. Regular reflection on assessment practices allows educators to refine their approaches and adapt to evolving student needs.

Conclusion: Advancing Assessment Practices in High School Education

As we journey through the subsequent chapters exploring quality indicators, educational rankings, and emerging trends in high school education, the insights gained from alternative assessment methods serve as a testament to the dynamic and multifaceted nature of evaluating student learning. By embracing a diverse range of assessment approaches, educators and policymakers can pave the way for a more inclusive, personalized, and effective high school education system.

Chapter 10: Standardized Testing: Pros and Cons
Advantages of Standardized Testing: Illuminating Educational Landscapes

Standardized testing, despite its controversies, has been a longstanding feature of educational systems worldwide. This section explores the advantages of standardized testing, shedding light on its potential benefits for students, educators, and policymakers. By examining the positive aspects, we aim to provide a nuanced understanding of the role standardized testing plays in shaping high school education.

Introduction: The Role and Rationale of Standardized Testing

Before delving into the advantages of standardized testing, the introduction sets the stage by establishing the role and rationale behind the use of standardized tests in education. Acknowledging the criticisms, it emphasizes the importance of recognizing the potential benefits that contribute to the broader educational landscape.

Standardized Testing as an Objective Measurement Tool

Fair and Consistent Evaluation:

One of the primary advantages of standardized testing is its ability to provide a fair and consistent evaluation of student performance. The use of a standardized format ensures that all students are assessed under the same conditions, minimizing potential biases and creating a level playing field.

Comparability Across Populations:

Standardized tests facilitate comparability across diverse populations, allowing educators, policymakers, and researchers to analyze and compare performance across different demographic groups. This comparative data can inform targeted interventions and resource allocation to address educational disparities.

Efficient Assessment Process:

Standardized testing provides an efficient method of assessing large numbers of students within a relatively short timeframe. This scalability is especially valuable for systems that need to evaluate the performance of a significant student population, such as nationwide assessments.

Informing Educational Policy and Reform

Data-Driven Decision Making:

Standardized test results offer a wealth of data that can inform data-driven decision-making at various levels of the education system. Policymakers and educators can use this information to identify strengths, weaknesses, and areas in need of improvement, guiding the development of evidence-based interventions.

Accountability Measures:

Standardized testing contributes to accountability measures in education. Schools and educators can be held accountable for student performance, providing a mechanism for ensuring transparency and incentivizing improvement efforts.

Policy Reforms and Targeted Interventions:

Analysis of standardized test data often prompts policy reforms and targeted interventions. By identifying areas of underperformance, policymakers can implement reforms that address specific challenges and improve overall educational outcomes.

College Admissions and Opportunities

Objective College Admissions Criteria:

Standardized tests, such as the SAT and ACT, serve as standardized criteria for college admissions. These tests provide colleges with a consistent measure to evaluate students from different high schools, regions, and backgrounds, helping ensure a fair and objective admissions process.

Access to Higher Education Opportunities:

Standardized testing can facilitate access to higher education opportunities, particularly for students from underrepresented or disadvantaged backgrounds. By providing a standardized metric, these tests can help identify talented students who may not have had access to other resources or opportunities.

Scholarship Eligibility:

Many scholarship programs use standardized test scores as eligibility criteria. This practice ensures that scholarship decisions are based on a standardized measure of academic achievement, promoting fairness in the distribution of educational resources.

Efficient Resource Allocation and Systemic Improvement

Identifying Areas for Improvement:

Standardized testing results allow educational stakeholders to identify specific areas for improvement within schools, districts, or entire education systems. This targeted approach helps allocate resources efficiently, focusing interventions where they are most needed.

Evaluating Educational Effectiveness:

The comparative nature of standardized testing allows for the evaluation of the effectiveness of different educational interventions, programs, or teaching methods. Educators and policymakers can use this information to make informed decisions about the allocation of resources and the adoption of best practices.

Global Competitiveness:

In an increasingly globalized world, standardized testing can provide insights into a country's educational competitiveness on the international stage. Comparative data allows nations to assess their standing in global education rankings and identify areas where improvement is needed to remain competitive.

Facilitating Research and Educational Studies

Data for Research and Analysis:

Standardized testing generates large datasets that can be used for educational research and analysis. Researchers can explore trends, correlations, and factors influencing student performance, contributing valuable insights to the broader academic community.

Longitudinal Studies:

The standardized nature of tests allows for the collection of longitudinal data, enabling researchers to track student progress over time. Longitudinal studies can provide insights into the impact of educational policies, interventions, and societal changes on academic outcomes.

Predictive Validity:

Standardized tests, particularly those used in college admissions, have demonstrated predictive validity in forecasting students' success in higher education. This predictive power helps colleges make informed decisions about admissions and supports students in making appropriate academic choices.

Conclusion: Recognizing the Potential Advantages of Standardized Testing

As we navigate the complexities of standardized testing in the subsequent chapters, exploring its limitations, criticisms, and evolving trends, it is crucial to recognize the potential advantages that contribute to the multifaceted landscape of high school education. While acknowledging the need for a balanced and nuanced approach, understanding these advantages can inform ongoing discussions about the role of standardized testing in shaping educational outcomes globally.

Limitations and Criticisms: Navigating the Complexities of Assessment

While standardized testing has its advantages, it is not without its share of criticisms and limitations. This section delves into the multifaceted challenges associated with standardized testing, exploring the nuances that shape the ongoing debate around its efficacy and impact on high school education.

Introduction: The Dual Nature of Standardized Testing

The introduction sets the stage by acknowledging the dual nature of standardized testing—its role as a tool for assessment and accountability, as well as its susceptibility to criticisms and limitations. This section aims to provide a comprehensive understanding of the complexities surrounding standardized testing.

Standardized Testing and Educational Inequity

Disparities in Access and Preparation:

One of the central criticisms of standardized testing revolves around disparities in access and preparation. Students from affluent backgrounds often have greater access to test preparation resources, coaching, and tutoring, creating an uneven playing field that may not accurately reflect their inherent abilities.

Cultural and Linguistic Bias:

Standardized tests may exhibit cultural and linguistic biases that disadvantage certain groups of students. The content, language, and cultural references within the tests may be more familiar to students from specific backgrounds, potentially leading to inequitable outcomes.

Limited Representation of Skills:

Critics argue that standardized tests offer a limited representation of students' skills and capabilities. The emphasis on specific types of reasoning and knowledge may neglect other valuable skills, such as creativity, critical thinking, and problem-solving, which are essential for success in the real world.

Narrowing Curriculum and Teaching to the Test

Teaching to the Test:

The pressure to perform well on standardized tests can lead to a phenomenon known as "teaching to the test." Educators may focus narrowly on the content and format of the test, potentially neglecting broader educational goals and a more comprehensive understanding of subjects.

Narrow Curriculum Emphasis:

The need to align curriculum with test content may result in a narrowing of educational emphasis. Subjects and skills not directly assessed by the standardized tests may receive less attention, limiting the overall educational experience for students.

Impact on Creativity and Critical Thinking:

Critics argue that the rigid structure of standardized tests may stifle creativity and critical thinking. The emphasis on selecting the "correct" answer from predetermined choices may not adequately assess students' abilities to think critically, solve problems, or generate innovative ideas.

Standardized Testing and Student Stress

High-Stakes Testing Anxiety:

The high-stakes nature of standardized tests, particularly those with significant implications for students' academic futures, can contribute to testing anxiety. This anxiety may affect performance and well-being, potentially providing an inaccurate reflection of students' true abilities.

Pressure on Teachers and Schools:

Educators and schools may also experience stress and pressure associated with high-stakes testing. The accountability measures tied to test results can influence teaching methods, school policies, and even teacher morale, with potential consequences for the overall educational environment.

Test-Induced Stress and Mental Health:

Critics highlight the potential negative impact of standardized testing on students' mental health. The stress associated with test preparation, performance expectations, and the perceived importance of test outcomes can contribute to mental health challenges among students.

Validity and Reliability Concerns

Limited Content Validity:

Critics raise concerns about the limited content validity of standardized tests, particularly in assessing complex and multifaceted skills. The test items may not adequately represent the full spectrum of knowledge and abilities within a given subject, leading to questions about the validity of the results.

Reliability Challenges:

While standardized tests aim for reliability, external factors such as test-taking conditions, personal circumstances, and socio-economic background can introduce variability. The reliability of the tests may be compromised if external factors significantly influence students' performance.

One-Size-Fits-All Approach:

Critics argue that the one-size-fits-all approach of standardized testing may not account for individual differences in learning styles, preferences, or intelligences. The diversity of students is not fully captured by a uniform testing model, potentially misrepresenting their true abilities.

Standardized Testing and Erosion of Instructional Time

Test Preparation Time:

The time dedicated to test preparation within the school year can detract from valuable instructional time. Critics contend that the focus on preparing students for standardized tests may come at the expense of a more holistic and enriching educational experience.

Shift in Educational Priorities:

The emphasis on standardized testing can lead to a shift in educational priorities. Schools may prioritize improving test scores over fostering a love for learning, critical thinking, and the development of well-rounded individuals.

Diminished Classroom Autonomy:

Educators may experience diminished autonomy in the classroom as the pressure to align instruction with standardized test content increases. This shift may limit the ability of teachers to adapt their teaching methods to the unique needs and interests of their students.

Conclusion: Navigating the Complex Terrain of Standardized Testing

As we navigate the nuanced landscape of standardized testing, acknowledging both its advantages and limitations is crucial for fostering informed discussions about its role in high school education. The subsequent chapters will further explore evolving trends, alternative assessment methods, and the potential for balancing standardized testing within a more comprehensive educational framework. By recognizing and addressing the criticisms, policymakers and educators can work towards refining assessment practices that align with the diverse needs and aspirations of students globally.

Impact on Educational Policy: Shaping Systems and Priorities

Standardized testing plays a significant role in shaping educational policies at various levels, from individual schools to entire nations. This section explores how the results of standardized tests influence policy decisions, the challenges associated with this impact, and the broader implications for the high school education landscape.

Introduction: The Interplay of Testing and Policy

The introduction sets the stage by highlighting the interconnectedness of standardized testing and educational policy. It outlines the various ways in which test results influence policy formulation and implementation, underscoring the importance of understanding this dynamic relationship.

Influencing Accountability Measures

Establishing Benchmarks for Accountability:

One of the primary ways standardized testing impacts educational policy is by establishing benchmarks for accountability. Test results often serve as key metrics for evaluating the performance of schools, districts, and even individual teachers. Policymakers use this data to identify underperforming entities and implement interventions to drive improvement.

High-Stakes Consequences for Schools:

Standardized testing introduces a high-stakes dimension to educational accountability. Schools may face consequences, such as funding reductions or even closure, based on their performance in these tests. This accountability-driven approach aims to incentivize schools to focus on improving educational outcomes.

Linking Teacher Evaluations to Test Scores:

Educational policies may tie teacher evaluations to student test scores. This linkage is intended to hold educators accountable for their impact on student learning. However, it raises concerns about the fairness and validity of using test scores as a sole measure of teacher effectiveness.

Informing Curriculum Development and Resource Allocation

Curriculum Alignment with Test Content:

Standardized testing often influences the alignment of school curricula with the content and format of the tests. Policymakers may encourage or mandate that schools align their instructional material with the topics covered in standardized tests. This alignment is seen as a way to ensure that students are adequately prepared for the assessments.

Resource Allocation Based on Test Results:

Educational policies may allocate resources based on standardized test results. Schools with lower scores may receive additional funding, targeted interventions, or specialized support to address identified weaknesses. This resource allocation aims to address educational disparities and improve overall student outcomes.

Impact on Instructional Time and Priorities:

The emphasis on standardized testing can influence how instructional time is allocated within schools. Teachers may feel compelled to dedicate more time to preparing students for the specific content and format of the tests, potentially narrowing the overall educational experience.

Driving Education Reforms and Interventions

Identifying Areas for Improvement:

Standardized testing serves as a diagnostic tool, helping policymakers identify specific areas for improvement within the education system. Test results can highlight disparities in performance across demographic groups, subjects, or regions, guiding the development of targeted reforms and interventions.

Policy Reforms Based on Test Data:

The data generated by standardized tests often prompts policy reforms at both the state and national levels. Policymakers may use the insights gained from test results to implement changes in curriculum, instructional methods, and assessment practices. These reforms are intended to enhance overall educational quality and outcomes.

Strategic Interventions for Underperforming Schools:

Underperforming schools, as identified by standardized testing, may become the focus of strategic interventions. These interventions could include additional funding, professional development opportunities for educators, and targeted support services for students. The goal is to uplift struggling schools and improve their overall performance.

Impact on College Admissions Policies

Standardized Testing in College Admissions:

The results of standardized tests, such as the SAT and ACT, have a significant impact on college admissions policies. Many colleges and universities use these test scores as a crucial component in their admissions decisions. This reliance on standardized testing raises questions about its fairness and relevance as a predictor of college success.

Debates on Test-Optional Policies:

In response to concerns about the equity and validity of standardized testing, some educational institutions have adopted test-optional admissions policies. These policies allow applicants to choose whether to submit their test scores. The debate surrounding the effectiveness and fairness of test-optional policies highlights the ongoing evolution of college admissions practices.

Broader Implications for College Access:

Educational policies related to standardized testing can have broader implications for college access, particularly for underrepresented and disadvantaged students. The reliance on test scores may inadvertently limit opportunities for certain groups, leading to discussions about the fairness and equity of college admissions processes.

Challenges and Concerns in Policy Impact

Balancing Accountability and Flexibility:

One of the key challenges associated with the impact of standardized testing on educational policy is striking a balance between accountability and flexibility. Policymakers must navigate the tension between holding schools accountable for outcomes and allowing flexibility for diverse teaching methods and student needs.

Equity Concerns and Disparities:

The reliance on standardized testing in educational policy raises equity concerns, as students from different socio-economic backgrounds may have unequal access to resources for test preparation. Policymakers must grapple with these disparities and seek ways to mitigate the impact of such inequities on policy outcomes.

Unintended Consequences of High-Stakes Policies:

High-stakes policies tied to standardized testing can have unintended consequences. The pressure to meet performance benchmarks may lead to practices such as teaching to the test or focusing narrowly on tested subjects, potentially undermining the broader goals of education.

Public Perception and Accountability Pressures

Public Perception of Educational Quality:

Standardized testing results often contribute to public perceptions of the quality of education within a region or country. Policymakers are aware of the role these perceptions play in shaping public opinion and may respond to test results by implementing policies aimed at improving educational outcomes.

Accountability Pressures on Policymakers:

Policymakers themselves face accountability pressures based on standardized testing outcomes. The performance of schools and districts, as reflected in test scores, can impact the political landscape. Policymakers may respond to these pressures by implementing reforms or interventions to demonstrate a commitment to improving education.

Conclusion: Navigating the Interconnected Realms of Testing and Policy

As we navigate the interconnected realms of standardized testing and educational policy, it is crucial to recognize the profound impact that test results have on shaping the priorities, practices, and outcomes of high school education. The subsequent chapters will explore alternative assessment methods, emerging trends, and the potential for more nuanced approaches to policy-making in the context of standardized testing. By understanding the complexities of this relationship, policymakers can work towards fostering an educational environment that prioritizes equity, flexibility, and holistic student development.

Evolving Trends in Standardized Testing: Navigating the Future of Assessment

Standardized testing, a cornerstone of educational evaluation, is experiencing notable transformations in response to evolving educational landscapes, technological advancements, and a growing awareness of its limitations. This section explores the changing trends in standardized testing, considering innovations, critiques, and alternative approaches that shape the future of assessment in high school education.

Introduction: Adapting to a Dynamic Educational Landscape

The introduction sets the stage by highlighting the need for standardized testing to adapt to the dynamic nature of contemporary education. It acknowledges the ongoing discussions about the limitations of traditional testing models and the quest for more inclusive, relevant, and equitable assessment methods.

Technological Advancements in Testing

Transition to Computer-Based Testing:

One significant trend in standardized testing is the transition from traditional paper-and-pencil tests to computer-based assessments. Computer-based testing offers advantages such as adaptive testing, immediate scoring, and enhanced test security. However, it also raises concerns about equitable access to technology and the potential impact on students' test-taking experiences.

Innovations in Online Proctoring:

The rise of online proctoring tools introduces new possibilities for remote testing. These technologies aim to maintain the integrity of online assessments by monitoring test-takers through webcams and other features. However, concerns about privacy, security, and the potential for technological glitches are important considerations in this evolving landscape.

Embracing Artificial Intelligence (AI):

The integration of artificial intelligence into standardized testing introduces possibilities for more adaptive and personalized assessments. AI algorithms can analyze individual performance patterns, tailor questions to students' abilities, and provide detailed insights for educators. Balancing the benefits of AI with ethical considerations and potential biases is a critical aspect of this trend.

Shift Towards Competency-Based Assessment

Competency-Based Education and Assessment:

An emerging trend in standardized testing is the shift towards competency-based assessment. This approach focuses on evaluating students based on their mastery of specific skills and knowledge rather than relying solely on traditional grade levels. Competency-based assessments aim to provide a more nuanced understanding of students' abilities and promote personalized learning experiences.

Micro-Credentials and Badging:

The trend towards competency-based assessment is accompanied by the rise of micro-credentials and digital badging. These credentials offer a granular representation of specific skills or achievements, providing a more comprehensive and flexible way to showcase a student's abilities. However, challenges related to standardization, recognition, and consistency must be addressed in implementing this trend.

Portfolio Assessment and Project-Based Learning:

To capture a more holistic view of students' capabilities, some educational institutions are exploring portfolio assessment and project-based learning as alternatives to traditional testing. These methods allow students to showcase their skills through real-world projects and demonstrations, promoting creativity, critical thinking, and practical application of knowledge.

Criticisms of High-Stakes Testing and Calls for Reform

Movement Towards Test-Optional Admissions:

In response to concerns about the fairness and equity of standardized testing, an increasing number of colleges and universities are adopting test-optional admissions policies. This trend acknowledges the limitations of relying on test scores as a sole measure of academic potential and aims to provide more inclusive pathways for college admission.

Advocacy for Holistic Admissions:

Educational institutions and advocates for education reform are calling for a shift towards holistic admissions processes. This approach considers a broader range of factors, including extracurricular activities, personal essays, and letters of recommendation, alongside standardized test scores. The goal is to create a more comprehensive evaluation that aligns with the diverse strengths and talents of students.

Exploration of Multiple Measures:

Recognizing the limitations of a singular reliance on standardized tests, there is a growing movement towards embracing multiple measures of assessment. This includes a combination of standardized testing, teacher evaluations, project-based assessments, and other indicators to provide a more comprehensive and nuanced understanding of student abilities.

Global Efforts to Address Educational Inequities

International Collaboration on Assessment Practices:

Efforts are underway to foster international collaboration on assessment practices. Organizations, such as the Organization for Economic Co-operation and Development (OECD), are working towards developing more inclusive and culturally sensitive assessment tools. This trend acknowledges the diverse educational landscapes across countries and aims to create assessments that consider a broader spectrum of student experiences.

Equity-Centric Assessment Policies:

A shift towards equity-centric assessment policies is gaining traction globally. Policymakers are increasingly focused on developing assessment tools that consider and address the unique challenges faced by disadvantaged and marginalized groups. This includes a commitment to minimizing cultural biases, providing additional support resources, and promoting fairness in assessment practices.

Access to Education in Low-Income Countries:

In low-income countries, efforts are being made to improve access to education and assessments. Innovations such as mobile-based assessments and open educational resources aim to overcome infrastructure challenges and provide educational opportunities to a broader population. This trend highlights the global commitment to ensuring that assessment practices contribute to, rather than hinder, efforts to address educational inequities.

Consideration of Socio-Emotional Skills and Well-Being

Integration of Socio-Emotional Skills:

Recognizing the importance of socio-emotional skills in student development, there is a growing emphasis on integrating assessments that evaluate traits such as resilience, teamwork, and adaptability. This trend reflects a broader understanding of education as not only about academic achievement but also about nurturing well-rounded individuals equipped for success in various aspects of life.

Focus on Student Well-Being:

As educational policies evolve, there is an increased emphasis on considering the impact of assessments on student well-being. High-stakes testing and the associated pressures can contribute to stress and anxiety among students. Policymakers are exploring ways to mitigate these negative effects and promote a positive and supportive learning environment.

Assessment of 21st-Century Skills:

The evolving landscape of standardized testing includes a shift towards assessing 21st-century skills. These skills, such as critical thinking, creativity, and digital literacy, are seen as essential for success in the modern world. The trend involves developing assessments that capture a student's ability to apply knowledge in real-world scenarios and navigate complex challenges.

Conclusion: Navigating the Future of Assessment in Education

As standardized testing undergoes transformative shifts, educators, policymakers, and stakeholders in education are navigating a landscape marked by innovation, critique, and a commitment to inclusivity. The subsequent chapters will delve into alternative assessment methods, the implications of these evolving trends for educational policy, and the potential for a more balanced and nuanced approach to assessment in high school education. By embracing these changes, the educational community can move towards a future where assessment practices align more closely with the diverse needs, aspirations, and potentials of students worldwide.

Chapter 11: Quality Indicators in Education

Key Indicators of Educational Quality: Navigating the Path to Excellence

Ensuring educational quality is a multifaceted challenge that involves assessing various dimensions of the learning environment. This section explores the key indicators that serve as benchmarks for evaluating the quality of high school education. From infrastructure to teaching methods, these indicators provide a comprehensive framework for understanding and improving educational quality.

Introduction: The Imperative of Educational Quality

The introduction establishes the significance of educational quality and its role in shaping the learning experiences of students. It highlights the complex interplay of factors that contribute to a high-quality education and introduces the key indicators that will be explored in the subsequent sections.

Physical Infrastructure and Learning Spaces

Modernized Classroom Facilities:

A key indicator of educational quality is the physical infrastructure of schools, including modernized classroom facilities. Well-designed and equipped classrooms contribute to a conducive learning environment, facilitating engagement and collaboration among students. The presence of adequate technology, comfortable seating, and appropriate lighting are essential components of modern classrooms.

State-of-the-Art Laboratories and Libraries:

Quality education is often associated with access to state-of-the-art laboratories and libraries. These facilities provide students with hands-on experiences, fostering scientific inquiry and research skills. Libraries stocked with a diverse range of resources contribute to a rich intellectual environment, supporting independent learning and research.

Sustainable and Safe School Buildings:

The sustainability and safety of school buildings are critical indicators of educational quality. Schools that prioritize environmentally friendly practices and adhere to safety standards create a secure and healthy atmosphere for both students and educators. Sustainable practices may include energy-efficient infrastructure, waste reduction initiatives, and eco-friendly landscaping.

Effective Teaching and Learning Practices

Highly Qualified and Engaging Teachers:

The presence of highly qualified and engaging teachers is a foundational indicator of educational quality. Qualified educators with expertise in their subject areas contribute significantly to students' academic success. Beyond qualifications, engaging teaching practices that stimulate critical thinking, creativity, and active participation enhance the overall quality of education.

Student-Centered Learning Approaches:

Educational quality is often associated with student-centered learning approaches. These approaches prioritize the individual needs and learning styles of students, fostering a more personalized and interactive educational experience. Methods such as project-based learning, cooperative learning, and inquiry-based instruction align with the principles of student-centered education.

Innovative Use of Technology in Instruction:

The integration of technology into instructional practices is an evolving indicator of educational quality. Schools that leverage technology effectively can enhance the learning experience, providing students with access to resources, interactive tools, and collaborative platforms. The thoughtful incorporation of educational technology aligns with the demands of the digital age.

Inclusive and Diverse Learning Environments

Promotion of Inclusivity and Diversity:

Educational quality is closely tied to the promotion of inclusivity and diversity within the learning environment. Schools that actively foster a sense of belonging for students from various backgrounds contribute to a more enriching educational experience. Inclusive practices may involve diverse curriculum representation, anti-bias education, and support for students with diverse learning needs.

Culturally Relevant Curriculum:

A culturally relevant curriculum is an important indicator of educational quality. It reflects the diversity of the student body and ensures that students encounter content that is representative of various cultures, perspectives, and historical narratives. Culturally relevant education promotes a more comprehensive understanding of the world and encourages critical thinking.

Support for Special Education and Diverse Learning Needs:

High-quality education is inclusive and addresses the diverse learning needs of all students, including those with special education requirements. Schools that provide adequate support services, personalized learning plans, and inclusive classroom practices contribute to an educational environment that values the unique strengths and challenges of every learner.

Assessment and Feedback Mechanisms

Effective Assessment Practices:

The effectiveness of assessment practices is a key indicator of educational quality. Assessments that align with learning objectives, provide timely and constructive feedback, and promote a growth mindset contribute to a culture of continuous improvement. Balanced assessment methods that include formative, summative, and authentic assessments offer a comprehensive view of student progress.

Individualized Feedback and Progress Tracking:

Educational quality is enhanced by individualized feedback and progress tracking mechanisms. Teachers who provide personalized feedback to students, highlighting strengths and areas for improvement, support a growth-oriented mindset. Progress tracking systems, whether through digital platforms or other means, enable educators, students, and parents to monitor academic development.

Use of Assessment Data for Improvement:

Schools that actively use assessment data for continuous improvement demonstrate a commitment to educational quality. Data-informed decision-making allows educators and administrators to identify trends, assess the effectiveness of instructional strategies, and implement targeted interventions to address areas of concern. This indicator emphasizes a culture of evidence-based practice.

Parent and Community Engagement

Collaborative Partnerships with Parents:

Educational quality extends beyond the classroom, involving collaborative partnerships with parents. Schools that actively engage parents in the educational process, providing clear communication, involvement opportunities, and support resources, create a holistic learning environment. Parental engagement contributes to a shared commitment to student success.

Community Involvement and Support:

The involvement of the broader community is a vital indicator of educational quality. Schools that actively collaborate with local businesses, community organizations, and civic groups contribute to a rich ecosystem of support for students. Community involvement can provide additional resources, mentorship opportunities, and real-world connections for students.

Transparent Communication and Accountability:

Educational quality is reinforced by transparent communication and accountability practices. Schools that communicate openly with parents and the community, sharing information about educational goals, policies, and outcomes, build trust and accountability. Transparency fosters a sense of shared responsibility for the quality of education within the broader community.

Conclusion: Navigating the Complexity of Educational Quality Indicators

As we navigate the complex landscape of educational quality, these key indicators serve as guideposts for understanding, assessing, and improving high school education. The subsequent chapters will delve into the correlation between these indicators and academic success, exploring the challenges and opportunities in implementing quality-driven educational policies. By focusing on these indicators, educators, policymakers, and stakeholders can collaborate to create high school environments that prioritize excellence, equity, and the holistic development of every student.

Correlation with Academic Success: Unraveling the Impact of Educational Quality Indicators

Understanding the correlation between quality indicators and academic success is essential for shaping effective educational policies and practices. This section explores how key indicators, ranging from physical infrastructure to teaching methods, influence students' academic achievements. By unraveling these connections, educators and policymakers can design strategies that foster an environment conducive to academic excellence.

Introduction: The Intersection of Quality Indicators and Academic Success

The introduction establishes the significance of exploring the correlation between quality indicators and academic success. It highlights the interconnected nature of educational quality and students' ability to excel academically. The ensuing discussion will delve into various quality indicators and their direct and indirect impacts on academic outcomes.

Physical Infrastructure and Learning Spaces

Modernized Classroom Facilities:

Modernized classroom facilities play a pivotal role in shaping academic success. Studies indicate that well-designed and equipped classrooms contribute to increased student engagement and improved academic performance. Adequate lighting, comfortable seating, and access to technology create an environment that supports effective teaching and learning.

State-of-the-Art Laboratories and Libraries:

Access to state-of-the-art laboratories and libraries correlates positively with academic success. These facilities provide students with opportunities for hands-on learning and in-depth research, fostering critical thinking and analytical skills. A well-equipped library with diverse resources contributes to enhanced self-directed learning, positively impacting academic achievement.

Sustainable and Safe School Buildings:

The sustainability and safety of school buildings are foundational to academic success. Students in environmentally sustainable and safe schools exhibit better attendance and improved concentration, contributing to overall academic achievement. A secure and healthy physical environment positively influences students' mental well-being, creating a conducive atmosphere for learning.

Effective Teaching and Learning Practices

Highly Qualified and Engaging Teachers:

The presence of highly qualified and engaging teachers is a key determinant of academic success. Research consistently demonstrates a positive correlation between teacher qualifications and student achievement. Teachers who effectively engage students, foster a love for learning, and provide clear instruction significantly impact academic outcomes.

Student-Centered Learning Approaches:

Student-centered learning approaches are closely linked to academic success. These methods, such as project-based learning and inquiry-based instruction, promote deeper understanding and application of knowledge. Students actively engaged in their learning process are more likely to develop critical thinking skills and achieve academic milestones.

Innovative Use of Technology in Instruction:

The integration of technology in instruction has a positive correlation with academic success. Educational technology enhances access to resources, facilitates interactive learning experiences, and prepares students for a digitally driven world. Schools that effectively leverage technology often witness improved student outcomes, including higher test scores and increased motivation to learn.

Inclusive and Diverse Learning Environments

Promotion of Inclusivity and Diversity:

Inclusive and diverse learning environments contribute to academic success. Research suggests that students who feel a sense of belonging and inclusivity perform better academically. Exposure to diverse perspectives and cultures enhances cognitive skills and prepares students to navigate an interconnected global society, positively influencing academic achievement.

Culturally Relevant Curriculum:

A culturally relevant curriculum correlates with increased academic success. When students see their cultural identities reflected in the curriculum, they are more likely to be engaged and motivated. Culturally relevant education fosters a deeper understanding of subject matter and promotes a positive attitude toward learning, impacting academic performance.

Support for Special Education and Diverse Learning Needs:

Schools that provide support for special education and diverse learning needs contribute to academic success for all students. Tailored interventions, personalized learning plans, and inclusive practices create an environment where every student can thrive academically. Addressing diverse learning needs positively influences overall academic outcomes.

Assessment and Feedback Mechanisms

Effective Assessment Practices:

Effective assessment practices are integral to academic success. Assessments aligned with learning objectives and providing timely, constructive feedback contribute to student understanding and improvement. Well-designed assessments, including formative and summative methods, play a crucial role in gauging academic progress and informing instructional decisions.

Individualized Feedback and Progress Tracking:

Individualized feedback and progress tracking positively impact academic success. When students receive personalized feedback on their strengths and areas for improvement, they are better equipped to set goals and make progress. Systems that enable students, parents, and educators to track academic development enhance overall academic outcomes.

Use of Assessment Data for Improvement:

Schools that actively use assessment data for improvement witness positive effects on academic success. Data-informed decision-making allows educators to identify areas of strength and weakness, tailor interventions, and enhance teaching strategies. Continuous improvement based on assessment data contributes to sustained academic excellence.

Parent and Community Engagement

Collaborative Partnerships with Parents:

Collaborative partnerships with parents correlate with increased academic success. When parents are actively engaged in their children's education, providing support, encouragement, and involvement, students are more likely to excel academically. Open communication and shared goals between schools and parents positively influence academic outcomes.

Community Involvement and Support:

Community involvement and support contribute to academic success. Schools that collaborate with local businesses, community organizations, and civic groups create a supportive network for students. Community resources, mentorship opportunities, and additional support services enhance the overall learning experience, positively impacting academic achievement.

Transparent Communication and Accountability:

Transparent communication and accountability practices positively influence academic success. Schools that communicate openly with parents and the community, sharing information about educational goals, policies, and outcomes, foster a sense of shared responsibility. Transparency builds trust and accountability, contributing to improved academic outcomes.

Conclusion: Enhancing Academic Success Through Quality Indicators

As we unravel the correlation between quality indicators and academic success, it becomes evident that a holistic approach to education, encompassing physical infrastructure, effective teaching practices, inclusivity, assessment methods, and community engagement, fosters an environment where students thrive academically. The subsequent chapters will delve into the challenges and opportunities in implementing policies that enhance these quality indicators, with a focus on creating a foundation for sustained academic success in high schools worldwide.

Infrastructure, Spending, and Educational Outcomes: Unveiling the Nexus

Understanding the relationship between infrastructure, spending, and educational outcomes is pivotal for shaping effective education policies. This section explores the impact of physical infrastructure and financial investments on educational quality and academic achievements. By unraveling this intricate nexus, educators and policymakers can devise strategies that optimize resources to enhance educational outcomes.

Introduction: The Crucial Role of Infrastructure and Spending in Education

The introduction establishes the critical importance of examining the relationship between infrastructure, spending, and educational outcomes. It underscores the multifaceted impact of physical learning environments and financial investments on the overall quality of education. The ensuing exploration will delve into the nuanced connections between infrastructure, spending, and academic achievements.

Physical Infrastructure and Learning Spaces

Modern and well-designed physical infrastructure is foundational to creating an environment conducive to effective teaching and learning. The quality of learning spaces directly influences educational outcomes in various ways.

Modernized Classroom Facilities:

Modernized classroom facilities contribute significantly to educational outcomes. Adequate lighting, comfortable seating, and the integration of technology create an environment that fosters engagement and active participation. Studies suggest that students in well-designed classrooms exhibit improved academic performance, highlighting the direct correlation between physical infrastructure and educational success.

State-of-the-Art Laboratories and Libraries:

Access to state-of-the-art laboratories and libraries positively influences educational outcomes. These facilities provide students with hands-on learning experiences and access to diverse resources. Well-equipped laboratories enhance practical understanding, while libraries support independent research and a broader understanding of subjects. Schools with such facilities are likely to witness improved academic achievements among their students.

Sustainable and Safe School Buildings:

The sustainability and safety of school buildings contribute significantly to educational outcomes. Research indicates that students in environmentally sustainable and safe schools exhibit better attendance and increased focus on learning. A secure and healthy physical environment positively influences students' mental well-being, creating a conducive atmosphere for academic success.

Financial Investments and Educational Spending

The allocation and utilization of financial resources in education play a crucial role in shaping the quality of learning experiences and, consequently, educational outcomes.

Teacher Salaries and Professional Development:

Investing in competitive teacher salaries and professional development positively impacts educational outcomes. Well-compensated teachers are more likely to be motivated and committed to their roles, leading to improved teaching quality. Ongoing professional development ensures that educators stay abreast of best practices, enhancing their effectiveness in the classroom and, consequently, contributing to better educational outcomes.

Curriculum Development and Learning Resources:

Allocating funds for curriculum development and learning resources is essential for ensuring a high-quality education. Up-to-date curriculum materials, textbooks, and supplementary resources enhance the learning experience, providing students with the tools they need to succeed academically. Schools with sufficient resources for curriculum development often witness positive correlations with improved educational outcomes.

Technology Integration and Infrastructure Investments:

Investments in educational technology and overall infrastructure positively influence educational outcomes. Schools that allocate funds for the integration of technology into instruction and maintain a robust technological infrastructure create opportunities for interactive learning experiences. Technology integration aligns with the demands of the digital age, preparing students for success in a technology-driven world and positively impacting academic achievements.

Special Education and Support Services:

Allocating resources for special education and support services is crucial for inclusive education and improved educational outcomes. Schools that invest in specialized support for students with diverse learning needs create an environment where every student can thrive. Adequate resources for special education positively correlate with improved academic achievements for students with diverse learning requirements.

Community Engagement and Financial Support

The involvement of the community, along with financial support, further enhances the overall educational outcomes of a school.

Community Fundraising and Local Contributions:

Communities that actively engage in fundraising efforts and make local contributions to schools provide additional financial support. These contributions can be used to enhance extracurricular activities, provide additional learning resources, or support infrastructure improvements. Schools benefiting from strong community financial support often experience positive correlations with improved educational outcomes.

Public-Private Partnerships:

Engaging in public-private partnerships can significantly impact educational outcomes. Collaborations with businesses, NGOs, and other private entities can bring additional financial resources and expertise to schools. These partnerships may lead to the development of specialized programs, mentorship opportunities, and access to resources that positively influence academic achievements.

Transparent Budgeting and Financial Accountability:

Transparent budgeting practices and financial accountability are critical for optimizing the impact of financial investments on educational outcomes. Schools that communicate openly about budget allocations, expenditures, and financial priorities build trust within the community. Transparent financial practices contribute to accountability and ensure that funds are directed toward initiatives that positively impact educational success.

Conclusion: Maximizing Educational Outcomes Through Strategic Investments

As we unravel the intricate connections between infrastructure, spending, and educational outcomes, it becomes evident that strategic investments are essential for creating an environment where students can thrive academically. The subsequent chapters will delve into the challenges and opportunities in implementing policies that optimize these investments, with a focus on maximizing educational outcomes for high schools globally.

Challenges in Implementing Quality Indicators: Navigating the Roadblocks to Educational Excellence

While quality indicators in education offer a roadmap to enhance learning environments, their implementation is not without challenges. This section explores the hurdles faced by educational institutions and policymakers in effectively incorporating and sustaining quality indicators. Understanding these challenges is crucial for devising strategies to overcome obstacles and ensure a continuous commitment to educational excellence.

Introduction: The Complex Landscape of Implementing Quality Indicators

The introduction sets the stage by emphasizing the significance of quality indicators in education and the pivotal role they play in shaping the learning experience. It introduces the idea that despite their importance, implementing these indicators comes with its own set of challenges. The subsequent exploration will delve into the various obstacles faced by educational stakeholders in integrating and maintaining quality indicators.

Resistance to Change: Institutional and Cultural Barriers

Resistance to change poses a significant challenge in implementing quality indicators. Educational institutions, often deeply rooted in traditional practices, may face resistance from faculty, staff, and administrators. Cultural norms and established routines can create barriers to adopting new indicators, hindering the swift implementation of improved practices.

Addressing this challenge requires a strategic approach that includes transparent communication, stakeholder engagement, and professional development programs. Cultivating a culture of openness to change and emphasizing the benefits of quality indicators can help overcome institutional and cultural resistance.

Resource Constraints: Financial and Infrastructural Limitations

Financial and infrastructural limitations present formidable challenges in implementing quality indicators. Many educational institutions, especially those in economically disadvantaged areas, may lack the necessary financial resources to invest in modern infrastructure, technology, or teacher training programs.

Creative solutions, such as seeking external funding, engaging in public-private partnerships, and prioritizing resource allocation based on identified needs, can help mitigate resource constraints. Policymakers must explore innovative financing models and advocate for increased investment in education to address these challenges effectively.

Lack of Professional Development Opportunities

The absence of robust professional development opportunities is a hindrance to implementing quality indicators. Teachers and administrators require continuous training to adapt to evolving educational practices, integrate technology effectively, and implement new teaching methodologies aligned with quality indicators.

Establishing comprehensive professional development programs, including workshops, seminars, and online courses, can empower educators to embrace change and incorporate quality indicators into their practices. Collaboration with educational experts and mentorship initiatives can further enhance professional development opportunities.

Data Collection and Analysis Challenges

Collecting and analyzing data to measure the effectiveness of quality indicators can be a complex task. Educational institutions may lack the necessary tools, expertise, or systematic processes for efficient data collection and analysis. This challenge hampers the ability to assess the impact of implemented indicators accurately.

Investing in data infrastructure, training staff in data collection and analysis techniques, and utilizing technology for streamlined processes can address this challenge. Collaborating with educational research institutions and leveraging external expertise can enhance the capacity of educational institutions to gather and interpret relevant data.

Inconsistencies in Implementation Across Regions

Inconsistencies in the implementation of quality indicators across different regions and educational systems pose a significant challenge. Diverse cultural, socio-economic, and political contexts may lead to variations in the interpretation and execution of quality indicators, affecting the overall effectiveness of these measures.

Harmonizing standards and indicators at a global or national level, while allowing for contextual adaptations, can help mitigate inconsistencies. Regular monitoring, evaluation, and feedback mechanisms can ensure alignment with overarching educational goals while accommodating regional nuances.

Overemphasis on Standardized Testing

An overemphasis on standardized testing can undermine the holistic implementation of quality indicators. Relying solely on test scores may lead to a narrow focus on academic outcomes, neglecting other crucial aspects of education, such as creativity, critical thinking, and socio-emotional development.

Balancing the use of standardized testing with alternative assessment methods, such as project-based assessments, portfolios, and collaborative projects, is essential. Policymakers must promote a comprehensive approach to evaluation that considers diverse facets of student learning and development.

Resistance from Stakeholders: Parents, Students, and Community

Resistance from various stakeholders, including parents, students, and the community, can impede the implementation of quality indicators. Misunderstandings or misconceptions about the purpose and benefits of these indicators may lead to skepticism or opposition.

Engaging stakeholders through transparent communication, informational campaigns, and involvement in decision-making processes can alleviate resistance. Establishing feedback mechanisms and showcasing tangible benefits of quality indicators can help build trust and garner support from the community.

Limited Integration of Technology in Education

Limited integration of technology in education poses a challenge to the effective implementation of quality indicators. In an increasingly digital age, leveraging technology for enhanced learning experiences is crucial. However, not all educational institutions have the infrastructure or expertise to integrate technology seamlessly.

Providing training for educators on technology integration, ensuring access to digital resources, and promoting partnerships with technology experts can address this challenge. Policymakers should prioritize initiatives that facilitate the integration of technology into educational practices.

Conclusion: Navigating Challenges for a Future of Educational Excellence

As we navigate the challenges in implementing quality indicators, it becomes evident that a multi-faceted approach is necessary. By addressing resistance, overcoming resource constraints, fostering professional development, and embracing technological advancements, educational stakeholders can create a foundation for sustained improvement. The subsequent chapters will delve into the opportunities and strategies for overcoming these challenges, ultimately paving the way for a future of educational excellence on a global scale.

Chapter 12: Global Educational Rankings
Overview of Ranking Systems: Decoding the Metrics of Educational Excellence

Educational rankings serve as benchmarks that offer insights into the performance of education systems globally. This section provides a comprehensive exploration of the various ranking systems, shedding light on their methodologies, criteria, and implications. Understanding the nuances of these rankings is essential for policymakers, educators, and the public to make informed decisions about educational priorities and improvements.

Introduction: The Significance of Global Educational Rankings

The introduction emphasizes the importance of global educational rankings in providing a comparative analysis of education systems worldwide. It sets the stage for an in-depth exploration of different ranking systems, acknowledging their influence on educational policies, resource allocation, and international perceptions of educational excellence.

Defining Educational Rankings

Educational rankings are assessments that assign numerical or categorical positions to educational institutions, systems, or countries based on predefined criteria. These criteria typically encompass a range of factors, including academic performance, research output, faculty quality, and infrastructure.

Diversity of Ranking Systems

International Ranking Systems:

Global ranking systems assess the performance of countries' education systems on an international scale. Examples include the Programme for International Student Assessment (PISA) and the Trends in International Mathematics and Science Study (TIMSS). These assessments primarily focus on students' academic achievements in core subjects, providing insights into the relative strengths and weaknesses of different national education systems.

University Rankings:

University rankings evaluate higher education institutions based on various criteria such as academic reputation, faculty quality, research output, and internationalization. Prominent examples include the QS World University Rankings, Academic Ranking of World Universities (ARWU), and Times Higher Education World University Rankings. These rankings play a crucial role in shaping institutional strategies, attracting students and faculty, and influencing funding decisions.

Subject-Specific Rankings:

Some rankings focus on specific academic disciplines, providing a nuanced assessment of universities or programs within a particular field. For instance, the QS World University Rankings by Subject and the Shanghai Ranking's Global Ranking of Academic Subjects offer insights into the strengths of institutions in areas like engineering, medicine, or social sciences.

Methodologies of Global Ranking Systems

PISA Methodology:

PISA, conducted by the Organisation for Economic Co-operation and Development (OECD), assesses the knowledge and skills of 15-year-old students in reading, mathematics, and science. The assessment emphasizes real-world problem-solving and critical thinking. PISA's methodology involves a sample of students from participating countries, providing a comparative analysis of their performance.

TIMSS Methodology:

TIMSS evaluates the mathematical and scientific knowledge of students in fourth and eighth grades. The assessment aims to measure students' understanding of fundamental concepts and problem-solving abilities. TIMSS employs a rigorous sampling method to ensure a representative sample of students, allowing for cross-country comparisons.

University Ranking Methodologies:

University rankings use diverse methodologies, often combining quantitative and qualitative indicators. Common criteria include academic reputation, faculty-to-student ratio, research output, international collaboration, and citations per faculty member. Each ranking organization may assign different weights to these factors, leading to variations in the final rankings.

Subject-Specific Ranking Methodologies:

Subject-specific rankings consider criteria relevant to the discipline, such as academic reputation, research impact, and employer feedback. For example, the QS World University Rankings by Subject incorporates surveys of academics and employers, research citations, and the H-index to assess the strength of university programs in specific academic fields.

Critiques of Global Ranking Systems

Limitations of PISA and TIMSS:

Critics argue that PISA and TIMSS focus excessively on standardized testing and may not capture the broader goals of education, such as creativity, critical thinking, and socio-emotional skills. Additionally, cultural and linguistic biases in the test design may impact the validity of the results.

University Ranking Criticisms:

University rankings face criticism for their reliance on subjective indicators, such as academic reputation surveys, which may be influenced by institutional prestige. Critics argue that focusing on research output may prioritize quantity over quality and neglect teaching and societal impact.

Subject-Specific Ranking Challenges:

Subject-specific rankings may face challenges in defining clear criteria for each discipline. The diversity of academic disciplines makes it challenging to create a one-size-fits-all methodology, and the weight assigned to different criteria may not accurately reflect the unique aspects of each subject area.

Impact of Rankings on Educational Policies and Practices

Policy Influence:

Global educational rankings have a substantial impact on national and institutional policies. Countries or universities that perform well in rankings may experience increased funding, international recognition, and a boost in student enrollment. Conversely, lower-ranking entities may face pressure to implement reforms and improve their standing.

Resource Allocation:

The rankings influence resource allocation, guiding governments and institutions in directing funds toward areas deemed essential for improvement. Institutions may prioritize hiring renowned faculty, investing in research infrastructure, or enhancing international collaboration based on ranking criteria.

Internationalization Strategies:

Universities often incorporate ranking indicators into their internationalization strategies. Achieving a high position in global rankings can attract a diverse student body, faculty, and research collaborations. Institutions may actively seek to improve specific aspects that impact their rankings to enhance their global standing.

Conclusion: Navigating the Complex Landscape of Educational Rankings

As we navigate the intricate world of global educational rankings, it becomes clear that these assessments play a significant role in shaping educational landscapes. Understanding the methodologies, critiques, and impacts of these rankings is essential for policymakers, educators, and the public. Subsequent chapters will delve deeper into specific ranking systems, exploring their implications and providing insights into how educational stakeholders can use this information to drive positive changes in high school education globally.

Criteria Used in Educational Rankings: Unveiling the Metrics of Excellence

Educational rankings serve as powerful tools for assessing the performance of education systems, institutions, and programs. The criteria employed in these rankings play a pivotal role in shaping perceptions of educational quality and guiding policy decisions. This section delves into the diverse criteria used in global educational rankings, exploring their significance, limitations, and implications for stakeholders in the field of education.

Introduction: The Foundations of Educational Rankings Criteria

The introduction sets the stage by highlighting the central role of criteria in shaping educational rankings. It emphasizes the multifaceted nature of education and the challenge of capturing its richness through specific metrics. As we delve into the various criteria employed in global rankings, it becomes evident that these metrics not only influence perceptions but also drive institutions and policymakers to prioritize certain aspects of education.

Academic Reputation: A Pillar of Excellence

Academic reputation is a cornerstone criterion in many global educational rankings. It often relies on surveys and peer assessments to gauge how institutions or programs are perceived within the academic community. This criterion reflects the esteem in which an educational entity is held by its peers, contributing significantly to its overall ranking.

Significance of Academic Reputation:

Academic reputation is considered a proxy for the quality of education and research output. A positive reputation can attract top faculty, students, and collaborative opportunities. For universities, it serves as a measure of their standing in the global academic landscape.

Limitations and Criticisms:

Critics argue that relying heavily on reputation surveys may perpetuate existing hierarchies and neglect emerging institutions with innovative approaches. The subjective nature of perceptions may also introduce biases based on regional, cultural, or linguistic factors.

Research Output and Impact: Quantifying Scholarly Contributions

Research output and impact metrics assess the quantity and influence of scholarly work produced by an institution or program. This criterion often considers factors such as the number of publications, citations, and the h-index, reflecting the institution's contribution to the advancement of knowledge.

Importance of Research Metrics:

Research metrics signal an institution's commitment to producing valuable contributions to academic knowledge. A high level of research activity is often associated with institutions at the forefront of innovation, making significant contributions to their fields.

Challenges and Controversies:

While research output is a valuable criterion, overemphasizing it may lead to a focus on quantity over quality. Critics argue that a narrow emphasis on research metrics may marginalize institutions that prioritize teaching, community engagement, or applied research.

Faculty Quality and Student-Faculty Ratio: Nurturing Academic Excellence

The quality of faculty and the student-faculty ratio are indicators used to assess the caliber of teaching and the level of individualized attention students receive. These criteria recognize the importance of a qualified and engaged faculty in delivering a high-quality education.

Role of Faculty Quality:

The expertise, reputation, and engagement of faculty members are critical factors in shaping the learning experience. Top-notch faculty can attract students, foster a culture of academic excellence, and contribute to an institution's overall standing in global rankings.

Significance of Student-Faculty Ratio:

A low student-faculty ratio is often associated with better opportunities for interaction, personalized attention, and mentorship. Institutions with a favorable ratio are perceived as more able to provide a supportive and engaging learning environment.

Challenges in Measuring Faculty Quality:

Quantifying faculty quality is complex and may involve subjective assessments. Research output, awards, and academic reputation surveys are common indicators, but these may not capture the full spectrum of teaching excellence and dedication to student success.

Internationalization and Diversity: Fostering a Global Perspective

Internationalization criteria assess an institution's efforts to promote diversity, cross-cultural collaboration, and a global perspective in its educational programs. These criteria recognize the importance of preparing students for a world that is increasingly interconnected.

Components of Internationalization:

Factors such as the proportion of international students and faculty, the availability of global exchange programs, and partnerships with institutions worldwide contribute to an institution's score in internationalization metrics.

Benefits of a Global Perspective:

A commitment to internationalization enriches the educational experience by exposing students to diverse perspectives, cultures, and ideas. It prepares them for a globalized workforce and fosters a more inclusive and interconnected academic community.

Challenges and Criticisms:

Criticisms often revolve around the potential for superficial internationalization, where institutions prioritize quantity over quality in their global initiatives. The criteria may also favor institutions with greater financial resources for international programs.

Student Success and Graduation Rates: Gauging Educational Impact

Student success and graduation rates assess an institution's ability to guide students through their academic journey successfully. High retention and graduation rates are indicative of an institution's commitment to providing adequate support and resources for student achievement.

Importance of Student Success Metrics:

The ability to retain and graduate students reflects the effectiveness of an institution in delivering a high-quality education. It suggests that students are receiving the support they need to navigate academic challenges and complete their programs successfully.

Challenges in Measurement:

Measuring student success can be challenging, as it involves understanding the diverse factors that contribute to student outcomes. Socioeconomic, cultural, and individual differences may impact graduation rates, necessitating a nuanced approach to interpretation.

Infrastructure and Facilities: Creating a Conducive Learning Environment

Infrastructure and facilities criteria evaluate the physical resources available to students, including libraries, laboratories, technological infrastructure, and recreational spaces. These criteria recognize the importance of a well-equipped environment in facilitating effective teaching and learning.

Role of Infrastructure in Education:

Modern and well-maintained facilities contribute to a positive learning experience, providing students with the tools and spaces needed for academic and extracurricular activities. Infrastructure criteria highlight an institution's commitment to creating a conducive learning environment.

Equity and Accessibility Considerations:

Critics argue that an emphasis on infrastructure may disproportionately benefit institutions with greater financial resources, potentially exacerbating existing disparities in education. Balancing investments in facilities with a focus on inclusivity is essential.

Conclusion: Navigating the Complex Landscape of Educational Criteria

As we navigate the intricate landscape of educational criteria in global rankings, it becomes evident that these metrics shape perceptions, drive institutional priorities, and influence policy decisions. The multifaceted nature of education requires a careful consideration of various criteria to provide a comprehensive understanding of educational excellence. Subsequent chapters will delve into specific ranking systems, exploring how these criteria impact the global assessment of high school education and offering insights into the complexities of achieving and sustaining educational excellence on a global scale.

Implications for Educational Policy: Guiding Decision-Making in a Globalized Landscape

Educational rankings, with their diverse criteria and methodologies, wield considerable influence over the shaping of educational policies. This section explores the implications of global educational rankings on the formulation and implementation of policies at national and institutional levels. As we unravel these implications, it becomes evident that rankings are not merely reflective but instrumental in driving systemic changes.

Introduction: The Interplay Between Rankings and Educational Policies

The introduction underscores the dynamic relationship between global educational rankings and policy decisions. It highlights the dual role of rankings as both mirrors reflecting the current state of education and catalysts propelling institutions and governments to strive for higher standards. Understanding this interplay is crucial for policymakers seeking to navigate the complex landscape of education on a global scale.

Influence on Resource Allocation: Shaping Budgetary Priorities

Educational rankings have a significant impact on resource allocation, shaping the budgetary priorities of both governments and institutions. Institutions that achieve higher rankings often receive increased funding, enabling them to invest in faculty development, research infrastructure, and other factors contributing to their success.

Rationale Behind Resource Allocation:

Governments and institutions allocate resources based on the criteria emphasized in rankings. For example, if research output and faculty quality are heavily weighted, institutions may direct funds toward research initiatives and faculty recruitment. This strategic allocation is driven by a desire to enhance the factors that contribute most to improved rankings.

Potential Drawbacks and Criticisms:

While aligning resource allocation with ranking criteria can drive excellence, it also raises concerns. Critics argue that overemphasis on specific criteria may lead to a skewed focus, neglecting essential aspects of education such as teaching quality, inclusivity, and community engagement. Striking a balance between ranking-driven priorities and holistic educational goals is a constant challenge for policymakers.

Impact on Institutional Strategies: Aligning with Ranking Indicators

Institutions often tailor their strategies to align with the indicators emphasized in global rankings. The pursuit of higher rankings becomes a strategic goal, influencing decisions related to faculty recruitment, program development, and internationalization efforts.

Recruitment of High-Quality Faculty:

To improve rankings, institutions prioritize the recruitment of high-caliber faculty members, often with strong research profiles. This not only enhances academic reputation but also contributes to research output, reinforcing the institution's standing in global rankings.

Program Development and Enhancement:

Institutions may invest in the development and enhancement of programs that align with criteria valued in rankings. For example, if internationalization is a key indicator, institutions may establish more robust exchange programs, fostering a diverse and globally connected student body.

Internationalization Initiatives:

The internationalization of education, a criterion in many rankings, becomes a strategic focus for institutions. Partnerships with global institutions, recruitment of international students and faculty, and the expansion of study abroad opportunities are commonly adopted strategies to enhance internationalization indicators.

Policies to Address Weaknesses: A Response to Ranking Deficiencies

When institutions or countries identify weaknesses through lower rankings, they often implement policies to address these deficiencies. The rankings act as diagnostic tools, guiding policymakers in identifying areas for improvement and formulating targeted interventions.

Reform Initiatives and Educational Policies:

Governments may institute educational reforms and policies aimed at addressing specific challenges identified through rankings. For instance, if a country lags in research output, policies promoting research funding, collaboration, and innovation may be introduced.

Quality Assurance and Accreditation:

Institutions may prioritize accreditation processes and quality assurance measures to demonstrate adherence to global standards. Achieving accreditation can positively impact rankings, signaling a commitment to maintaining high educational standards.

Investment in Research and Innovation:

Countries and institutions aspiring to improve their research-related rankings may increase investments in research and innovation. Funding schemes, grants, and infrastructure development aimed at fostering a culture of research may be introduced.

Competitive Dynamics: Fostering a Global Educational Marketplace

Global rankings contribute to the creation of a competitive educational marketplace where institutions and countries vie for prominence. This competition can drive innovation, excellence, and collaboration while also fostering a climate of accountability.

Attracting International Students and Faculty:

Higher-ranked institutions become magnets for international students and faculty. The competitive advantage associated with a favorable ranking attracts a diverse and talented pool of individuals, contributing to the institution's global reputation.

International Collaborations and Partnerships:

Institutions and countries may actively seek international collaborations and partnerships to enhance their global standing. Collaborative research initiatives, joint programs, and strategic alliances become avenues to bolster rankings and compete on a global scale.

Impact on Educational Diplomacy:

Rankings influence the diplomatic efforts of countries, shaping their educational diplomacy strategies. Countries with higher-ranked institutions may use their educational standing as a diplomatic tool, fostering international relations and collaborations.

Challenges in Achieving Balance: Addressing Trade-offs and Unintended Consequences

While rankings offer valuable insights, achieving a balance between their influence and broader educational goals poses challenges. Policymakers must navigate trade-offs and mitigate unintended consequences to ensure that the pursuit of higher rankings aligns with the overarching mission of providing quality education.

Trade-offs Between Teaching and Research:

A common challenge is balancing the emphasis on research output with the importance of effective teaching. Policies that incentivize research may inadvertently shift focus away from teaching quality, impacting the overall educational experience.

Inclusivity and Diversity Challenges:

The pursuit of rankings may lead to unintended consequences related to inclusivity and diversity. Institutions focused on specific criteria may inadvertently neglect efforts to create inclusive learning environments and diverse student populations.

Pressure on Institutions and Students:

The intense competition driven by rankings may create pressure on institutions and students. Institutions may prioritize metrics that boost rankings at the expense of broader educational goals, while students may experience heightened stress due to the competitive nature of the educational environment.

Conclusion: Navigating the Intersection of Rankings and Policy

As we navigate the intersection of global educational rankings and policy decisions, it becomes evident that rankings are powerful drivers shaping the landscape of education. The influence on resource allocation, institutional strategies, and policy formulation underscores the need for a nuanced and balanced approach. Policymakers must continually assess the implications of rankings, addressing challenges and leveraging the positive aspects to foster a global educational environment that prioritizes excellence, inclusivity, and innovation. Subsequent chapters will delve into specific ranking systems, offering a deeper understanding of their unique contributions and challenges in the context of high school education globally.

Criticisms and Alternatives to Ranking Systems: Navigating the Complexities of Assessment

While global educational rankings provide valuable insights, they are not without their share of criticisms. This section explores the various critiques leveled against ranking systems, delving into their limitations and potential drawbacks. Additionally, it examines alternative approaches and emerging models that aim to address some of the challenges inherent in traditional ranking methodologies.

Introduction: Acknowledging the Limitations of Ranking Systems

The introduction sets the stage by acknowledging the widespread use and impact of global educational rankings while recognizing the need for a critical examination of their methodologies. It highlights the complexities of assessing educational quality on a global scale and introduces the diverse criticisms and alternatives that will be explored in the subsequent sections.

Criticisms of Global Educational Rankings

1. Lack of Holistic Assessment:

One prominent criticism of ranking systems is their tendency to oversimplify the complex nature of education. By predominantly focusing on quantitative metrics such as research output, faculty-to-student ratios, and internationalization efforts, rankings may overlook qualitative aspects of education, such as teaching quality, student engagement, and community impact.

2. Subjectivity in Metrics:

The subjective nature of certain metrics, especially those related to academic reputation and peer assessments, introduces an element of bias. Cultural, linguistic, and regional biases can influence perceptions, potentially disadvantaging institutions from certain parts of the world.

3. Reinforcement of Inequality:

Critics argue that rankings can reinforce existing inequalities in the global educational landscape. Institutions with greater financial resources may have a competitive advantage, as they can invest heavily in areas prioritized by ranking criteria, further widening the gap between well-funded and resource-constrained institutions.

4. Overemphasis on Research:

Many ranking systems heavily weight research-related metrics, potentially sidelining the importance of effective teaching and community engagement. This bias may lead institutions to prioritize research output at the expense of a balanced and comprehensive educational experience.

5. Lack of Consideration for Regional Contexts:

The one-size-fits-all approach of many ranking systems may not adequately account for the diverse educational contexts and priorities across regions. Metrics that hold significant weight in Western contexts may not accurately reflect the strengths and contributions of institutions in other parts of the world.

Alternatives to Traditional Ranking Systems

1. Multidimensional Assessments:

An alternative approach involves adopting multidimensional assessments that consider a broader range of factors. Instead of relying solely on quantitative metrics, this model incorporates qualitative indicators, such as teaching effectiveness, student satisfaction, and community engagement, providing a more holistic view of educational quality.

2. Stakeholder Engagement:

Incorporating the perspectives of various stakeholders, including students, alumni, employers, and local communities, offers a more comprehensive assessment of an institution's impact. Surveys and feedback mechanisms can provide valuable qualitative data that goes beyond the metrics commonly used in traditional ranking systems.

3. Regionalized Ranking Systems:

Recognizing the diversity of educational priorities and contexts, some advocate for the development of regionalized ranking systems. These models take into account regional nuances and emphasize criteria that align with the specific strengths and challenges of educational institutions within a particular geographic area.

4. Transparency and Accountability:

Promoting transparency in the methodology of ranking systems and holding them accountable for the impact of their assessments can mitigate some criticisms. Clear communication about how metrics are weighted and calculated allows institutions to understand their rankings and work toward improvement more effectively.

5. Impact Assessment:

Shifting the focus from outputs to outcomes, an impact assessment approach evaluates the real-world contributions of educational institutions. This model considers factors such as social mobility, community development, and the success of graduates in their careers, providing a more nuanced understanding of an institution's overall impact.

Case Studies: Exploring Innovative Approaches

1. QS Stars Rating System:

The QS Stars Rating System, developed by QS Quacquarelli Symonds, takes a more holistic approach to assessment. It evaluates institutions based on a broader set of criteria, including teaching quality, employability, social responsibility, inclusiveness, and facilities. The system awards stars in each category, providing a multidimensional view of an institution's strengths.

2. Times Higher Education (THE) University Impact Rankings:

THE University Impact Rankings assess universities' contributions to achieving the United Nations' Sustainable Development Goals. This approach shifts the focus from traditional metrics to factors such as social and economic impact, environmental sustainability, and commitment to global goals.

3. U-Multirank:

U-Multirank takes a multidimensional approach, allowing users to compare institutions based on various indicators, including teaching and learning, research, knowledge transfer, international orientation, and regional engagement. This tool enables a personalized assessment based on individual preferences and priorities.

Challenges in Implementing Alternatives

1. Data Availability and Consistency:

One of the challenges in implementing alternative models is the availability and consistency of data. Traditional ranking systems often rely on easily quantifiable metrics, while alternative approaches may require more nuanced and context-specific information, posing challenges in data collection and standardization.

2. Resistance to Change:

The academic community, accustomed to traditional ranking systems, may resist embracing alternative models. Resistance to change, coupled with concerns about the comparability and validity of new assessment methods, can impede the adoption of innovative approaches.

3. Balancing Quantitative and Qualitative Data:

Finding the right balance between quantitative and qualitative data in alternative models is a complex task. While qualitative indicators offer valuable insights, they may be subjective and challenging to standardize, requiring careful consideration in the design of assessment frameworks.

Conclusion: Navigating the Evolving Landscape of Educational Assessment

As we navigate the complexities of global educational rankings, it becomes evident that criticisms have spurred innovation in assessment methodologies. Alternative approaches aim to address the limitations of traditional models, offering more nuanced, context-aware, and inclusive assessments. While challenges exist in the implementation of these alternatives, the ongoing dialogue about the future of educational assessment encourages a shift toward more comprehensive and meaningful evaluations of educational institutions worldwide. Subsequent chapters will further explore specific ranking systems, examining their unique features, contributions, and adaptations in the realm of high school education globally.

Chapter 13: Emerging Trends and Future Prospects
Evolving Landscape of High School Education: Navigating Change and Embracing Innovation

The introduction sets the stage for exploring the evolving landscape of high school education. It emphasizes the dynamic nature of education and the need for continuous adaptation to meet the challenges and opportunities that lie ahead. As we delve into emerging trends, this chapter aims to provide insights into the future prospects of high school education globally.

Shifts in Pedagogy and Teaching Methodologies

Inquiry-Based Learning:

One of the notable trends in the evolving landscape of high school education is the shift towards inquiry-based learning. This approach emphasizes active student engagement, critical thinking, and problem-solving. High schools are increasingly adopting inquiry-based methods to cultivate a deeper understanding of subjects and foster a lifelong love for learning.

Blended Learning Environments:

Advancements in technology have paved the way for blended learning environments, where traditional classroom instruction integrates seamlessly with online resources. This hybrid approach allows for personalized learning experiences, catering to diverse student needs and preferences. High schools are exploring innovative ways to leverage technology without compromising the essential elements of face-to-face interaction.

Project-Based Learning Initiatives:

Project-based learning has gained prominence as an effective way to connect theoretical knowledge with real-world applications. High schools are incorporating project-based initiatives into their curricula to enhance students' problem-solving skills, teamwork, and creativity. These hands-on experiences contribute to a more holistic educational journey.

Embracing Technological Integration

Digital Literacy as a Core Competency:

In response to the increasing role of technology in modern society, high schools are recognizing the importance of digital literacy as a core competency. Beyond basic computer skills, digital literacy encompasses the ability to critically assess information, navigate online platforms responsibly, and leverage technology for effective communication and collaboration.

Integration of Artificial Intelligence (AI) and Machine Learning:

The integration of artificial intelligence (AI) and machine learning into high school education is an emerging trend with transformative potential. AI-powered tools can provide personalized learning experiences, adaptive assessments, and data-driven insights to educators. High schools are exploring ways to leverage these technologies to enhance teaching efficiency and student outcomes.

Online Learning Platforms and Massive Open Online Courses (MOOCs):

The accessibility of online learning platforms and Massive Open Online Courses (MOOCs) has expanded educational opportunities beyond traditional boundaries. High schools are exploring partnerships with reputable online platforms to offer a broader range of courses, enabling students to pursue diverse subjects based on their interests and career aspirations.

Global Collaboration and Cultural Exchange

Virtual Exchange Programs:

Global collaboration and cultural exchange are becoming integral components of high school education.

Virtual exchange programs allow students to connect with peers from different parts of the world, fostering cultural awareness, language proficiency, and a global perspective. High schools are actively seeking opportunities to incorporate virtual exchanges into their curricula.

International Collaborative Projects:

High schools are engaging in international collaborative projects that transcend geographical boundaries. Students collaborate on research, community service initiatives, and cultural exchanges, providing a rich and immersive learning experience. These projects contribute to the development of global competencies and interpersonal skills.

Focus on Holistic Development

Emotional Intelligence and Well-being Programs:

Recognizing the importance of holistic development, high schools are increasingly incorporating programs that focus on emotional intelligence and well-being. These initiatives aim to support students' mental health, resilience, and social-emotional skills, creating a positive and supportive learning environment.

Inclusive Education Practices:

Inclusive education practices are gaining prominence, emphasizing the importance of accommodating diverse learning needs. High schools are adopting strategies to create inclusive classrooms, providing additional support for students with disabilities, and fostering a sense of belonging for all learners.

Career-Ready Education:

The evolving landscape of high school education places a strong emphasis on preparing students for future careers. Career-ready education involves aligning curricula with industry needs, providing practical skills development, and offering experiential learning opportunities such as internships and mentorship programs.

Assessment and Evaluation Reforms

Competency-Based Assessments:

Moving away from traditional standardized testing, high schools are exploring competency-based assessments. These assessments focus on evaluating students' mastery of specific skills and knowledge, providing a more comprehensive understanding of their capabilities.

Portfolio Assessments and Project Portfolios:

Portfolio assessments and project portfolios are gaining popularity as alternative methods of evaluating students' progress. These approaches allow students to showcase their achievements, projects, and reflections, offering a more holistic representation of their learning journey.

Environmental Sustainability Education

Integration of Environmental Sustainability into Curricula:

In response to global environmental challenges, high schools are integrating environmental sustainability into their curricula. Students are exposed to topics such as climate change, conservation, and sustainable practices, fostering a sense of environmental responsibility and awareness.

Green School Initiatives:

High schools are embracing green school initiatives that promote environmentally friendly practices. These initiatives may include energy-efficient infrastructure, waste reduction programs, and outdoor learning spaces that connect students with nature.

Conclusion: Charting the Course for the Future

As high school education continues to evolve, educators, policymakers, and stakeholders play a crucial role in shaping its trajectory. The trends highlighted in this chapter represent a dynamic landscape where innovation, adaptability, and a commitment to holistic development are central. By navigating these changes and embracing emerging opportunities, high schools can prepare students not only for academic success but also for the complex and interconnected challenges of the future. Subsequent chapters will delve into specific case studies and examples that illustrate the implementation of these emerging trends in various educational contexts globally.

Anticipated Changes and Challenges: Navigating the Path Forward in High School Education

The introduction sets the stage for examining anticipated changes and challenges in high school education. It emphasizes the need for foresight in adapting to the evolving educational landscape and introduces the key themes that will be explored in this chapter.

Anticipated Changes in High School Education

1. Personalized Learning Journeys:

One of the anticipated changes in high school education is a continued shift towards personalized learning journeys. Advances in technology, including adaptive learning platforms and artificial intelligence, enable educators to tailor instruction to individual student needs. This move towards personalization aims to enhance engagement, cater to diverse learning styles, and foster a deeper understanding of subjects.

2. Competency-Based Education:

Anticipated changes include a broader adoption of competency-based education, where students progress based on their mastery of specific skills and knowledge rather than traditional grade levels. This approach aligns with the idea of individualized learning, allowing students to advance at their own pace and ensuring a more comprehensive understanding of the material.

3. Integration of Emerging Technologies:

The integration of emerging technologies is poised to transform the high school education landscape. Virtual reality (VR), augmented reality (AR), and immersive simulations are expected to play a more significant role in creating interactive and engaging learning experiences. These technologies have the potential to bring abstract concepts to life and provide students with hands-on, experiential learning opportunities.

4. Interdisciplinary Learning:

Anticipated changes also include a growing emphasis on interdisciplinary learning. Recognizing the interconnected nature of knowledge, high schools may increasingly integrate subjects, fostering a holistic understanding of complex issues. Interdisciplinary learning prepares students for the interdisciplinary challenges they are likely to encounter in higher education and the workforce.

5. Continued Emphasis on Soft Skills:

In response to the evolving demands of the workplace, high schools are anticipated to place a continued emphasis on the development of soft skills. Communication, critical thinking, collaboration, and adaptability are crucial skills that contribute to students' overall success in their academic and professional journeys.

Challenges on the Horizon

1. Technological Accessibility and Equity:

While emerging technologies offer exciting possibilities, a significant challenge lies in ensuring equitable access to these resources. Disparities in technological infrastructure and access to devices may exacerbate educational inequalities. Addressing these disparities is crucial to ensuring that all students can benefit from the opportunities presented by technological advancements.

2. Teacher Professional Development:

The successful integration of emerging trends and technologies relies heavily on the professional development of educators. High schools face the challenge of providing ongoing training and support to teachers, helping them adapt to new pedagogical approaches, implement technology effectively, and navigate the evolving demands of education.

3. Balancing Standardization and Personalization:

Achieving a balance between standardized assessments and personalized learning approaches poses a challenge. While personalized learning allows for tailored experiences, standardized assessments remain a widely accepted measure of academic achievement. Striking the right balance between these two approaches is essential to ensure that educational outcomes are meaningful and universally recognized.

4. Managing Data Privacy and Security:

The increased use of technology in high school education raises concerns about data privacy and security. Safeguarding sensitive student information and ensuring compliance with privacy regulations become paramount. High schools must implement robust data protection measures and policies to mitigate the risks associated with the collection and storage of student data.

5. Adequate Resources and Funding:

Implementing anticipated changes in high school education requires adequate resources and funding. Schools may face challenges in securing the necessary financial support for infrastructure upgrades, technology integration, and professional development initiatives. Ensuring equitable distribution of resources is crucial to prevent further disparities in educational opportunities.

6. Reimagining Assessment Models:

Shifting towards competency-based education and personalized learning necessitates a reimagining of traditional assessment models. Designing assessments that effectively measure diverse skills and knowledge levels, while maintaining validity and reliability, is a complex challenge. High schools must explore innovative assessment methods that align with evolving educational paradigms.

7. Navigating Cultural and Societal Expectations:

Anticipated changes in high school education may challenge existing cultural and societal expectations. As education evolves, schools must navigate potential resistance to change, addressing concerns from parents, students, and other stakeholders. Effective communication and collaboration are essential to garner support for progressive educational practices.

Conclusion: A Call to Navigate Change Responsibly

As high school education stands at the cusp of significant transformation, it is imperative to approach anticipated changes and challenges with foresight and responsibility. Embracing innovation while addressing potential pitfalls requires a collaborative effort from educators, policymakers, parents, and students. By navigating these changes responsibly, high schools can lay the foundation for an educational landscape that prepares students for the complexities of the future. Subsequent chapters will delve into specific case studies and examples that illustrate how high schools are addressing these anticipated changes and challenges in diverse global contexts.

Opportunities for Global Collaboration: Building Bridges in High School Education

The introduction sets the stage for exploring the opportunities for global collaboration in high school education. It emphasizes the transformative potential of connecting classrooms across borders, fostering cross-cultural understanding, and preparing students for the challenges of a globally interconnected world.

Connecting Classrooms Across Continents

In an era where communication knows no geographical boundaries, high schools have a unique opportunity to connect classrooms across continents. Global collaboration opens avenues for students to engage in meaningful exchanges, sharing perspectives, and gaining insights into different cultures, societies, and educational systems.

International Exchange Programs:

International exchange programs remain a cornerstone of global collaboration in high school education. These programs provide students with the opportunity to immerse themselves in a different cultural context, learn a new language, and develop a deeper appreciation for diversity. The exchange of students fosters lifelong connections and contributes to the development of global citizens.

Virtual Collaboration Platforms:

Advancements in technology have given rise to virtual collaboration platforms that facilitate real-time interactions between students from different parts of the world. These platforms offer a space for collaborative projects, joint research endeavors, and cultural exchanges. Through virtual collaboration, high schools can overcome geographical constraints and create meaningful connections.

Joint Projects and Collaborative Research Initiatives

1. Joint Academic Projects:

High schools can collaborate on joint academic projects that transcend borders. From science experiments to literary analyses, students from different countries can work together on projects that not only deepen their subject knowledge but also enhance their collaborative skills.

2. Collaborative Research Initiatives:

Collaborative research initiatives provide an opportunity for high school students to engage in meaningful research projects with peers from other countries. Whether it's addressing global challenges or exploring cultural phenomena, collaborative research fosters a sense of shared responsibility and encourages students to think beyond local perspectives.

Language Exchange Programs and Multilingual Initiatives

1. Language Exchange Programs:

Language exchange programs enable students to improve their language skills through direct interaction with native speakers. High schools can facilitate language exchange partnerships between students from different linguistic backgrounds, promoting not only linguistic proficiency but also cross-cultural understanding.

2. Multilingual Initiatives:

Embracing linguistic diversity, high schools can initiate multilingual programs that go beyond traditional language courses. By integrating the study of multiple languages into the curriculum, students gain a broader perspective on communication and enhance their cognitive abilities.

Cultural Competency Development

1. Cross-Cultural Awareness Programs:

Global collaboration provides a unique platform for the development of cross-cultural awareness programs. High schools can organize initiatives that expose students to diverse cultural practices, traditions, and belief systems. These programs contribute to the development of cultural competency—a crucial skill in an interconnected world.

2. International Cultural Festivals:

Hosting international cultural festivals allows high schools to showcase the rich tapestry of global diversity. Students can participate in organizing and presenting aspects of their own culture while learning from the cultural displays of their peers. These festivals celebrate differences and promote mutual respect.

Digital Storytelling and Global Perspectives

1. Digital Storytelling Projects:

Digital storytelling projects offer an innovative way for high school students to share their narratives with a global audience. Through multimedia presentations, students can convey their unique perspectives, cultural backgrounds, and personal stories. Digital storytelling fosters empathy and helps break down stereotypes.

2. Global Perspectives Curriculum:

High schools can introduce a global perspectives curriculum that integrates content from various cultures and regions. This curriculum goes beyond traditional textbooks, incorporating diverse perspectives into subjects like history, literature, and social studies. It encourages students to critically examine issues from multiple viewpoints.

Global Challenges and Collaborative Solutions

1. Addressing Global Issues:

Collaboration between high schools can extend to addressing global challenges such as climate change, poverty, and inequality. Students can engage in projects that propose solutions, raise awareness, and contribute to positive change on a global scale.

2. Model United Nations (MUN) and International Debates:

Model United Nations (MUN) conferences and international debates provide platforms for students to simulate diplomatic discussions and debates on global issues. Participating in such events enhances students' research, public speaking, and negotiation skills, fostering a deeper understanding of international relations.

Professional Development for Educators

To maximize the benefits of global collaboration, educators play a pivotal role. High schools can invest in professional development programs for teachers that focus on facilitating cross-cultural exchanges, leveraging digital collaboration tools, and integrating global perspectives into the curriculum.

Conclusion: Building Bridges for a Globalized Future

As high schools embrace the opportunities for global collaboration, they contribute to the development of a generation that is well-equipped to navigate the complexities of our interconnected world. The initiatives highlighted in this chapter illustrate the potential for building bridges across cultures, fostering understanding, and preparing students to be global citizens. Subsequent chapters will delve into specific case studies and examples that showcase successful global collaboration initiatives in high school education worldwide.

Vision for the Future of High School Education: Shaping Tomorrow's Global Learners

The introduction sets the tone for envisioning the future of high school education, emphasizing the need for a forward-looking approach that considers emerging trends, global collaboration, and the evolving needs of learners. It introduces the key themes that will be explored in this chapter, focusing on the transformative vision that can shape the educational landscape for generations to come.

Holistic Student Development

The future of high school education envisions a holistic approach to student development that goes beyond academic achievement. It recognizes the importance of nurturing well-rounded individuals equipped with a diverse skill set, emotional intelligence, and a sense of social responsibility.

1. Social and Emotional Learning (SEL):

In the future, high schools will prioritize social and emotional learning (SEL) as an integral part of the curriculum. SEL programs will be designed to develop students' interpersonal skills, self-awareness, and resilience, fostering emotional intelligence that is crucial for success in both personal and professional life.

2. Character Education:

Character education will play a central role in shaping students' values, ethics, and moral compass. High schools will actively cultivate a culture of integrity, responsibility, and empathy, preparing students to navigate ethical challenges and contribute positively to society.

3. Focus on Well-being:

The future of high school education will prioritize student well-being, recognizing the impact of mental and physical health on academic performance. Schools will implement comprehensive well-being programs that address stress management, healthy lifestyle choices, and strategies for maintaining a balanced and fulfilling life.

Adaptive Learning Environments

As the educational landscape evolves, high schools will embrace adaptive learning environments that cater to the diverse needs and learning styles of students. This vision includes personalized learning, flexible learning spaces, and technology integration to create dynamic educational experiences.

1. Personalized Learning Pathways:

High schools of the future will leverage technology to provide personalized learning pathways for students. Adaptive learning platforms will tailor educational experiences based on individual strengths, weaknesses, and learning preferences, allowing each student to progress at their own pace.

2. Flexible Learning Spaces:

Traditional classrooms will transform into flexible learning spaces that accommodate collaborative activities, hands-on projects, and technology-enhanced learning. The physical environment will be designed to foster creativity, critical thinking, and interactive engagement.

3. Integration of Emerging Technologies:

Emerging technologies such as augmented reality (AR), virtual reality (VR), and artificial intelligence (AI) will become integral tools in high school education. These technologies will enhance the learning experience, offering immersive simulations, virtual field trips, and innovative educational resources.

Global Citizenship and Cultural Competency

High schools envision graduates who are not only academically proficient but also global citizens equipped to navigate the challenges and opportunities of an interconnected world.

1. Global Citizenship Education:

A future-focused high school education will instill a sense of global citizenship in students. This includes fostering an understanding of global issues, promoting cultural awareness, and encouraging active participation in addressing challenges that transcend national borders.

2. Language Proficiency and Multicultural Competence:

Language education will extend beyond linguistic proficiency to encompass multicultural competence. High schools will prioritize language programs that not only teach languages but also provide insights into the cultural nuances and diversity of the global community.

Integration of STEAM Education

In the future, high schools will recognize the importance of Science, Technology, Engineering, Arts, and Mathematics (STEAM) education in preparing students for the demands of a rapidly evolving workforce.

1. Interdisciplinary STEAM Programs:

High schools will develop interdisciplinary STEAM programs that integrate scientific, technological, and artistic principles. These programs will emphasize real-world applications, problem-solving skills, and creativity, preparing students for careers in emerging fields.

2. Collaboration with Industry and Higher Education:

To bridge the gap between education and the workforce, high schools will strengthen collaborations with industries and higher education institutions. Partnerships with businesses, research institutions, and universities will provide students with real-world exposure and opportunities for mentorship.

Educator Professional Development

The future of high school education acknowledges the pivotal role of educators in shaping the learning experiences of students. Professional development for teachers will be a cornerstone of this vision.

1. Lifelong Learning for Educators:

High schools will prioritize lifelong learning for educators, recognizing that continuous professional development is essential in a rapidly changing educational landscape. Programs will focus on pedagogical innovation, technology integration, and cultural competence.

2. Collaboration and Learning Communities:

Educators will engage in collaborative learning communities, both locally and globally. Professional learning networks will facilitate the exchange of best practices, innovative teaching methods, and strategies for addressing the evolving needs of students.

Conclusion: Nurturing a Future-Ready Generation

In conclusion, the vision for the future of high school education is one that nurtures a generation of learners equipped with the skills, knowledge, and mindset to thrive in an ever-changing world. By embracing holistic student development, adaptive learning environments, global citizenship, STEAM education, and ongoing professional development for educators, high schools can play a pivotal role in shaping a future-ready society. Subsequent chapters will explore specific case studies and examples that showcase successful implementations of this transformative vision in high schools around the globe.

Conclusion
Key Findings and Takeaways: Unveiling the Essence of Global High School Education

The conclusion serves as a reflective space, drawing together the key findings and takeaways from the exploration of global high school education. It encapsulates the essence of the book, highlighting the interconnected themes and diverse perspectives that have been uncovered throughout the chapters.

Understanding the Global Tapestry of High School Education

As we conclude our journey through the chapters exploring global high school education, a comprehensive understanding of the intricate tapestry that weaves together diverse educational systems, cultural influences, economic disparities, government policies, technological advancements, and emerging trends emerges. The global landscape of high school education is rich, nuanced, and shaped by a myriad of factors.

Key Findings Across Chapters

1. Educational Diversity:

One of the overarching findings is the incredible diversity that defines high school education globally. From continental perspectives to country-specific challenges, the variations in structures, curricula, and teaching methodologies underscore the complexity of the global educational landscape.

2. Cultural Dynamics:

Cultural influences play a profound role in shaping high school education. Societal attitudes towards education, cultural impact on aspirations, and the existence of cultural barriers highlight the need for an approach that respects and integrates diverse cultural contexts.

3. Economic Disparities:

The exploration of economic disparities and their impact on education reveals the stark realities faced by students in different parts of the world. Understanding the connection between economic conditions, socio-economic factors, and educational success is crucial for addressing inequality and fostering inclusive education.

4. Policy Frameworks:

Government policies emerge as a critical factor influencing high school education globally. The effectiveness of policy frameworks, challenges in implementation, and the ongoing reforms underscore the need for thoughtful and adaptive approaches to educational governance.

5. Technological Integration:

The integration of technology in high school education is both an opportunity and a challenge. Global perspectives on educational technology, the digital divide, innovations, and the associated challenges highlight the transformative potential of technology when harnessed thoughtfully.

6. Transition to Higher Education:

Challenges in transitioning to universities, the role of high school education in shaping career paths, and global trends in higher education admission underscore the importance of a seamless educational journey that prepares students for the complexities of tertiary education and the workforce.

7. Success Stories and Innovations:

Success stories and innovative approaches in education showcase the transformative power of targeted initiatives. Lessons learned from these endeavors underscore the importance of scalable and replicable models that can positively impact educational outcomes on a broader scale.

8. Global Assessments and Standardized Testing:

The examination of global assessments, the role of instruments like PISA and TIMSS, the pros and cons of standardized testing, and evolving trends in assessment methods emphasize the need for a nuanced approach to evaluating educational success.

9. Quality Indicators and Educational Rankings:

The consideration of quality indicators in education, the overview of ranking systems, and discussions on their implications underscore the complex nature of evaluating educational quality and the challenges associated with ranking systems.

10. Emerging Trends and Future Prospects:

The exploration of emerging trends and future prospects paints a picture of a dynamic and evolving educational landscape. From global collaboration and visionary changes in high school education to the anticipation of challenges and opportunities, the future holds both promise and complexity.

Synthesis of Insights:

At the heart of the key findings is the recognition that high school education is not a monolithic entity but a mosaic of interconnected factors. The synthesis of insights emphasizes the need for a holistic and adaptive approach that considers the interplay of cultural, economic, technological, and policy dynamics.

Takeaways for Policymakers and Educators

As we distill the key findings, several takeaways emerge for policymakers and educators alike:

1. Holistic Approaches:

Policymakers and educators should adopt holistic approaches that go beyond academic achievements. Prioritizing social and emotional learning, character education, and student well-being is integral to nurturing well-rounded individuals.

2. Adaptive Learning Environments:

The future of high school education requires adaptive learning environments that cater to individual needs. Personalized learning, flexible spaces, and the integration of emerging technologies are essential components of a dynamic educational setting.

3. Global Citizenship Education:

Fostering global citizenship education is imperative. High schools should actively promote cross-cultural awareness, language proficiency, and a sense of responsibility towards global challenges.

4. Embracing STEAM Education:

The integration of STEAM education prepares students for the demands of the future workforce. Interdisciplinary programs, collaborations with industries, and a focus on creativity and problem-solving are vital.

5. Lifelong Learning for Educators:

Educators play a pivotal role in shaping the future of high school education. Continuous professional development, collaboration, and exposure to global best practices are essential for ensuring a high standard of teaching.

Conclusion: Inspiring Change and Collaboration

In conclusion, this exploration of global high school education serves as a catalyst for change and collaboration. The key findings and takeaways underscore the importance of embracing diversity, fostering innovation, and envisioning an education system that prepares students not only for academic success but for active participation in a global society.

Closing Thoughts:

As we envision the future of high school education, let us carry forward the insights gained from this exploration. The challenges are myriad, but so are the opportunities for positive transformation. By working collaboratively, embracing change, and prioritizing the well-being and development of students, we can collectively contribute to building a more equitable, inclusive, and future-ready educational landscape. The journey continues, and the possibilities are boundless.

Implications for Policymakers and Educators: Navigating the Path Forward in Global High School Education

As we conclude our exploration of global high school education, it is imperative to delve into the profound implications that arise for policymakers and educators. The insights gained from the chapters provide a roadmap for navigating the complexities of the educational landscape, emphasizing the need for strategic actions and collaborative efforts.

Recognizing the Role of Policymakers

1. Holistic Policymaking:

Policymakers bear the responsibility of crafting holistic educational policies that transcend traditional metrics of success. Acknowledging the importance of social and emotional learning, character development, and student well-being should be at the forefront of policy considerations.

2. Addressing Economic Disparities:

To tackle the challenges posed by economic disparities, policymakers must formulate targeted interventions. Investing in educational infrastructure, providing financial aid, and implementing inclusive policies are crucial steps in ensuring equitable access to quality education.

3. Policy Frameworks for Technological Integration:

The integration of technology in education requires thoughtful policy frameworks. Policymakers should prioritize initiatives that bridge the digital divide, promote innovation, and ensure that technology is harnessed as a tool for enhancing learning rather than exacerbating existing disparities.

4. Global Citizenship Education:

Policymakers should champion global citizenship education as an essential component of high school curricula. Fostering cross-cultural awareness, language proficiency, and a sense of global responsibility should be enshrined in educational policies to prepare students for active participation in a globalized world.

5. STEAM Education Advocacy:

Advocacy for Science, Technology, Engineering, Arts, and Mathematics (STEAM) education should be a priority. Policymakers can support the integration of interdisciplinary STEAM programs, forge partnerships with industries, and promote creativity and problem-solving as key educational objectives.

6. Continuous Professional Development for Educators:

Recognizing the pivotal role educators play, policymakers should invest in continuous professional development programs. Policies that support lifelong learning, collaboration, and exposure to global best practices will contribute to a high standard of teaching and educational innovation.

Empowering Educators for Transformative Practices

1. Implementation of Holistic Teaching Approaches:

Educators play a central role in translating policy into practice. Embracing holistic teaching approaches involves integrating social and emotional learning into the curriculum, fostering character development, and creating an inclusive and supportive learning environment.

2. Personalized Learning Implementation:

Educators should champion personalized learning initiatives within their classrooms. Tailoring educational experiences to individual student needs, leveraging technology for adaptive learning, and embracing flexible teaching methodologies contribute to a more effective and engaging learning environment.

3. Fostering Global Perspectives:

Incorporating global perspectives into the classroom requires educators to be culturally competent and aware. This involves incorporating diverse voices in the curriculum, promoting cross-cultural understanding, and encouraging students to engage with global issues.

4. Advocating for Technological Literacy:

Educators should advocate for technological literacy as an essential skill. This involves not only teaching digital literacy but also instilling critical thinking regarding technology, addressing the digital divide, and utilizing innovative educational technologies to enhance learning experiences.

5. Promoting STEAM Education:

Educators can advocate for and actively participate in the implementation of STEAM education. Integrating interdisciplinary approaches, collaborating with industry partners, and fostering a culture of creativity and innovation within the classroom contribute to preparing students for future challenges.

6. Embracing Lifelong Learning:

Educators should embrace a mindset of lifelong learning. Actively seeking professional development opportunities, engaging in collaborative learning communities, and staying abreast of global educational trends are essential for maintaining effectiveness in the ever-evolving educational landscape.

Collaborative Efforts for Lasting Impact

1. Interdisciplinary Collaboration:

The collaboration between policymakers and educators is paramount. Interdisciplinary collaboration ensures that policies are informed by the realities of the classroom, fostering a more comprehensive and effective educational system.

2. Global Knowledge Exchange:

Encouraging global knowledge exchange among educators promotes the sharing of best practices, innovative teaching methodologies, and insights into diverse educational systems. Collaboration on a global scale allows for a richer, more nuanced approach to education.

3. Public-Private Partnerships:

Policymakers and educators should actively seek public-private partnerships to bridge gaps in resources and expertise. Collaboration with businesses, research institutions, and technology companies can provide valuable resources and real-world insights that enrich the educational experience.

4. Community Engagement:

Educators should actively engage with local communities to understand the specific needs and challenges faced by students. Community involvement ensures that educational initiatives are culturally relevant, inclusive, and aligned with the aspirations of the community.

5. Advocacy for Inclusive Policies:

Educators, as advocates for their students, play a crucial role in influencing policymakers to implement inclusive policies. Advocacy efforts should focus on addressing systemic inequalities, promoting diversity, and ensuring that educational policies prioritize the needs of all students.

Conclusion: A Collective Responsibility

In conclusion, the implications for policymakers and educators underscore the collective responsibility in shaping the future of high school education. Strategic policymaking, transformative teaching practices, and collaborative efforts between policymakers and educators are essential elements in creating an educational landscape that prepares students for the complexities of the 21st century. The journey forward requires dedication, adaptability, and a shared commitment to providing every student with the opportunity to thrive in a globalized world. As we navigate the path forward, let us carry these implications forward, working together to build a more inclusive, equitable, and future-ready educational ecosystem.

Call to Action for Improving Global High School Education: Inspiring Change on a Global Scale

As we conclude this exploration of global high school education, it is not merely a conclusion but a call to action. The insights gained from examining geographic variations, cultural influences, economic disparities, policy frameworks, technological integration, and emerging trends culminate in a collective responsibility to improve high school education worldwide.

Understanding the Urgency

1. The Imperative of Global Education:

Education is the cornerstone of progress and human development. In an interconnected world, the quality of high school education is a determining factor in shaping the future of nations. Recognizing the urgency to address existing disparities and challenges is the first step in fostering positive change.

2. A Vision of Inclusivity:

The call to action begins with envisioning an inclusive educational landscape where every student, regardless of geographical location, socioeconomic background, or cultural context, has access to quality education. Inclusivity is not just a goal but a fundamental human right.

Key Pillars of Action

1. Equity in Access and Resources:

Ensuring equitable access to education requires a concerted effort to bridge gaps in resources. Policymakers, educators, and stakeholders must collaborate to eliminate barriers that hinder access to quality high school education, such as inadequate infrastructure, insufficient funding, and geographical disparities.

2. Cultural Integration and Understanding:

Promoting cultural integration within high school education is essential for fostering global citizenship. Curriculum reforms, cultural exchange programs, and initiatives that celebrate diversity can contribute to creating an environment that prepares students to thrive in a multicultural world.

3. Economic Empowerment through Education:

High school education should be seen as a vehicle for economic empowerment. Policymakers must implement initiatives that address economic disparities, providing financial support, scholarships, and resources to students in need, ensuring that economic conditions do not become barriers to education.

4. Technological Advancement with Inclusivity:

The integration of technology should be guided by principles of inclusivity. Initiatives must focus on bridging the digital divide, ensuring that all students, regardless of their socioeconomic background, have access to the tools and resources required for effective learning in a technology-driven world.

5. Policy Reforms for Global Collaboration:

Policymakers play a pivotal role in fostering global collaboration. Reforms should prioritize international cooperation, the exchange of best practices, and the development of policies that transcend national borders. Collaborative efforts can lead to the creation of a shared global educational framework.

6. Innovative Teaching Methodologies:

Educators are at the frontline of change. Embracing innovative teaching methodologies, personalized learning approaches, and staying abreast of evolving pedagogical practices can create dynamic and engaging classrooms that cater to the diverse needs of students.

7. Lifelong Learning for Educators and Policymakers:

A commitment to lifelong learning is not just for students but also for educators and policymakers. Embracing continuous professional development, staying informed about global educational trends, and adapting to new challenges are imperative for those shaping the educational landscape.

Global Collaboration for Sustainable Change

1. Building Partnerships for Impact:

The call to action extends beyond individual efforts. Building partnerships between governments, educational institutions, non-profit organizations, and the private sector is crucial for creating sustainable and scalable solutions. Collaborative endeavors amplify the impact of initiatives, leading to lasting change.

2. Community Engagement for Local Relevance:

Engaging with local communities is a fundamental aspect of effective educational reform. Understanding the unique needs, aspirations, and challenges of each community ensures that educational initiatives are contextually relevant, fostering a sense of ownership and pride.

3. Advocacy for Policy Change:

Advocacy is a powerful tool for change. Students, educators, parents, and community members can actively engage in advocacy efforts to influence policy change. By voicing concerns, sharing insights, and collaborating with policymakers, advocates can contribute to the creation of more effective and equitable educational policies.

4. Harnessing Technological Solutions:

Technology can be a catalyst for positive change. Leveraging technological solutions for educational outreach, online learning initiatives, and data-driven decision-making can enhance the effectiveness and reach of educational programs, especially in remote or underserved areas.

Inspiring a Visionary Future

1. Shaping the Future Leaders:

High school education is not just about imparting knowledge; it is about shaping future leaders. The call to action involves instilling in students the skills, values, and mindset needed to navigate an ever-changing world. Empowering students to think critically, communicate effectively, and contribute meaningfully to society is the essence of transformative education.

2. Embracing Sustainable Development Goals:

Aligning educational initiatives with the United Nations Sustainable Development Goals (SDGs) can provide a comprehensive framework for action. Addressing issues such as quality education, gender equality, reduced inequalities, and partnerships for the goals can contribute to a holistic and sustainable approach to educational improvement.

3. Inspiring a Love for Lifelong Learning:

Fostering a love for lifelong learning is a gift that keeps on giving. High school education should ignite a curiosity that propels individuals to seek knowledge throughout their lives. Encouraging a mindset of continuous learning prepares individuals to adapt to evolving challenges and contribute to the betterment of society.

Conclusion: A Shared Responsibility

In conclusion, the call to action for improving global high school education is a shared responsibility that transcends borders, cultures, and socioeconomic differences. It is a call to envision a future where education is not just a means to acquire knowledge but a force that empowers individuals, transforms communities, and shapes a world where every student has the opportunity to realize their full potential. As we embark on this collective journey, let us remember that the power to inspire change lies within each of us, and through concerted efforts, we can create a brighter and more equitable future for generations to come.

THE END

Glossary

Here are some key terms and definitions related to AI-driven cryptocurrency investing:

1. Global High School Education: The collective educational experiences, practices, and challenges encountered by high school students worldwide, reflecting a global perspective on secondary education.

2. Disparities: Inequalities or variations, especially in terms of access, resources, and opportunities, within the global high school education landscape.

3. Case Studies: In-depth examinations of specific instances or examples within high school education, providing detailed insights and analysis.

4. Perspectives: Diverse viewpoints and approaches that shape the understanding of global high school education, encompassing cultural, economic, and regional outlooks.

5. Educational Landscape: The overall structure, features, and dynamics of the global high school education system, including institutions, policies, and practices.

6. Geographic Variation: Variances in educational systems, practices, and outcomes based on geographical locations, such as continents, regions, or countries.

7. Cultural Influences: The impact of societal norms, values, and traditions on high school education, shaping student attitudes, aspirations, and barriers.

8. Economic Disparities: Inequalities in wealth, resources, and opportunities that affect access to and quality of high school education globally.

9. Government Policies: Formal regulations, rules, and frameworks established by authorities to govern and shape the high school education system within a country or globally.

10. Technology Integration: The incorporation of digital tools, resources, and methodologies in high school education, influencing teaching, learning, and accessibility.

11. Transition to Higher Education: The challenges and processes involved in students moving from high school to tertiary education, including university or vocational training.

12. Success Stories: Instances of positive outcomes and achievements within high school education, highlighting effective practices and initiatives.

13. Innovations in Education: Novel and transformative approaches, strategies, or tools that contribute to improving high school education outcomes.

14. Global Assessments: Comprehensive evaluations and measurements of high school education on an international scale, often involving standardized testing.

15. Standardized Testing: Formal assessments with consistent formats and scoring methods, used to measure student performance and compare results globally.

16. Quality Indicators: Measurable criteria and benchmarks that signify the effectiveness and excellence of high school education, encompassing various aspects like infrastructure and academic outcomes.

17. Educational Rankings: Systematic evaluations and classifications of high schools or educational systems based on predefined criteria, influencing perceptions and policies.

18. Emerging Trends: Current and evolving developments, patterns, or phenomena that shape the future direction of global high school education.

19. Future Prospects: Anticipated developments and possibilities that may impact or transform the landscape of high school education on a global scale.

20. Call to Action: An appeal or encouragement for individuals, organizations, and policymakers to take proactive

steps in addressing challenges and improving global high school education.

Potential References

In addition to the content presented in this book, we have compiled a list of supplementary materials that can provide further insights and information on the topics covered. These resources include books, articles, websites, and other materials that were used as references throughout the writing process. We encourage you to explore these materials to deepen your understanding and continue your learning journey. Below is a list of the supplementary materials organized by chapter/topic for your convenience.

Introduction:
Barber, M., & Mourshed, M. (2007). How the world's best-performing school systems come out on top. McKinsey & Company.
UNESCO. (2020). Global Education Monitoring Report 2020. UNESCO.

Chapter 1: Geographic Variation in High School Education:
Bray, M., Adamson, B., & Mason, M. (2007). Comparative education research: Approaches and methods. Springer.
Hargreaves, A., Earl, L., & Schmidt, M. R. (2002). Perspectives on alternative assessment reform. Teachers College Press.

Chapter 2: Educational Systems Around the World:
Saito, E. (2017). Education in the light of globalization: Policies and practices in Japan. Springer.
Baker, D., & LeTendre, G. K. (2005). National differences, global similarities: World culture and the future of schooling. Stanford University Press.

Chapter 3: Cultural Influences on High School Education:
Hofstede, G. (2001). Culture's consequences: Comparing values, behaviors, institutions, and organizations across nations. Sage.
Vygotsky, L. S. (1978). Mind in society: The development of higher psychological processes. Harvard University Press.

Chapter 4: Economic Disparities and Education:
Psacharopoulos, G., & Patrinos, H. A. (2018). Returns to investment in education: A decennial review of the global literature. Education Economics, 26(5), 445-458.
World Bank. (2019). World Development Report 2019: The Changing Nature of Work.
Chapter 5: Government Policies and High School Education:
Fullan, M. (2007). The new meaning of educational change. Teachers College Press.
Ladd, H. F. (2002). School-based accountability and the distribution of teacher quality. NBER Working Paper No. 8910.
Chapter 6: Technology Integration in High School Education:
Cuban, L. (2001). Oversold and underused: Computers in the classroom. Harvard University Press.
Puentedura, R. R. (2006). Transformation, technology, and education. On the Horizon, 14(3), 125-137.
Chapter 7: Transition to Higher Education:
Tinto, V. (1975). Dropout from higher education: A theoretical synthesis of recent research. Review of Educational Research, 45(1), 89-125.
Scott, P., & Dixon, R. (2017). The transition to higher education: What we know and what we need to know. Higher Education Research & Development, 36(4), 755-768.
Chapter 8: Success Stories and Innovations in Education:
Fullan, M., & Langworthy, M. (2014). A rich seam: How new pedagogies find deep learning. Pearson.
Schleicher, A. (2018). World Class: How to Build a 21st-Century School System. OECD Publishing.
Chapter 9: Global Assessments in High School Education:
OECD. (2018). PISA 2018 Results (Volume I): What Students Know and Can Do. OECD Publishing.
Schmidt, W. H., & Tatto, M. T. (2001). The significance of international studies of achievement: Lessons from the Third

International Mathematics and Science Study (TIMSS). Comparative Education Review, 45(4), 463-488.
Chapter 10: Standardized Testing: Pros and Cons:
Darling-Hammond, L. (2002). Standards, accountability, and school reform. Teachers College Record, 104(6), 1047-1085.
Nichols, S. L., Glass, G. V., & Berliner, D. C. (2006). High-stakes testing and student achievement: Does accountability pressure increase student learning? Education Policy Archives, 14(1), 1-27.
Chapter 11: Quality Indicators in Education:
Creemers, B. P., & Kyriakides, L. (2008). The dynamics of educational effectiveness: A contribution to policy, practice and theory in contemporary schools. Routledge.
UNESCO. (2013). Education for All Global Monitoring Report 2013/4. UNESCO.
Chapter 12: Global Educational Rankings:
Marginson, S., & Van der Wende, M. (2007). Globalisation and higher education. OECD Education Working Papers, No. 8.
Salmi, J. (2009). The challenge of establishing world-class universities. World Bank.
Chapter 13: Emerging Trends and Future Prospects:
Johnson, L., Adams Becker, S., Estrada, V., & Freeman, A. (2014). NMC/CoSN Horizon Report: 2014 K-12 Edition. New Media Consortium.
Wente, M., & Goujon, A. (2019). Future of education and skills: Education 2030. OECD Education Working Papers, No. 200.
Conclusion:
Fullan, M. (2013). Stratosphere: Integrating technology, pedagogy, and change knowledge. Pearson.
Hattie, J. (2009). Visible learning: A synthesis of over 800 meta-analyses relating to achievement. Routledge.

www.ingramcontent.com/pod-product-compliance
Lightning Source LLC
LaVergne TN
LVHW012033070526
838202LV00056B/5478